Sukuk
Securities

The Wiley Finance series contains books written specifically for finance and investment professionals as well as sophisticated individual investors and their financial advisors. Book topics range from portfolio management to e-commerce, risk management, financial engineering, valuation and financial instrument analysis, as well as much more. For a list of available titles, visit our Web site at www.WileyFinance.com.

Founded in 1807, John Wiley & Sons is the oldest independent publishing company in the United States. With offices in North America, Europe, Australia and Asia, Wiley is globally committed to developing and marketing print and electronic products and services for our customers' professional and personal knowledge and understanding.

Sukuk Securities

New Ways of Debt Contracting

MEYSAM SAFARI
MOHAMED ARIFF
SHAMSHER MOHAMAD

WILEY

Cover image: Wiley
Cover design: ©iStock.com/javarman3

Copyright © 2014 by John Wiley & Sons Singapore Pte. Ltd.

Published by John Wiley & Sons Singapore Pte. Ltd.
1 Fusionopolis Walk, #07-01, Solaris South Tower, Singapore 138628

Other Wiley Editorial Offices
John Wiley & Sons, 111 River Street, Hoboken, NJ 07030, USA
John Wiley & Sons, The Atrium, Southern Gate, Chichester, West Sussex,
P019 8SQ, United Kingdom
John Wiley & Sons (Canada) Ltd., 5353 Dundas Street West, Suite 400,
Toronto, Ontario, M9B 6HB, Canada
John Wiley & Sons Australia Ltd., 42 McDougall Street, Milton,
Queensland 4064, Australia
Wiley-VCH, Boschstrasse 12, D-69469 Weinheim, Germany

ISBN 978-1-118-93787-7 (Hardcover)
ISBN 978-1-118-94375-5 (ePDF)
ISBN 978-1-118-94374-8 (ePub)
ISBN 978-1-119-02923-6 (oBook)

Typeset in 10/12 pt, Sabon LT Std by Aptara

Printed in Singapore by C.O.S Printers Pte Ltd.

10 9 8 7 6 5 4 3 2 1

As often happens with new topics of investigation, writers benefit from ideas that come from many unexpected sources. So we want to acknowledge the many who, through their discourses with the authors of this book, have provided seminal ideas that are part of the growing literature on Islamic debt instruments. We dedicate this book to all those people first because we owe them all a collective debt. Next, we dedicate this book to the researchers and practitioners who are day by day expanding our understanding of what constitutes Islamic finance.

Contents

Preface xi

Acknowledgments xiii

List of Tables xv

List of Figures xvii

About the Authors xix

PART ONE

The Foundation of *Sukuk* Securities 1

CHAPTER 1
Introduction to *Sukuk* Markets 3
    Islamic (Participation) Debt Securities 4
    The Origin of *Sukuk* Structures 6
    Contemporary *Sukuk* Securities 9
    How *Sukuk* Securities Are Priced 10
    The Structure of This Book 12

CHAPTER 2
***Sukuk* Securities: Definitions, Classification, and Pricing Issues** 13
    Fundamental Principles 14
    Definitions and Regulations 20
    Classification Based on Practices 22
    Conclusion 29

CHAPTER 3
Pragmatic and Idealistic Approaches to Structuring *Sukuk* 31
    Shari'ah: The Basic Foundations of Islamic Finance and *Sukuk* 32
    Islamic Financial Principles 35

Three Approaches to Islamic Finance   40
The History of *Sukuk*   41
Sukuk Structures: Pragmatic and Idealistic Approaches   44
Conclusion   55

CHAPTER 4
Contract Design and the Structure of Common *Sukuk*
Securities Issued to Date   **57**
Mudarabah (Partnership)   57
Musharakah (Profit Sharing)   59
Murabahah (Markup)   62
Ijarah (Leasing)   64
Salam (Futures)   67
Istisna (Working Capital)   69
Conclusion   70

CHAPTER 5
Samples of *Sukuk* Issued   **71**
Sukuk Simpanan Rakyat (Malaysia)   71
Central Bank of Bahrain   73
Khazanah Nasional Berhad (Malaysia)   74
Qatar Central Bank   74
Nakheel Sukuk (UAE)   75
Mahan Airline Company (Iran)   75
Conclusion   76

CHAPTER 6
Contract Design and the Structure of *Sukuk* Securities Yet Issued   **77**
Wakalah (Agency)   77
Manfaah (Usufruct)   78
Muzarah (Farmland Leasing)   78
Musaqah (Orchard Leasing)   79
Muqarasah (Tree Leasing)   79
Conclusion   79

CHAPTER 7
***Sukuk* Securities and Conventional Bonds**   **81**
Comparison of the Yields of Islamic Securities and Bonds   82
Yield Curves   86
The Granger Causality Test for the Yields of *Sukuk* and
    Conventional Bonds   90
Conclusion   94

PART TWO

Sukuk **Securities in Practice**   **97**

CHAPTER 8
Regulations with a Difference   **99**
Regulating *Sukuk*   99
Conclusion   105

CHAPTER 9
Securitization, Trading, and Rating   **107**
Sukuk Trading   107
Sukuk Rating Methodologies   113
Conclusion   123

CHAPTER 10
Worldwide *Sukuk* Markets   **125**
The Geographical Location of *Sukuk* Securities   128
The Effect of Geographical Location on
     Contract Specifications   137
Conclusion   139

CHAPTER 11
Regulatory Issues for *Sukuk* Financial Products   **141**
The Current *Sukuk* Market   142
Regulation and *Shari'ah* Issues in the
     Current *Sukuk* Market   143
Current *Sukuk* Structures   145
Possible Developments and Implications   151

PART THREE

Payoff Structures and *Sukuk* Valuation   **161**

CHAPTER 12
The Foundation and Principles of Islamic Finance   **163**
Foundation   163
Principles   164
Conclusion   167

CHAPTER 13
Cash-Flow Identification and Pattern Recognition for
Theoretical Valuation Models **169**
Zero-Promised Regular-Payment *Sukuk* 169
Fixed-Promised Regular-Payment *Sukuk* 171
Variable-Promised Payment *Sukuk* 172
Undetermined-Promised Payment *Sukuk* 174
Conclusion 175

CHAPTER 14
A Matter of Choice: *Sukuk* or Bond? **177**
The Economics of Conventional Bond-Based Funding 178
World Markets for Conventional Loans 181
The Case against Interest-Based Debt with No Risk Shared 182
Are *Sukuk* an Alternative to Bonds? 185
Conclusion 187

CHAPTER 15
Challenges and Future Developments **189**
Valuation 189
Liquidity 190
Market Widening and Market Depth 191
Cost of Issuance 191
Variation in Schools of Thought 192
Educating More Experts in *Sukuk* 193
Regulatory Sufficiency 194
Conclusion 195

Bibliography **197**

Index **209**

Preface

This book is about an emerging financial market that promises to provide effective funding for *production activities* under a set of safe risk-sharing and profit-sharing finance principles built into the design, and trading of a wholly new form of fixed-income securities called *sukuk*. In a speech on October 13, 2013, announcing new laws to get London to join *sukuk* trading, British prime minister David Cameron said that the new investments are possible "because of the unique openness of the city of London and because of our commitment to help London lead the way in Islamic finance across the world, just as it has led the way in global finance across the ages."

Sukuk contracts are based on an entrepreneur and a financier taking a business risk together and sharing the profits while being prepared to incur losses together if the venture goes bust. The *sukuk* securities market is found in 12 countries, as of 2014. *Sukuk* trading started in 1998 on a small scale and has grown to its present size of close to US$1.2 trillion. When fully developed, it offers an alternative mode of fund-raising for all users of funds as long as the specific needs are taken into account and a *sukuk* contract is provided that meets those needs.

There is no literature dedicated solely to introducing these revolutionary securities markets to the readers in a comprehensive manner or, equally important, to providing a technical introduction to market players to what is described by the financial press as the Islamic (participation) debt market.

Given the endorsement of the World Bank for this new form of financing for developing countries, the value of new issues has grown 45 percent per year from 2011 to 2013, compared with a 17 percent growth per year from 1998 to 2010. The markets for this new form of debt are becoming more attractive to corporations, which are increasing players in all 12 markets. Governments are substantial players in sourcing infrastructural development funding. Agencies such as central banks and public works and energy firms are also seeking to raise funds in this new form.

This book attempts to answer a number of questions for both novices and experts in these marketplaces: What is a *sukuk* security? How should it be classified vis-à-vis bond markets? How is it designed? What are the different types of *sukuk* contracts that uniquely match the needs of farmers, on the one hand, and the working capital of a manufacturer, on the other hand? How big is the market? Why is its targeted funding mode superior to the general-purpose borrowing through conventional bond funding? How is this market different from the common bond market?

Commentators have hailed this form of financing with full asset backing as having the potential to reduce the appetite for debt. By design, borrowers could not borrow more than 100 percent of the value of their assets. We look at this new debt instrument in the context of debt overload in both the public and private sectors in the first two decades of the current century. Since 2008, debt has been decreased by governments, corporations, and individuals because the world has taken on too much debt per capita in the last quarter century. According to the World Bank criterion, debt should not be more than 80 percent of the gross domestic product (GDP) for the economy to be sustainable.

Since the onset of the global financial crisis as well as the Eurozone debt crisis, economic agents are quickly limiting debt across the world to make their economies crisis-resistant. The design features explained in this book on *sukuk* offer a better choice than the radical idea of fully backed banks or the idea of returning banks to the same mode as corporations in backing equity at about 30 percent of total assets. These calls are being made by analysts to stabilize the financial system without examining the merits of *sukuk* as an alternative to the same malady.

This new debt instrument locks the producer and the financier to the profit-and-loss outcomes of a project before asking for rewards from a venture. Such a mode of finance, along with the limiting of loans to no more than 100 percent of the asset value of a borrower, is extolled by many scholars and international institutions as a solution to the debt overload at current period. It appears that this debt overload is the servitude of humanity to modern financial corporations predicted by Thomas Jefferson in the 19th century at the birth of fractional banking. Under fractional banking, banks create money with very little asset backing compared to the 100 percent asset backing by the borrower when a *sukuk* contract is made.

In a sermon in August 2013, Pope Benedict XVI commented that modern lending practices are basically faulty in logic and harmful to the world order and natural justice. Could the new form of debt described in this book be a long-term solution to the ills of modern debt practices based on one-sided contracts in which risk is not shared?

Acknowledgments

This book is a result of a major scholarship grant from the Khazanah Nasional Holding (a Sovereign Wealth Fund) to the University Putra Malaysia. This led to an international collaboration, with one of the authors of this book coming from Australia to Malaysia over a seven-year period to do joint research. Apart from our sincere gratitude to this funding source, our sincere gratitude is also extended to the Maybank Endowment at the University Putra Malaysia, which facilitated the joint research.

Several industry people extended their helping hands. Two we would like to name are Meor Amri Meor Ayob of Bond Pricing Agency Malaysia and Dr. Yeah Kim Leng of Bond Rating Agency Malaysia, both of whom made it possible for us to access data and expertise at their respective firms. Mervyn Lewis, in Adelaide, Australia, and Michael Skully and Abdullah Saeed, both in Melbourne, Australia, deserve a special mention for their continued joint work on Islamic finance research that has added a fair amount of new knowledge to this fledgling field of study.

To the numerous others who participated in the making of this book, we owe an intellectual debt for sharing their ideas, time, and expertise.

We owe an intellectual debt to Peter Casey for his permission to reproduce a chapter on regulatory lessons (Chapter 11). He is an experienced regulator of *sukuk* markets with experience in the United Kingdom and United Arab Emirates. Equally important, we thank Abdullah Saeed and Omar Salah for their elucidation in Chapter 3 on the theoretical aspects of *sukuk* structures. They have all added great insights on the regulatory framework.

The professional staff at John Wiley & Sons has been very helpful in the long process of converting the manuscript into a book. We would like to specially mention the four whom we got to know: Nick Wallwork, Jeremy Chia, Gladys Ganaden in Singapore, and Kimberly Monroe-Hill in Hoboken, New Jersey, United States of America.

List of Tables

Table 5.1   List of Notable *Sukuk* Issuances in Malaysia

Table 7.1   Paired Sample *t*-Test Results between Bonds and *Sukuk* with Similar Features of Issuer and Tenure

Table 7.2   Results of Pairwise Granger Causality Tests

Table 9.1   Summary of Risk Characteristics of *Sukuk* Structures

Table 9.2   Main Risk Factors Pertaining to *Musharakah* and *Mudarabah Sukuk*

Table 10.1   *Sukuk* Securities Issued Based on Country of Domicile

Table 10.2   *Ijarah Sukuk* Securities Issued Based on Country of Domicile

Table 10.3   *Istisna Sukuk* Securities Issued Based on Country of Domicile

Table 10.4   *Mudarabah Sukuk* Securities Issued Based on Country of Domicile

Table 10.5   *Murabahah Sukuk* Securities Issued Based on Country of Domicile

Table 10.6   *Musharakah Sukuk* Securities Issued Based on Country of Domicile

Table 10.7   *Sukuk* Securities Issued Based on Issuing-Country Risk

Table 10.8   *Ijarah Sukuk* Securities Issued Based on Issuing-Country Risk

Table 10.9   *Istisna Sukuk* Securities Issued Based on Issuing-Country Risk

Table 10.10   *Mudarabah Sukuk* Securities Issued Based on Issuing-Country Risk

Table 10.11   *Murabahah Sukuk* Securities Based on Issuing-Country Risk

Table 10.12   *Musharakah Sukuk* Securities Based on Issuing-Country Risk

Table 12.1   Expansion of the Islamic Financial Services Industry

List of Figures

Figure 2.1   Fundamental Principles of *Sukuk* Security Compared to Conventional Debt Security

Figure 2.2   Classification Based on Cash-Flow Payoff Patterns of *Sukuk* Securities

Figure 2.3   A Simple Classification of Long-Term and Short-Term *Sukuk* Securities

Figure 2.4   Classification of *Sukuk* Contracts Based on Their Financial Characteristics

Figure 2.5   *Sukuk* Based on Their Underlying Contractual Structure

Figure 3.1   Structure of *Ijarah Sukuk*

Figure 3.2   Structure of Hybrid *Sukuk*

Figure 3.3   Structure of *Mudarabah Sukuk*

Figure 4.1   Diminishing *Musharakah Sukuk* Structure

Figure 4.2   *Ijarah Sukuk* Structure

Figure 4.3   *Salam Sukuk* Structure

Figure 7.1   Yield Curve of Government-Issued Securities (Conventional Bonds versus *Sukuk*)

Figure 7.2   Yield Curve of Government Agency–Issued Securities (Conventional Bonds versus *Sukuk*)

Figure 7.3   Yield Curve of AAA-Rated Financial Institution–Issued Securities (Conventional Bonds versus *Sukuk*)

Figure 7.4   Yield Curve of AAA-Rated Corporate-Issued Securities (Conventional Bonds versus *Sukuk*)

Figure 9.1   Formation of an SPC

Figure 10.1   Number of Worldwide *Sukuk* Issues

Figure 10.2   *Sukuk* Issuance by Country, 2011

Figure 10.3   *Sukuk* Securities Issued Based on the Country of Domicile

Figure 10.4   *Ijarah Sukuk* Securities Issued Based on the Country of Domicile

Figure 10.5   *Mudarabah Sukuk* Securities Issued Based on the Country of Domicile

Figure 10.6   *Musharakah Sukuk* Securities Issued Based on the Country of Domicile

Figure 10.7   *Sukuk* Securities Based on the Issuing-Country Risk

Figure 10.8   *Ijarah Sukuk* Securities Based on the Issuing-Country Risk
Figure 10.9   *Mudarabah Sukuk* Securities Based on the Issuing-Country
                      Risk
Figure 13.1   Zero-Promised Regular-Payment Cash-Flow Pattern of
                      Sukuk Securities
Figure 13.2   Fixed-Promised Regular-Payment Cash-Flow Pattern of
                      Sukuk without Promised Maturity Payment
Figure 13.3   Cash-Flow Pattern for *Sukuk* with Fixed-Promised Regular
                      Payments and Promised Maturity Payment
Figure 13.4   Growing-Promised Regular-Payment Pattern with
                      Predetermined-Promised Maturity Payment
Figure 13.5   Declining-Promised Payment Cash-Flow Pattern
Figure 13.6   Undetermined-Promised Payment Cash-Flow Pattern

About the Authors

Meysam Safari, PhD, is a senior lecturer at SEGi University, Malaysia. With a scholarship from Khazana Holdings Malaysia, he spent five years researching the topic of *sukuk* under the guidance of the other two authors at the University Putra Malaysia. He holds an undergraduate engineering degree and a doctoral degree in finance from the University Putra Malaysia.

Mohamed Ariff, PhD, a professor of finance at the Bond University, Australia (and the University Putra Malaysia), is widely considered a specialist on Asian Pacific finance and Islamic finance. He served in 2004–2007 as the elected president of the 26-year-old Asian Finance Association. He is a coauthor of *Investments*, a leading McGraw-Hill textbook, and has authored or coauthored 33 other books. His scholarly articles have appeared in leading economics and finance journals.

Shamsher Mohamad, PhD, is a professor at the International Centre for Education in Islamic Finance, also known as INCEIF. He has served in various capacities over 31 years, rising to his last position as dean of the economics faculty at the University Putra Malaysia. He has authored or coauthored several books (including *Efficiency of the Kuala Lumpur Stock Exchange* and *Stock Pricing in Malaysia*). He has published scholarly papers in finance journals.

One

The Foundation of *Sukuk* Securities

CHAPTER 1

Introduction to *Sukuk* Markets

On Christmas Eve 2013, Pope Francis, in his first apostolic exhortation, pleaded for "a return of economics and finance to an ethical approach which favors human beings." Instituting an ethical approach to finance is the purpose of Islamic financial markets, which have created securities that conform to Islamic scripture and traditions. In some countries this form of contracting has been dubbed *participation finance* to emphasize the profit-sharing aspect of this new market practice. Islamic securities are specially tailored financial products that conform to the set of ethical and common law–based financial transaction principles laid out in *Shari'ah*, or Islamic law. *Shari'ah* literally means "the way," and it takes its body of principles from the Quran and the *Sunnah* (an account of the normative behavior of the Prophet Muhammad). Those principles are strictly applied when designing the financial contracting terms that cover such products. Compliance is assured by a committee of experts working at each financial institution, and the institutions must abide by the rulings of both the national and international committees on compliance standards.

Although sovereign laws enacted by various governments originated with some strong ethical foundations in order to protect people, these were watered down in recent centuries by the power of the moneyed class, which includes modern banks. The result is that some of the high moral edicts that governed the financial behavior of human societies are no longer taken into consideration in the design, marketing, and sale of financial products. There has been a call in recent years to go back to human ethics, since the world has witnessed how new and untested financial innovations could wreck the wealth of societies. It is a call for finance that favors human beings against the interests of the moneyed class.

For example, in the environment of close to zero percent interest rates that has prevailed since 2010, banks are now going back to the old bad habit of offering bets on future events to entice bank depositors to bring their savings to the banks with a "bet." If the bets are won, the contracted low interest rate will be increased by the banks. Of course, the experience of depositors in the United States in 1994–2008 was that bets like these made lots of people lose money. Although such bets are just another form of gambling, bank regulators have yet to move aggressively to outlaw these contracts being offered by regular (versus investment) banks that cater to the common person with little savings.

ISLAMIC (PARTICIPATION) DEBT SECURITIES

Islamic financial instruments, constructed with some extra elements of ethical precepts, have helped to form a niche market for financial products in 76 countries today. The total assets of this niche market are no more than a small fraction of the world's conventional securities markets. These Islamic securities may be classified into four major groups: stocks, mutual funds, money markets, and *sukuk* (bonds that comply with *Shari'ah* requirements).

Sukuk certificates are Islamic debt securities held by the lenders. This book is about these new instruments, which are currently issued and traded in 12 markets; the first public issue was in 1998. In October 2013, Britain announced its intention to start a *sukuk* market in 2014–2015. This book describes the foundation of *sukuk* as Islamic securities, sometimes also called *participation debt certificates* or *participation debt securities* to connote the risk-sharing aspect of *sukuk* debt contracting.

The principles to which Islamic securities adhere are quite different from those used in the design of conventional securities, but some modern terms are shared by the two practices, borrowed from conventional financial contracting. The modern financial principles that guide the design of conventional debt securities evolved over two and a half centuries without much reference to the type of ethical principles that have been applied in designing Islamic financial products in historical times as well as today.

The vast majority of the lending for production funding was secured by the invention of fractional reserve banking around 1850 CE. This new form of banking was revolutionary, and it has secured widespread acceptance from regulators. This revolution started about four decades after the papal edict that made lending at interest permissible for the adherents of the Roman Catholic Church.

Production funding that existed before this papal edict was not based on interest, nor did it shirk risk sharing in lending. Loans were based on profit sharing and risk sharing, but this slowly gave way to a one-way contract in which the return and risk of a production loan became divorced from the outcomes of lending. The voyages of Christopher Columbus were designed as risk-sharing and profit-loss-sharing contracts. Queen Isabella and King Ferdinand of Spain secured 70 percent of Columbus's profits on goods, including slaves, that managed to survive the risk of transatlantic navigation.

Today's mode of funding is based on the entrepreneur taking the *full risk* of a venture; the lender takes no risk of failure but is assured of a prenegotiated reward if the venture succeeds. Fractional banks can therefore offer much cheaper loans than the risk-shared loans of historical times.

This is not the case with Islamic financial securities. The financial contracts designed under the Islamic (participation) label require strict adherence to some fundamentally different principles for all kinds of securities, be they publicly traded bills, shares, debtlike *sukuk*, stocks and derivatives, or privately traded instruments.

Islamic financial instruments can be classified into four core types of contracts:

1. *Musharakah* **securities.** Ownership and control of a firm's assets through the purchase of shares of stock makes this class very similar to common stock ownership. The shares of stocks are securities that give the owner a claim to the profits only if the profits are earned after the risk of the project has been shared.
2. *Sukuk* **securities.** These are mostly finite-period debt (rarely equity) or funding arrangement contracts, mostly without managerial control of the project funded but with unique fractional ownership of a set of income-producing assets of a borrower. These assets are set aside by the borrower as asset-backed or asset-based contracts held in a special purpose company (SPC) owned by the fund providers, whose payoff is based on profit sharing from the assets of the SPC.
3. *Takaful* **(insurance).** *Takaful* contracts are risk-transfer arrangements that contain the provision that the insurance premiums collected from the insured parties are to be invested only in approved (i.e., permissible by *Shari'ah*) securities. *Takaful* uses mutual insurance principles; hence, the excess profits of the insurance operator are distributed at regular intervals to members based on a prenegotiated profit ratio.
4. **Islamic mutual funds.** These are investment funds managed on behalf of clients for a fee and recovery of the costs incurred in managing the portfolios. Return of profits occurs after the management costs are recovered. These funds are to be invested only in socially beneficial production activities, not antisocial (as defined by *Shari'ah*) projects.

This simple four-category division of Islamic financial products may resemble the conventional security classes of stocks, bonds, insurance, and mutual funds. However, there are significant differences in their structure, in the mode of pricing them, in collateralization, and in what economic production activities may have access to the funds.

For example, the pricing of Islamic securities is done through profit-sharing and risk-sharing contracts under the ethical principle of giving rewards only after the risks are shared. Conventional securities are priced by interest-based payments to investors, usually prenegotiated, with no risk shared. Some Islamic securities may even have special features, such as a strange form of diminishing principal repayments with profit sharing. Thus, profit payments are reduced as the entrepreneur takes more control of the production. This is called diminishing *musharakah*. There are other exotic contracts, all tied to the specific funding needs in the production process.

These and other characteristics make participatory financial instruments very different from conventional instruments. The appearance of similarity is somewhat exaggerated by critics not knowing that the important structural differences are meant to safeguard both borrowers and lenders and to ensure ethics-based funding arrangements.

Since Islamic securities, once issued as publicly traded instruments, are also traded in financial markets, we have to also include two more categories of Islamic financial instruments: Islamic capital markets, and private equity (or private *sukuk*, private *takaful*, or private mutual funds). The latter category is a separate group of securities when such securities are not traded in public markets, so we may also call them *nontraded* private Islamic securities.

Thus, we have six categories of Islamic financial transaction modes. We have provided these introductory remarks to set the stage for our discussion of only one of these classes, *sukuk*, in the rest of the book. We now proceed with this task by examining *sukuk* securities as a class by itself.

THE ORIGIN OF *SUKUK* STRUCTURES

Historical research in the Mediterranean region, traditionally known as the cradle of civilization, indicates that lending for production purposes was done through profit-sharing *and* risk-sharing contracts. Further, the loan was given only if the borrower had some assets or was likely to acquire some as a result of the financing. The exception to this rule was borrowing by kings and governments and perhaps also by the moneyed class as well as those in financial difficulty.

Historical records allude to the creation of *sukuk* as a borrowing instrument that Islamic legal scholars in the Turkish empire helped to design for public financing when the emperor needed to borrow large sums of money for reconstruction after the devastation of the empire after five crusades that ended in 1285 CE. The innovation of fund-raising consistent with Islamic ethics of borrowing differed considerably from Christian practices at that time, which were based on Babylonian and Greco-Roman laws.

A financial contract must have the following characteristics under the Islamic participatory finance principles of borrowing and funding. Ownership and control contracts must be based on profit sharing by participating in the risk of the project so that the profit accrues to lenders *after* the fund is used for the project. The outcome of such funding is the profit earned, which is shared in proportion by the financier and the business. The important issue is that it is a shared arrangement even though the *sukuk* is a borrowing instrument for a limited period. One brings the capital and the other entrepreneurship to make things useful for the society under a joint arrangement.

The rewards to the financier depend on the outcome of the funds being applied, which includes a small chance of losses. The parties have a mutual interest in securing a good outcome of the business activity; the project risk is not shifted entirely to the entrepreneur. This enhances society's welfare. The interests of the moneyed class engaged in the lending are thus subject to the welfare of the community in which the moneyed class resides.

When no ownership and control is involved with the assets of an enterprise, a *sukuk* instrument is agreed upon as follows: (1) The fund provider has a share of that part of the borrower's assets transferred to a special legal body, the SPC, to be owned by the lenders; (2) the borrower earns rewards from the income of the set-aside assets to service the borrowed money at the end of the contract period; and (3) the earnings of the SPC assets could provide periodic incomes to be paid as rewards if the contracts provided for such payoffs at regular intervals as ordinary annuity.

In a sense, then, to borrow, a producer firm must have part of its assets removed from the producer firm's control so that the lender has income from those set-aside assets to service the fund provider. While the asset transfer makes such debt riskier, it also ensures that the borrower is limited to borrowing only to the extent that the assets have value. The principle is "Have assets, can borrow."

Borrowing for any purpose other than economic usefulness to society is discouraged. The setting aside of assets of a producer firm ensures an income as return to the lender, which is meant to make the borrowing contract more secure—two-sided or asynchronous. That is not the case in current conventional bond markets, although without risk sharing with prenegotiated interest payments, conventional debt contracts may still be less risky.

Borrowing in conventional bond markets is usually based on the good credit reputation of the borrowers. Certainly, the assets are not owned from day one of the funding, nor are risks shared before payoffs occur. Under the modern laws applying to conventional lending, a lender may still have to take the borrower to court under the provisions of the corporate laws to make a claim for the assets owned by the borrower, the producing firm. This is a costly process.

A *sukuk* contract, in contrast to a conventional bond, was agreed upon by the Turkish emperor to raise money by setting aside some of the treasury assets to be owned by the lending public to rebuild the infrastructure of the empire.

Another characteristic in *sukuk* funding is that the reward that the fund provider gets from investment is from income from the assets set aside by the borrower in order to pay an agreed-upon return (regular payoffs, if such a term is contracted) based on profit share and to repay the borrowed funds at the end of the term of the loan contract.

Although *sukuk* funding as described above is a producer loan, another class of borrowing is individuals borrowing for sustenance, in which case funds are lent without any promised payoff (the so-called increase or *commenda*) above the sum lent. This form of Islamic lending is based on repayment of the principal lent, nothing more. This is called *qard hassan*, or benevolent loan, which is a form of lending with no interest. Repayment of the principal by the borrower is a must, however. *Qard hassan* is mandated solely to fund household funding needs. This form of borrowing is an insignificant portion of the total market.[1]

This form of funding is similar to the papal lending that occurred in Italy during periods of famine and war; the Church lent money generously without any interest and with no expectation of the principal being repaid. Though the principal is to be repaid, forgiving the return of principal is advised in the Quran. Lending for sustenance without an expectation of reward—and even the forgoing of the principal amount—is clearly lauded as an act of piety in the Torah, the Bible, and the Quran. There is a shared Abrahamic moral ethos for consumption lending, but this should not be confused with production lending based on shared risk and profits.

---

[1] For example, the National Australia Bank (the second-largest Australian bank in 2014) has made available a large sum of money to a Muslim financial cooperative to lend to needy families to buy household durables without any interest payments. Traditionally, this form of lending has been widely practiced in communities in which society, a bank, or a rich individual provides interest-free loans to needy families to obtain productive assets. Some reports indicate that banks do lend about 1/25 of their funds for this purpose in Iran, for example.

CONTEMPORARY *SUKUK* SECURITIES

The current Islamic *sukuk* funding market in Malaysia was rediscovered about in 1990 when a private-sector firm, Shell Malaysia, issued a *sukuk* borrowing instrument to raise RM125 million (US$40 million) through a private issue in the Kuala Lumpur capital market (now Bursa Malaysia). Since then, and especially since 2000, this market has grown, with private-sector firms as well as government agencies raising money by issuing *sukuk* securities in Kuala Lumpur and 11 other countries. The Bank for International Settlements, which deals with both publicly traded and private issues, reports that the *sukuk* bond market around the world is worth about US$1,200 billion (about 1.2 percent of conventional bond issues).

Private issues dominate this market because the government issues amount to less than US$100 billion in open markets in the same 12 locations. The most active markets are found in just 6 of these locations: Malaysia, Kuwait, the United Arab Emirates (UAE), Oman, Qatar, and Saudi Arabia (in that order). *Sukuk* issues have grown in 23 years, and there is room for the further growth of this market.

Scholars have different opinions on the character of the assets transferred and jointly owned by the lenders in the form of SPCs. One school of thought is that as long as the assets transferred are not real assets, a *sukuk* contract is not likely to be secure. The majority opinion is that real assets must back funding contracts.[2] In the last two decades, this provision has been watered down so much that some institutions have gotten the approval of the *Shari'ah* regulators to consider any assets permissible as long as they are income producing. In practice, usufructs and incomes of financial assets are used as substitutes for real assets.

One school of thought is that the assets must be owned, and the other school is that the assets need not be owned, so that the contract could provide for asset-based contracting. In extreme cases, the assets transferred are recontracted to be owned by the borrower. This issue is addressed separately in Chapters 3 and 9.

The *sukuk* market has grown very fast in the six countries mentioned above, which offer new sources of funds for investors to fund both private and public projects. All these countries follow the profit-sharing formula and the SPC having ownership of income-producing assets held by the lenders, at least at the start of the lending process. The World Bank has endorsed this form of borrowing for large funds urgently needed to finance infrastructure

---

[2] U. M. Chapra, "The Major Modes of Islamic Finance," course in Islamic Economics, Banking, and Finance series, Islamic Foundation, Leicester, UK, 1998.

projects in developing countries. The self-liquidating nature of this form of long-term loan issued mostly in local currencies makes this form of financing cheaper than the megaloans denominated in major currencies structured in the six international bond markets: London, New York, Tokyo, Sydney, and several Swiss cities.

HOW *SUKUK* SECURITIES ARE PRICED

Thousands of years of financial history have provided human beings with new mechanisms to facilitate their lives through using some form of money. Among the very old practices is the concept of trade; this evolved from the simple mechanism of barter, which developed into the current means of paper currencies and coinage when China invented paper money 1,000 years ago. Paper currencies such as dollar are used to measure the value of virtually every tangible and intangible asset. However, the fundamental, hotly debated issue over time has been how to determine the true value or price of a particular asset.

Sukuk securities, as a relatively new class of financial instrument, are no exception to this concern. Over time, various methods were developed for pricing, which is the valuation of financial instruments leading to price discovery. Four methods are applicable in the case of *sukuk* securities. These methods are based on the foundation principles of commerce, which suggest that fair pricing should be used. Since there is no conflict between the concepts, general procedures, and rationality of these methods, on the one hand, and the ethical and religious requirements of Islam, on the other, one may apply these mechanisms. However, some adjustments might be required in the way that valuation is done for *sukuk*. Such adjustments are thoroughly discussed in Chapter 13.

The first method of valuation is the *public auction* pricing process. This method is based on the economic concepts of supply and demand. It suggests that the price would be a market clearing value in which the supply and demand for an item meets the funds available. We like to call this the cucumber theory: overproduction of cucumbers lowers their price, whereas shortages of cucumbers increase their price.

This method is widely used by practitioners for valuation of publicly traded *sukuk* securities, which is also similar for conventional bonds. In this process, the issuer, with the intermediation of an investment bank, structures a proposal for an issuance of *sukuk*. Through the public auction held by the investment bank, the price is discovered by the investors in the bidding, similar to how houses are auctioned to eager buyers. Investors bid for the highest price if they assume that there is value in it for them. Therefore, the *sukuk* would be sold to the investors with the highest bids.

Private negotiation is the second method of pricing *sukuk* securities. This method is used in private placements offered to a limited number of private investors. This process can be conducted as an over-the-counter solution offered by investment bankers (as middlemen) to cut a deal between the originator and the investors, or it can be conducted as a direct bilateral negotiated contract between the two parties (in the way a Masai herdsman buys his cattle).

This method is also similar to the bilateral negotiation of a lender and a borrower in a bank loan, but in the case of *sukuk* with Islamic contracting terms, these bilateral agreements are enforceable legal documents governing the prenegotiated terms of contract between the issuer and the investors. Such a method is suitable mostly for private *sukuk* placement, in the same way that private debt placement takes place in 125 conventional fixed-income markets around the world.

The third method of pricing is *convertible* pricing. Some of the *sukuk* securities have a convertible option feature embedded in their structure (e.g., Telekom Malaysia). Such structures provide their investors with the option to trade in their *sukuk* certificates with a certain amount of equity shares of the underlying firm (mostly the originator) after a predetermined time. Some of the *sukuk* placements in markets like London, Zurich, and Luxembourg are originated by firms listed in their local markets.

Hence, there are two special elements visible in such structures. First, their value is tied to the value of an underlying equity share, as a consequence of the convertible options featured in them; and second, the underlying equity share value represents a cross-market firm. Such placements therefore resemble the depository receipts of a foreign firm's stock in the market where the *sukuk* securities are traded. Thus, the existing mechanisms of pricing depository receipts become handy. Such forms of *sukuk* securities are, currently, a small fraction of the market; however, there is a growth potential for this form of fund-raising structure.

The first three pricing methods are mainly based on the outcomes of market-driven initiatives such as supply and demand and are therefore called the market value of the security. However, the actual pricing of conventional fixed-income securities are not limited to market price.

Theoretical modeling is the fourth method of pricing conventional debt securities. The absence of a theoretical pricing model has led to a focus on the market forces, and the underlying value of the security is thus partly overlooked. The lack of correct measures causes the mispricing commonly observed in the *sukuk* security market.

These two categories of methods—market based and theory based—when applied together will result in a more accurate price discovery for *sukuk* securities. The theoretical valuation modeling of *sukuk* securities is thoroughly discussed in Part III.

The principles of Islamic finance affect the pricing of Islamic instruments, and then all possible cash-flow patterns of different structures are generated based on their definitions. With the cash-flow patterns in hand, valuation models are developed. In order to develop correct valuation models and to make them more familiar for practitioners, a conventional pricing approach is first selected for experimentation to arrive at theoretical prices.

Sukuk securities that have identical cash-flow patterns as conventional bonds are priced with the same existing models. For instance, one form of *ijarah sukuk* (a lease contract) is identical to coupon-bearing collateralized bonds, so its price should be computed the same way. On the other hand, *musharakah sukuk* (profit sharing) is like no other bond security because its payoff is tied to the performance of the underlying firm (or the SPC). Thus, the cash flows are not predetermined, and modeling the security would be much more challenging in ways similar to the modeling of equity shares. These models are developed in the last part of the book.

THE STRUCTURE OF THIS BOOK

Introductory materials to define, describe, classify, and provide the structures of the various debt contracts are presented in Part I. Our aim in this part is to provide both the layperson and the specialist with an understanding of how this new security is designed and to show the structural differences among the six most commonly issued instruments. The theoretical grounds of *sukuk* markets are described in this part.

In Part II, our aim is to present evidence that the new debt market has a number of features that make it different from the conventional bond market, to which market players refer in trading *sukuk* securities. We show that *sukuk* securities yield significantly higher yields than their identical conventional counterparts. The yield differences are, in fact, quite substantial. We explain that this is a result of the higher risk inherent in risk-sharing and profit-sharing contracts, although this connection has yet been empirically verified.

Part III is concerned with the issue of how to map the payoffs in each of the instruments to identify the cash-flow patterns. This part describes a number of core types of payoff structures. These patterns can then be used to identify mathematical solutions as objective valuation models. Another feature of this part is the contribution of a chapter by a specialist in regulation on the issues confronting continued growth from regulatory shortcomings. The book ends with a discussion of the challenges for the continued growth of this form of debt structuring, which is only about 28 years old.

CHAPTER 2

Sukuk Securities: Definitions, Classification, and Pricing Issues

The foundation principles for *sukuk* certificates have developed in conformity with Islamic legal principles based on the Quran's commandments and elaborated in *Shari'ah* through 14 centuries of development. The word *sukuk* is not found in the Quran; it emerged as a development in the application of the Quran's principles to the real human act of debt funding.

The practice of borrowing and lending with asset backing (or assets that would be created from such debt) for specific production activities was widely known in the pre-Islamic Middle East and Mediterranean regions. Such debt transactions were practiced as risk-shared and profit-shared loans to be liquidated over mostly finite periods. The shorter the production process—for example, working capital loans (*istisna*) taken by producers of goods—the shorter the duration of lending. These practices were adapted by scholars who applied doctrinal provisions of Islam and refined them as Islamic debt instruments to make funding possible for economic activities.

By the late 19th century, which also coincided with the demise of Islamic empires in most parts of the world, the use of *sukuk* slowly waned, being replaced with modern banking practices and the introduction of modern financial instruments based on no risk sharing and prenegotiated interest payments. After about four decades, during which profit-sharing and risk-sharing banking was reintroduced, the Islamic debt instrument of *sukuk* appeared in the late 1990s in a number of countries.

The foundation principles are quite comprehensive as a guide to the parties in a contract. Examples of this are fairness in risk sharing, thus earning a permissible increase (*commenda*), and equity and full information provision (no asymmetric information, so both parties have the same information). Financial contracts are provided in a written form so they can be formally witnessed. In this chapter, we restrict our discussion of fundamental principles to those that affect *sukuk* securities.

FUNDAMENTAL PRINCIPLES

The word *sukuk* is plural for a certificate (*sakk*) of ownership of a given class of assets that a borrower gives to a lender as proof of ownership.[1] Therefore, *sukuk* securities are debt instruments that require the creation of assets in a separate entity, these assets being owned proportionally by the lenders, the fund providers. Full asset-backed lending is a fundamental principle of *sukuk* contracting.

In a sense, it suggests that without the lender being able to create an arm's length asset backing to a debt-funding arrangement to which the borrower has transferred income-producing assets, there cannot be any lending contract in an ethical financial transaction. This suggests that all *sukuk* securities have to have this safety net, so that from the start of the contract, the lenders have asset backing for their funding.

This makes *sukuk* security safer than conventional bonds because the lender in a conventional debt contract would need the permission of a court to obtain the right of ownership. That permission is given only if the issue is contested at the time of an actual default of the promised payoff.

A *sukuk* contract may thus be defined simply as a debt-funding arrangement agreed to between a party providing the funds (the investor) and the counterparty (a government or a firm, since individuals rarely issue *sukuk*) that is borrowing the funds to engage in permissible economic activities of production or service. Funding arrangements may vary, including an ownership and control basis, sharing-type securities, pure borrowing-type securities, and leasing-type securities. Because of this, it is inaccurate to describe *sukuk* as solely an Islamic *debt* instrument, as is the widespread practice of finance mass media.

Unlike in most *sukuk* issues, in sharing-type (*musharakah*) *sukuk* securities issued to investors, the fund providers get rewards only in the form of a portion of the profits based on a prenegotiated profit ratio. If the ownership is assigned to all the assets of the borrower, whether the ownership entails control or absence of control of the enterprise, this too is *musharakah sukuk*, a sharing-type funding arrangement for a finite period (an uncommon concept in modern finance).

It is very useful to get subordinated common stock with voting rights for a finite period. This type does not exist presently and may be thought of

---

[1] Historical references suggest that the word *sukuk* was used both as a singular term and as the plural form of *sakk*. In addition to its use in borrowing and lending, this mode of issuing certificates was practiced a millennium ago in Damascus as a form of check writing to pay for purchases. In this book, we use the term *sukuk* as both singular and plural, as the context indicates.

as a common share in a specific project with a finite period of life to produce an item for the fund to be paid back with profits. In conventional share funding, if another restriction were imposed to limit the use of such funds to produce permitted products or services, the result would be an Islamic common stock, whcich is the *musharakah* contract. If these were also issued for a finite period, this would be a new type of share unknown to date. All contracts with an infinite period and shared ownership and control of assets of the total enterprise are pure *musharakah* contracts.

A more common practice is for a borrower to set aside a portion of income-producing assets previously under the control of a producer into a special purpose company (SPC) and immediately make those assets available as owned by the investors in proportion to the funding ratio; this is a basic asset-backed *sukuk* contract. A simple *sukuk* security would be a funding arrangement for a finite period with the provision of ownership of part of the borrower's assets set aside as owned by an SPC, which would service the investors during the contract period using incomes produced by the SPC and, in cases of likely default, through the sale of assets.

Hence, one should consider a finite-period funding arrangement for debt as a characteristic of *sukuk* funding. Another characteristic is the removal of part of the borrower's assets into an SPC to be owned by the fund providers starting from the contract issue date. In recent years, a novel practice has somewhat altered asset-backing to *asset-based* contracting—instead of real assets, usufructs that produce incomes are accepted as assets.

Some scholars and regulatory regimes oppose this practice as a deviation, since there is no real asset in asset-based SPC. Asset backing is not the case with conventional bond-type lending, since the lenders have to contest in court only if nonpayment of prenegotiated interest payments occurs; the court has the discretion to permit creditors to access ownership of assets of the total firm. Not so in *sukuk* contracts. This makes Islamic funding arrangements a lot safer and prevents borrowers from borrowing without assets to back the funding.

Asset backing can be considered a fundamental principle. If there are no assets to back a loan made to a producer, there is no funding. This places quantity limits on excessive borrowing. Heavy reliance on borrowed funds has been associated with financial fragility in the economic policy literature, which concludes that excessive debt has been the root cause of many bankruptcies over the centuries as well as during crisis periods and business downturns.

New Zealand's central bank pioneered a new regulation in 2013 under which a bank will lose its license if more than 10 percent of its loans exceed 80 percent loan to asset backing. This rule is meant to slowly bring down the debt overload of governments, firms, and households.

A recent example of financial fragility is the global financial crisis, which developed from the nonrecourse to fund providers of real assets of major banks and financial firms. Had there been an ownership factor, there would not have been the credit bulge in 1994–2006, which has been blamed for the start of the global crisis. Debt gauging under *sukuk* would not exceed 100 percent of a debtor's assets, so there would be no question of debt overload if these principles were strictly followed.

Another characteristic is the use of profit ratio in the contract to determine the rewards to investors. Since profit or loss is known only after a span of time in which the borrowed fund has been applied to an economic activity, this introduces the very significant characteristic of Islamic fund providers sharing in the risk of a project before a reward can be mandated and decided on. One can see this quite clearly when a firm decides to pay dividends, in the case of common shares. Dividends are paid at quarterly periods in the United States and at half yearly periods in other countries. If there is no profit in a period (e.g., if there has been a fire that reduced the value of the real assets of an SPC), then there is no reward or just part reward for that period.

To the extent that the payment of reward is conditional on profits occurring, the nature of the payment is not fixed, so aggregate economic activities are relieved somewhat by producers and financiers sharing in the risk. Thus, to treat the rewards promised as fixed and apply a fixed-coupon-paying bond valuation model to value a *sukuk* security is not justifiable unless it is meant only as an approximate indicator of theoretical value.

There are specific *sukuk* contracts that require the amount of payoff to be fixed and paid periodically or that permit the payoff to grow at a constant rate. That payoff is fixed, but the incomes of the SPC may be higher or lower. There are two *sukuk* contracts that are exceptions to the general rule of payoffs being not fixed. These special arrangements are *ijarah* (lease-type) *sukuk* funding, with payoffs of a fixed rental-type arrangement; and *bai bithaman ajjal sukuk* (constant-growth profit sharing that starts with a fixed ratio), which provides for the payoff to increase by a constant factor in each subsequent periodic payment. The latter is a popular issue in Malaysia. It may be an arrangement in which the rental of the assets held by the SPC increases by a constant factor after the first ordinary annuity payment is made. There are four other types of *sukuk* securities that do not share this fixed or constant rate of growth characteristic, which will be described in a later section.

Another characteristic of *sukuk* funding is that when there is only an initial funding and no periodic rewards paid over the entire period of contract, the payoff is intended at the terminal period. Such contracts have different modes of design. Some are designed with a predetermined end-period payment formula, whereas others are designed with the end-period value based on the market value of the SPC assets at the terminal period. An example is a debtor's buyback arrangement at a price, to reduce the risk of the market price being volatile.

The conventional bond design does not permit this level of sophistication because the lender is treated as an outsider to the firm with no ownership of any part of the borrower's assets. To the extent there is ownership in *sukuk* contracting, though only to that portion of income-producing assets in the removed SPC, it is possible that there will be a market value (less or more, depending on the depreciation and replacement value of assets in the SPC). The important point is that the value of the payoffs could be in excess of the original funding to provide a return that is unspecified. Thus the payoff is stochastic (random), depending on the market value of assets in the SPC at a future date, unless a buyback arrangement limits this. That is, for valuation purposes, the final repayment is indeterminate and is not fixed (except in buyback contracting), and this introduces a new element in the valuation of such assets.

Finally, as in all Islamic financing contracts, the projects to which funding is supplied must be consonant with legally permitted, or halal, economic products and services. For example, there are doctrinal restrictions to funding firms engaged in gambling, the production of intoxicants for human consumption, prostitution, or the production of pork for human consumption. *Sukuk* financing will not be extended to such economic activities; this is an ethical principle very dear to most moral societies. Some conventional ethical mutual funds do not hold stocks of companies that produce intoxicants, weapons, or environmental degradation, for instance.

There are few other restrictions, one of which is that funding is made unavailable to firms engaging in usurious interest-based activities. We are not going to delve into other characteristics now but will discuss them in a later chapter. Figure 2.1 provides a comparison of the fundamental principles underlying the contract specifications of *sukuk* funding to conventional debt funding contracts as a summary of discussion to this point.

There are six main differences between Islamic *sukuk* funding arrangements and conventional bond-based or bank-lending arrangements. First, the pricing of the bond is based on how much of the profit share the borrower is willing to give, which, of course, depends on the riskiness of the project to which the fund is applied.

A letter of credit to import $1 million worth of wood product into a country may be less risky than to fund a project to build a toll road. Hence the profit ratio would be lower in the former case (in reality, it is a small fee) and higher in the latter case. In a conventional lending contract, be it a prenegotiated fixed or variable payoff (or fee-based) loan, the payoff

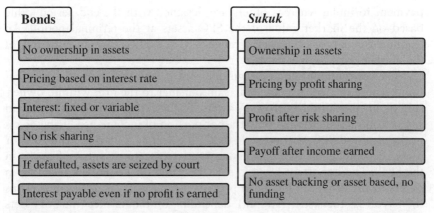

FIGURE 2.1 Fundamental Principles of *Sukuk* Security Compared to Conventional Debt Security

is lower in the former case and higher in the latter case. There is a subtle difference. The fund provider in *sukuk* agrees to take no rewards if in a particular year there is no profit, unless there is proof that the borrower has behaved fraudulently. That means that there is participation in the risk of the project. Even worse, the project may fail out of willful neglect of the entrepreneur, in which case the commercial court would adjudicate how the matter is settled.

These two favorable aspects, profit sharing and risk sharing, may make *sukuk* securities have a higher risk than is the case in prefixing a payoff in lower interest-based securities where there is no ownership of any assets until the project fails.

The second and third ways in which *sukuk* differs from a conventional contract are that a reward is given only if profits are earned, and if the project fails with no proof of willful negligence, the principal is lost to the extent of the market value of the assets in the SPC, which is owned by the fund providers. Having access to ownership of income-producing assets from day one of the contract limits the loss of the entire principal fund. In conventional bond-type lending, the reduction of debt settlement is applied to the entire firm's assets and not just the assets transferred to the SPC. The litigation costs charged by lawyers and accountants are huge in such cases. After almost 10 years, the lenders to the failed WorldCom Corporation have incurred a share of the court award—4 percent of the judgment amount, as reported in August 2013 in the financial press.

Hence, during crises, *sukuk* contracts tend to take away or waste fewer assets than would be the case in conventional funding. The firm could resume normal action with the assets not assigned to the SPC and avoid the expensive litigation costs.

The fourth characteristic is that for a *sukuk* funder, only the assets in the SPC are accessible for sale, not all the firm's assets. This provides a metaphorical halfway house before bankruptcy, whereas under conventional funding, bankruptcy is the only course under civil law in most countries. Even in the case of Chapter 11 protection (in which a firm can apply to continue to operate while all assets are being taken away by lenders), under bankruptcy laws the unavailability of this limited-damage recourse to settle dispute saves assets not transferred to the *sukuk* holders through the SPC.

Hence, at the aggregate level of the economy, there is no need to throw away large amounts of assets each time a crisis or recession occurs, because under *sukuk* contracting part of the loss is borne by the *sukuk* funders, and most assets are under the control of the owner of the firm. The extent to which debt settlement is reduced, known in the market as a *haircut*, is limited.

The fifth characteristic is that *sukuk* provides special structures to match the special needs of the project cash flow. For example, in a working capital *sukuk* (*istisna*), the customer who wants to produce an item over a finite period may provide funds for that period for production of an item by an entrepreneur even before the item is produced; this encourages entrepreneurship. The asset backing in this case is the revealed information about the future existence of the item to be produced as specified by the entrepreneur, who risks his or her labor, and the financier, who risks his or her working capital. But the contract must specify the exact nature of the product so that the future existence of that product could serve with reasonable probability as the value for the purpose of working capital funding.

There are other more exotic designs, such as that the original sum funding a project will be repaid both as profit sharing and as part principal repayment in what is called diminishing *musharakah sukuk* contracts. Complexity of product design is a desirable characteristic in finance, and the specificity of projects means that the firm cannot deploy funds to other than the approved purposes.

Finally, the doctrinal restrictions on the application of the funds to prosocial (i.e., halal) activities constitute the sixth distinguishing feature of Islamic finance in general. As noted earlier, religious doctrine dictates that gambling, prostitution, the production of intoxicants, and the production of pork for human consumption are not permitted. Therefore, no *sukuk* funding will be made available if the intended use of the fund is to produce those items or activities. This aspect introduces an embargo on financing antisocial production, even though an individual may use his or her own money to engage in such activities so that public funding is not made available.

This discussion then introduces a high moral purpose to debt contracting (as well as equity financing). This aspect is meant to starve the growth of antisocial activities by denying investments in prohibited economic activities. If one uses one's own funds to carry out these activities, then it is a different matter of taking personal responsibility for breaking the doctrine relating to prohibited activities. This is not an area for compromise under Islamic doctrine-based fundamental principles.

A brief examination suggests that *sukuk* are not bondlike funding contracts or bank lending based on the following: (1) prefixed or variable interest rates, (2) profit sharing, (3) non-risk-sharing contracting, or (4) a principal guaranteed to be returned at the terminal period. In addition, basic conventional funding is not easy to structure in complex ways because of the lack of an SPC, and there are no provisions under modern debt contracts for restricting antisocial economic activities.

DEFINITIONS AND REGULATIONS

Because *sukuk* is a relatively new product in only 12 markets, there is no consensus on its exact definition. Some international regulatory bodies—such as the Accounting and Auditing Organization for Islamic Financial Institutions (AAOIFI), the International Islamic Financial Market (IIFM), and the Islamic Financial Services Board (IFSB)—have attempted to define *sukuk*.

In 2004 the AAOIFI defined *sukuk* as "certificates of equal value representing, after closing subscription, receipt of the value of the certificates and putting it to use as planned, common title to shares and rights in tangible assets, usufructs and services, or equity of a given project or equity of a special investment activity."

In 2010 the IIFM defined *sukuk* as a "commercial paper that provides an investor with ownership in an underlying asset." It is asset-backed trust certificates evidencing ownership of an asset or its usufruct (earnings or fruits). It has a stable income and complies with the principle of *Shari'ah*. Unlike conventional bonds, *sukuk* needs to have an underlying tangible asset transaction either in ownership or in a master lease agreement.

The IFSB's 2009 definition of *sukuk* is as follows: "*Sukuk* (plural of *sakk*), frequently referred to as 'Islamic bonds,' are certificates with each *sakk* representing a proportional undivided ownership right in tangible assets, or a pool of predominantly tangible assets, or a business venture (such as a *mudarabah*). These assets may be in a specific project or investment activity in accordance with *Shari'ah* rules and principles." This definition of *sukuk* differs from conventional interest-based securities (i.e., bonds) in the following ways:

- The funds raised through the issuance of *sukuk* should be applied to investments in *specified* assets rather than for general unspecified purposes. This implies that identifiable assets should provide the basis for Islamic bonds.
- Since the *sukuk* are backed by the real underlying assets, income generated by the set-aside assets must be related to the purpose for which the funding is used.
- The *sukuk* certificate represents a proportionate ownership right over the set-aside assets in which the funds are being invested. The ownership rights are transferred, for a fixed period ending with the maturity date of the *sukuk*, from the original owner (the originator) to the *sukuk* holders.

Some authorities in Islamic countries, such as the Qatar Financial Center, require the authorized firms to comply with international definitions.[2] Others define *sukuk* in their own way. The Securities Commission of Malaysia, which has issued guidelines on the offering of Islamic securities, defines *sukuk* as "a document or certificate which represents the value of an asset."[3] The Liquidity Management Center in Bahrain defines *sukuk* as "a certificate of equal value representing undivided shares in ownership of tangible assets, usufruct, and services or (in the ownership of) the asset of particular projects or investment activity."[4]

As these definitions suggest, there is no time-limit specification for *sukuk*. In other words, *sukuk* may be issued for long-term financing as well as short-term financing. Short-term *sukuk* with maturities of as short as one month are issued by various issuers; this is akin to conventional bills or papers. One of the earliest issues of short-term *sukuk* was the 30- and 91-day *salam* (futures) *sukuk* issued by the Bahrain Monetary Agency in 2001.[5]

Bank Negara Malaysia, the central bank of Malaysia, also issues one-year short-term *ijarah sukuk*. Since the beginning of 1994, this bank has

---

[2] The Qatar Financial Center, in the *Islamic Finance Rulebook* under section 6.2.2, requires the authorized firm to comply with AAOIFI standards.

[3] Securities Commission of Malaysia, "Guidelines on the Offering of Islamic Securities," www.sc.com.my/main.asp?pageid=448.

[4] Liquidity Management Center, "About *Sukuk*," www.lmcbahrain.com/pdf/about-sukuk.pdf.

[5] In 2006 the Bahrain Monetary Agency was renamed the Central Bank of Bahrain.

introduced the Islamic Interbank Money Market (IIMM) as an intermediary to provide a ready source of short-term investment outlets based on *Shari'ah* principles. Although IIMM works under the concept of *mudarabah* (partnership) financing, the bank did not issue *sukuk* for this specific purpose.

The regulatory authorities in each regime in which *sukuk* are issued have clearly defined the *sukuk* security, and anyone may find these definitions on each regulator's website. In this chapter, we use the international standard-setting bodies' definitions of *sukuk* (cited earlier). The IIFM's definition of "paper" can be extended to any finite-period *sukuk*. The IFSB's definition is highly applicable to financial institutions, and it emphasizes asset transfer and ownership while ignoring trading aspects. These definitions, along with the AAOIFI's definition, identify several common themes: the existence of an SPC, asset ownership, and real assets, as well as usufructs.

CLASSIFICATION BASED ON PRACTICES

There is a tendency in the popular finance press to describe *sukuk* as "Islamic bonds." The reader should be aware by now that this is not an accurate description. First, there is a profit-sharing formula for pricing risk; second, there is ownership in set-aside assets; and third, the funds may lose all or part of the principal or profit if the project fails through no fault of the entrepreneur or when profits did not accrue in a particular payment period. These essential fundamentals are lost if *sukuk* is described as a bond. Thus, *sukuk* cannot be classified as Islamic bonds.

The *Shari'ah* literature has provided references to 14 different *sukuk* instruments, but only 6 are commonly used. These are classified in the literature in different ways. Our aim in this section is to discuss this issue and find a classification that is implicitly based on wider practice.

One popular classification is by reference to the issuer, as is also done with conventional bonds. This gives us the following: (1) risk-free government issues as Treasury *sukuk* (there are a few different ones here); (2) agency *sukuk* issued by an SPC, such as a government railway company; and (3) *sukuk* securities with higher risk than the last ones issued by private firms or institutions (such as the Islamic Development Bank or the World Bank). These private funding arrangements are rated by rating agencies such as Moody's, Standard & Poor's, and RAM of Malaysia.

The agencies give ratings of excellent (AAA to AA) or good (A to BBB) investment grade, both of which are similar to conventional bonds, and poor (BB to B), or not investment grade. Much has been learned from grafting these common rating processes onto *sukuk* securities in the last 15 years. The market accepts this rating process as reasonable for computing similarities and differences, and it has been widely accepted by regulators and *Shari'ah* supervisors.

Yet rating a *sukuk* security based on the existing criteria for the bond market is questionable. *Sukuk* have unique features that are not amenable to bond-type rating. There is good reason to believe that those widespread practices in the rating industry, though largely accepted at this stage of market development, needs to be modified at least for those contracts that do not fit squarely with the prenegotiated interest-based bond securities in which risk is not shared.

Another way *sukuk* have been classified is by market type. Primary issues are initial offers before being listed and traded. These are issued in the primary markets by investment banks after approval by regulatory authorities before being sold to any investors wanting to invest in a *sukuk* issue. Investment banking laws and rules are complied with as considered safe for investors, and the process of formal application may reveal the qualifications of the issuers during the book-building process and needs to be done before the balloting of applications.

Once issued, *sukuk* are traded in secondary markets, which are traded if the primary holders sell their holding in the market, either in stock exchanges or in the over-the-counter markets. Most *sukuk* securities are traded, but there are a few that cannot be traded, such as in Bahrain until 2012. Classification by market type is not meaningful because it does not reveal anything more than the fact that the listing has occurred.

We propose, therefore, to depart from these two classification methods by describing a way of classifying based on the intrinsic nature of the *sukuk* terms as these are marketed in practice. This is summarized in Figure 2.2. The classification is as follows:

- **Class I: *Musharakah sukuk*.** Sharelike securities are with full control either over an infinite period, in which case it is the risk-shared and profit-shared common share, or simply a *musharakah* contract. If the *musharakah* is over a finite period with some form of payoff based on profit sharing and risk sharing, with the payoff of rewards and the principal being repaid at a diminishing rate, then this is a diminishing *musharakah sukuk*.
- **Class II: Discount *sukuk*.** There is no payoff during intermediate periods; the payoff occurs at the end period. If that is less than one year, it is a bill, but if it is more than one year, it is a loan arrangement. There is no servicing of fund providers at regular periods in some of them. The SPC is responsible for providing a regular income that will ensure that

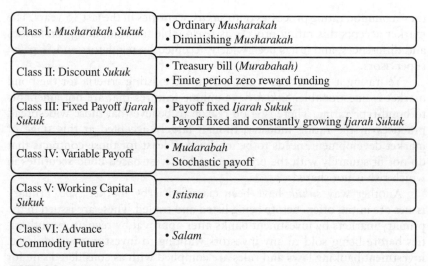

Class I: *Musharakah Sukuk*	• Ordinary *Musharakah* • Diminishing *Musharakah*
Class II: Discount *Sukuk*	• Treasury bill (*Murabahah*) • Finite period zero reward funding
Class III: Fixed Payoff *Ijarah Sukuk*	• Payoff fixed *Ijarah Sukuk* • Payoff fixed and constantly growing *Ijarah Sukuk*
Class IV: Variable Payoff	• *Mudarabah* • Stochastic payoff
Class V: Working Capital *Sukuk*	• *Istisna*
Class VI: Advance Commodity Future	• *Salam*

FIGURE 2.2   Classification Based on Cash Flow Payoff Patterns of *Sukuk* Securities

the end value is higher than the received fund (the principal). Obviously, the sum paid is indeterminate until the end period is reached and a price is discovered in the market for the SPC.

■ **Class III: Fixed and constant-growth payoff *sukuk*.** Under this arrangement, the payoff coming from the SPC is agreed to grow each period, after the first payment, at a constant growth rate. If the profit share is fixed at, for instance, US$100, each subsequent period's payment may increase at the rate of 5 percent. In that case the second payment would be $105, and so on. The SPC may have income far exceeding this amount, but the payoff is fixed at a constant growth rate.

■ **Class IV: Variable payoff *sukuk*.** This is determined by the income of the SPC. A *murabahah* contract, for example, provides for markup and not profit sharing and is appropriate if the bank buys an asset at a price, then sells the item to a borrower at a markup so that the funding is equal to the price plus markup recovered over a certain period. A mortgage-reducing type of payoff is worked out. In the case of a variable payoff, the regular payments are variable but are determinable from the profit ratio at each period of payoff. A contract may have specified profit sharing but not the amount. Since the SPC's profits are variable, the actual payoff at each payoff period will be different, based on some benchmark (the London Inter-Bank Offer Rate, or LIBOR, is used in 25 percent of *sukuk* contracts).

A *mudarabah sukuk* is another example of this type. There could be no reward for funding (such as in a sustenance loan), in which case the proceeds of sale of the SPC assets are used to pay the initial funded amount and the balance, if any is given back to the borrower. More commonly, a payoff is given, in which case the fund provider gets a payoff equal to the principal plus the profit share of the project as agreed.

- **Class V:** *Istisna sukuk.* This is a case of working capital funding in which a fund provider provides capital to manufacture an item. A full description of the item (e.g., a toll road) is known, and the payment is based on installments of the prenegotiated amount. The final payment will be the extra payment to make up the market value of the item manufactured.
- **Class VI:** *Salam sukuk.* In this contract, the item purchased will materialize in a future period but a payment is made now to secure ownership of that item. An example is paying a sum of money now for fruit still on trees that will be delivered as a ripe commodity in six months. This contract is widely used in agricultural and extracting industries.

Short-term securities and long-term securities issued could be the following: (1) equity-based *musharakah* contracts as *musharakah sukuk*, which is a common share–like issue for a finite period; (2) asset-based *sukuk* as *ijarah* or several others; or (3) pure *sukuk*, in which the payoffs are fixed for the term of the funding.

This simple three-way classification (see Figure 2.3) makes for an easy understanding of the six classes. We believe that the last two classifications are based on implicit provisions in *sukuk* instruments as traded in several

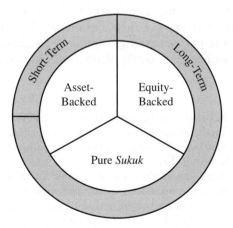

FIGURE 2.3 A Simple Classification of Long-Term and Short-Term *Sukuk* Securities

markets. It is also fruitful to have a simple classification based on the contract term.

In May 2003 the AAOIFI issued *Shari'ah* standard FAS 17 (Financial Accounting Standards No. 17), titled "Investment *Sukuk.*" The AAOIFI issued standards for 14 different types of *sukuk*, some of which are tradable and others are nontradable, based on the type and characteristics of the issued *sukuk*. The *sukuk* mentioned in the standard are *murabahah, istisna, salam, ijarah, mudarabah,* and *musharakah.*[6]

Proper classification of *sukuk* securities, similar to all other securities as well as any ideas or objects, enhances differentiation so that each can be clearly recognized. The current literature provides two types of classification for *sukuk*. The first is based on issuer type and includes sovereign *sukuk* (government or quasi-government) and corporate *sukuk*. The second classification is based on contract form and includes *mudarabah, musharakah, murabahah, ijarah, salam,* and *istisna*. The first two are sometimes considered major or primary modes of Islamic finance because they are based on profit-sharing and risk-sharing contracts—the profit or loss arising from assets financed by the *sukuk* issues is shared by the parties according to a predetermined ratio.

Another possible classification for *sukuk* is based on their financial characteristics, such as pure debt, equity based, asset backed, or discount.[7] Each of the main categories may then, if necessary, be subcategorized to accommodate various types of contracts. To accommodate various types of asset-backed *sukuk* contracts, and based on their intrinsic purpose, three more subcategories have been created: property-backed (semicollateralized) *sukuk*, advance- or deferred-payment *sukuk*, and project-financing *sukuk*. These classifications are summarized in Figure 2.4.

Like conventional firms, Islamic companies require funds to initiate, operate, promote, and expand their businesses. This need is addressed through either internal or external sources. External financing could be obtained by issuing new equity-share certificates (i.e., infinite-period

---

[6] Other types of *sukuk* that have been defined in this AAOIFI standard but are not widely used are *wakalah, muzarah, musaqah, muqarasah, ijarah, mowsufa bithimn, manfaah ijarah, manfaah ijarah mowsufa bithimn,* and *milkiyat al-khadamat*. (These will be defined in the text as they are discussed.)

[7] A *mudarabah* contract implies that one party provides funds to an entity and is entitled to the benefits and profits of the entity, but without any management role. This resembles the process of borrowing and lending, in which the lender does not have any managerial role in the way the funds are used. Hence, the term *pure debt* is used to illustrate this concept.

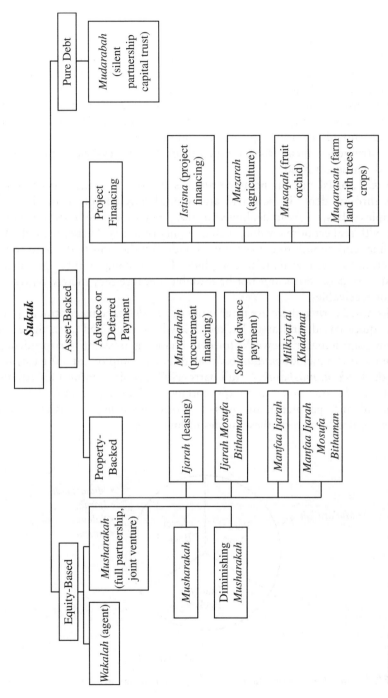

FIGURE 2.4 Classification of *Sukuk* Contracts Based on Their Financial Characteristics

musharakah) as an Islamic financial instrument, in the same way that conventional firms issue common stocks. This can also be achieved by issuing funding certificates (*sukuk*) as an Islamic finite-period "loan" arrangement, but such an instrument, as will be described later, is not the mere equivalent of a conventional bond.

The distinction between Islamic and conventional financing methods lies in the borrowing process, or the debt instruments they use. Islamic methods should not deal in payment or in receiving interest (*riba*), and the debt instrument is meant to share the risk of the business with a promise of reward that is not fixed.

Sukuk, or Islamic financing certificates, are one of many ways to raise funds through debt. These certificates should fully comply with *Shari'ah* principles. Thus, to avoid dealing with *riba*, they should be based on something with real economic value, such as equity or assets. There are modes of debt financing similar to conventional bonds, but they must adhere to some restrictions to become *Shari'ah*-compliant. The most important requirement is that pure-debt certificates not be tradable, because they merely represent debt or receivables.

As noted earlier, there are three types of *sukuk* financing contracts: pure debt, equity based, and asset backed. As will be explained later, there are various contractual frameworks for debt financing in Islamic jurisprudence. These contracts include *mudarabah* (silent partnership or capital trust) for pure-debt *sukuk*; *musharakah* (full partnership or joint venture) for equity-based *sukuk*; and *murabahah* (procurement financing), *ijarah* (leasing), *salam* (advance payment), and *istisna* (project financing) for asset-backed *sukuk*. Figure 2.5 depicts these modes of financing.

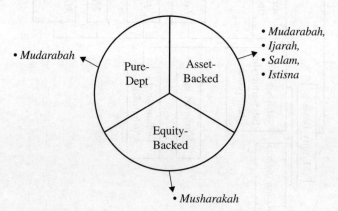

FIGURE 2.5   *Sukuk* Based on Their Underlying Contractual Structure

Mudarabah and *musharakah* are considered the primary modes of Islamic finance because they are based on the profit-sharing and risk-sharing paradigm fully endorsed under *Shari'ah*. In this paradigm, the outcome of investment (the actual amount of profit or loss) is completely based on the performance of the investment project and is not predetermined. The only predetermined factors are the duration of investment and the ownership or distribution ratio of each party in the profit or loss of the project.

In contrast to the primary modes of financing, in the secondary modes the outcome of investment for the investors is to some extent predetermined and is not fully tied to the performance of the investment project. For instance, in an *ijarah* contract, the investor will benefit from a predetermined rental fee for a certain period. However, for the secondary modes of finance to be *Shari'ah* compliant, the principal investment should not be guaranteed by the issuer.

CONCLUSION

Sukuk securities have been designed as Islamic financial instruments for funding the needs of producer firms, so we are dealing with funding production, not consumption, loans. These instruments are now offered and traded in 12 *sukuk* securities markets. These are mostly finite-period debt instruments designed for the specific funding needs of a producer firm and adhere to Islamic ethical principles. *Sukuk* securities can be differentiated from common bonds in a number of ways. The most important differences are risk and-profit sharing, asset backing, and symmetric information sharing.

CHAPTER 3

Pragmatic and Idealistic Approaches to Structuring *Sukuk*[*]

S*ukuk* are Islamic securities that are often translated as "Islamic bonds." However, that translation does not entirely cover the substance of *sukuk*. A closer look at *sukuk* shows that it has elements that might resemble both shares and bonds, depending on the applicable underlying Islamic financial contract terms and structures. In this chapter we will outline the background of *sukuk* to provide a better understanding of it as an Islamic financial instrument.

This chapter aims to illustrate the discrepancies in the idealistic approach toward *sukuk* structures. That is, how this financial product should ideally be structured from a *Shari'ah* participatory perspective is compared to the pragmatic approach that has been adopted at this early stage of the product's market development in 2014.

In order to place *sukuk* in context, some relevant concepts associated with *Shari'ah* will be briefly mentioned. These include key sources of *Shari'ah* as well as the concepts of *ijtihad*, *riba*, and *gharar* (defined later). In the following historical overview of *sukuk*, we provide particular focus on the origins of the word *sukuk*, its use in medieval times, and the recent history of *sukuk*, which are known today as new financial instruments in financial and capital markets. Finally, the development of several forms of *sukuk* will be described, and a number of structures and mechanisms will be explained that have been developed in practice over the years, highlighting

---

[*] This chapter was previously published in Mohamed Ariff, Munawar Iqbal, and Shamsher Mohamad, eds., Sukuk *Islamic Debt Securities: Theory, Practice, and Issues* (Cheltenham, UK: Edward Elgar, 2012). Permission of the copyright holder and the authors (Abdullah Saeed and Omar Saleh) has been obtained to reproduce this chapter in this book.

the tension between the idealistic and pragmatic approaches toward *sukuk* structures today.

SHARI'AH: THE BASIC FOUNDATIONS OF ISLAMIC FINANCE AND *SUKUK*

The raison d'être of *sukuk* lies in the *Shari'ah*. *Shari'ah* literary means "the way," and it is generally understood to be the body of Islamic religious law. Islamic law, in the context of Islamic finance, does not refer to a specific law of a particular jurisdiction. Instead, what is meant is a set of religious and moral principles, concepts, and rules as developed throughout Islamic history, based largely on the Quran and the *Sunnah*. *Fiqh* (Islamic jurisprudence) is the knowledge of the practical regulations and rules of *Shari'ah* acquired by detailed study of the sources.[1] Banking and financial activities form part of the economic activities that make up one area of *fiqh* called *fiqh al-mu'amalat*.

Sources of *Shari'ah*

In accordance with the classical theory of Islamic jurisprudence, there are two primary sources of Islamic law and a range of secondary sources. The primary source is the Quran, the holy scripture of Islam that Muslims believe was revealed to the Prophet Muhammad by the angel Gabriel. About 80 verses of the Quran refer to strictly legal matters, although it is unclear whether the legal injunctions in these verses are obligatory or permissible.[2] After the Quran, the second most important source is the *Sunnah* (an account of the normative behavior of the Prophet, as documented in the *hadith*, the record of his words and deeds). The secondary sources include *ijma'* (the consensus of the scholars), and *qiyas* (reasoning by analogy).

Ijtihad (defined next) is often referred to as a secondary source of Islamic jurisprudence. However, *ijtihad* is not strictly a source of law; rather, it is a method by which an individual interprets the legal meaning of the texts and rules of the Quran and the *Sunnah*. Although each individual has the freedom to propose interpretations of texts and rules, it is only when these

---

[1] S. H. Nasr, *The Heart of Islam: Enduring Values for Humanity* (New York: HarperOne 2002), 123.

[2] D. Pearl, *A Textbook on Muslim Law* (London: Croom Helm, 1979), 1.

interpretations are supported by a subsequent *ijma'*, or scholarly consensus, that they attain the necessary authority in Islamic law.

Sukuk are not referred to in the Quran or in the *Sunnah*. The ideas that have been developed in relation to *sukuk*, how they are to be structured and used, are the result of *ijtihad*.

Ijtihad

Given the importance of *ijtihad* for any exploration of *sukuk*, a deeper discussion of the concept is warranted.

The Classical View of Ijtihad

Ijtihad is the mechanism and the process by which the law revealed in the Quran and the *Sunnah* may be interpreted, developed, and kept alive in line with the intellectual, political, economic, legal, technological, and moral developments of society as it develops over time. Since the rules and instructions provided in the Quran and the *Sunnah* are limited in number, and Muslims face new situations and problems at all times and in all places, the revealed law may not always be able to provide specific answers. This ultimately determines the necessity for *ijtihad* and makes it an essential instrument in the development of Islamic law.

It may be argued that ideas about *sukuk* developed in such a context. The need for funding through the capital markets required an Islamic alternative to conventional bonds. Through the exercise of *ijtihad*, contemporary scholars, consulting with bankers and lawyers, developed *sukuk* as a *Shari'ah*-compliant (some would say still not consistent) alternative to conventional bonds.

Ijtihad began as an extremely flexible institution among the first two or three generations of Muslims. It gradually became more rigid with the development and writing down of *Shari'ah*—the *hadith*, exegesis, law, theology, history, and *usul al-fiqh* (principles of jurisprudence). In particular, the success of Imam Shafi'i (the Prophet Muhammad's cousin) in formulating and propagating his *usul* and the further development of this *usul* by later scholars led to a gradual decline in the flexibility available to scholars of all persuasions.

The early lack of formalism in the first century of Islam (beginning in 622 CE with the *hijra*, the flight of the Prophet from Mecca to Medina) thus gave way to a more systematic, formal, and rule-governed method. By the fourth century AH (*anno hijra*, the designation for the Islamic calendar), *usul al-fiqh* methodology was well-established in Islamic legal scholarship, and by the end of the sixth century it had reached its zenith in the works of eminent scholars such as al-Juwayni (d. 478 AH, or 1085 CE) and al-Ghazali

(d. 505 AH, or 1111 CE). In the following centuries, serious attempts to question major aspects of *usul* were made only in rare cases.[3]

Ijtihad in the Modern Period

Until the modern period, *ijtihad* remained a formalistic, legalistic, and literalistic practice. In the 19th and 20th centuries CE, faced with Western concepts such as rationalism, historical criticism, development, nationalism, and human rights, many Muslims, with varying degrees of skill in Islamic scholarship, began to question the suitability of the existing methods of *ijtihad*. This newfound awareness and critical attitude is now widespread throughout the Islamic world. Considerable diversity exists, and it would be foolish to claim that the concerns and perspectives of Muslim scholars throughout the world are all the same. Local circumstances have a strong influence; internal and external threats, demographics, levels of development, contact with different cultures, and educational opportunities all vary. Scholars differ in their perceptions of the social, economic, political, and legal problems facing their respective communities.

Today, three different forms of *ijtihad* can be identified. The first is text-based *ijtihad*. This was generally recognized in the classical period and is still practiced in traditional Islamic legal scholarship. It is based on the foundational texts as well as on *ijma'* and *qiyas* and relies on the rules and principles of *usul al-fiqh*. Each new legal problem is viewed largely in isolation and does not have to be considered as an element of a whole system. When a new problem emerges, the scholar identifies relevant texts of *Shari'ah* and attempts to apply the rules of *usul al-fiqh*. The new problem is then linked to an earlier ruling or a text, and a decision is made about its *Shari'ah*-compliance. The text could be a verse of the Quran, a *hadith*, or the view of an imam. Literal reading of texts, strict application of the rules of *usul*, and heavy emphasis on conformity and traditionalism are the hallmarks of this form of *ijtihad*.

The second form is eclectic *ijtihad*. A scholar faces a problem or an issue and must decide whether it is acceptable from an Islamic perspective.

---

[3] Notable exceptions are the attempts of 'Izz b. Abd al-Salam (d. 660 AH, or 1261 CE) and Shatibi (d. 790 AH, or 1388 CE) to understand the problem of *ijtihad* from an objective perspective without antagonizing the agreed-upon principles of *usul*. The Hanbali jurist Najm al-Din al-Tufi (d. 716 AH, or 1316 CE) is another exception. He went beyond any other jurist and declared that it is the public interest that should determine what is Islamic and what is not. Contrary to the generally accepted view, he argued that the public interest could override even a clear text of the Quran or the *Sunnah* in cases other than worship.

The scholar is already convinced of the *Shari'ah* compliance of the issue and attempts to justify his or her position by selecting texts such as verses, a *hadith*, or views of imams that support the scholar's preconceived position. Such a method is ad hoc and opportunistic and does not systematically follow principles or rules. No consideration is often given to *usul al-fiqh* methodology, and the scholar often ignores possible textual or historical evidences to the contrary. This is the most hazardous and problematic approach of all in terms of intellectual honesty—hazardous because it has no clear boundaries, signposts, or methods that can be conceptualized and followed. A number of examples of eclectic *ijtihad* are found in the emerging areas of Islamic economics, banking, and finance.

The third form is context-based *ijtihad*. Although it existed in an undeveloped form in early Islam, context-based *ijtihad* should be seen as a relatively new phenomenon. It is distinguished by the fact that it attempts to understand a problem in both its historical and its modern contexts. If a problem emerges for which an Islamic view is needed, the scholar first looks carefully at the problem, identifying its features, purpose, and function or role in today's society. If it is found that a related or similar problem existed in the time of the Prophet, the scholar will examine the historical problem as precedent for the modern one.

In this the scholar is often guided by the concept of *maslahah* (public interest or common good). The scholar is less concerned with the outward form of the problem, historical or modern. More emphasis is placed on the underlying objectives of *Shari'ah* in relation to the problem, such as fairness, justice, and equity. A decision will then be made about the attitude Muslims should adopt vis-à-vis the problem in today's environment. In context-based *ijtihad,* the scholar is not interested in specific *ijma'* formed in the classical period or in certain *usul*-based tools like *qiyas* but mainly conducts what a contextual analysis of both the modern situation and the classical period.

ISLAMIC FINANCIAL PRINCIPLES

Islamic law, in principle, recognizes contractual freedom. All contracts and contractual provisions are allowed unless explicitly prohibited in the foundation texts. The obvious and crucial questions, then, are what these explicit prohibitions are and how they pertain to financial transactions. The foundation texts identify two explicit prohibitions: (1) receiving and paying *riba* (interest or usury) and (2) *gharar* (uncertainty), to the extent possible.

Riba

Riba is often divided into three different forms: the *riba al-jahiliyya*, *riba al-fadl*, and *riba al-nasi'a*.[4] *Riba al-jahiliyya* is prohibited directly in the Quran, whereas *riba al-fadl* and *riba al-nasi'a* are prohibited in the *Sunnah*. *Riba al-jahiliyya* refers to the *riba* of the pre-Islamic period.[5] According to the practice in pre-Islamic Arabia, interest was charged at the maturity of debts from interest-free loans or credit sales and compounded at later maturity dates.[6] This form of *riba* has been prohibited in the Quran.[7] The Quran also mentions that Muslims should abandon all remaining *riba*.[8] One of the most discussed verses on the prohibition of *riba* in the Quran permits trade but prohibits *riba*:

> *Those who devour [riba] will not stand except as stand one whom the Evil one by his touch Hath driven to madness. That is because they say: "Trade is like [riba]," but Allah hath permitted trade and forbidden [riba]. Those who, after receiving direction from their Lord, desist shall be pardoned for the past; their case is for Allah (to judge); but those who repeat (the offense) are companions of the Fire: They will abide therein (forever).* [9]

The prohibitions of *riba al-fadl* and *riba al-nasi'a* (defined later) originate from the *Sunnah*.[10] There are several *hadith* that prohibit both, but the most quoted one is as follows:

> *[Ubada b. al-Samit] ([may] Allah be pleased with him) reported Allah's Messenger (may peace be upon him) as saying: Gold is to be*

---

[4] N. A. Saleh, *Unlawful Gain and Legitimate Profit in Islamic Law: Riba, Gharar, and Islamic Banking* (Cambridge, UK: Cambridge University Press, 1986), 13–14; M. A. El-Gamal, *Islamic Finance: Law, Economics, and Practice* (Cambridge, UK: Cambridge University Press, 2006), 49–50.

[5] Ibn Rushd, *The Distinguished Jurist's Primer*, vol. II: *Bidayat al-Mujtahid wa Nihayat al-Muqtasid*, trans. I. A. K. Nyazee (Reading, UK: Garnet, 1996), 158; Saleh, *Unlawful Gain*, 13–14; El-Gamal, *Islamic Finance*, 49–50.

[6] Ibn Rushd, *Distinguished Jurist's Primer*, 2:158; Saleh, *Unlawful Gain*, 13–14; El-Gamal, *Islamic Finance*, 49–50.

[7] Quran 3:130.

[8] Ibid., 2:275–279.

[9] Ibid., 2:275. The translation I have used is by Yusufali, University of Southern California's Center for Muslim-Jewish Engagement, www.usc.edu/schools/college/crcc/engagement/resources/texts/muslim/quran/002.qmt.html.

[10] Ibn Rushd, *Distinguished Jurist's Primer*, 2:158; Saleh, *Unlawful Gain*, 13.

paid for by gold, silver by silver, wheat by wheat, barley by barley, dates by dates, and salt by salt, like for like and equal for equal, payment being made hand to hand. If these classes differ, then sell as you wish if payment is made hand to hand. [11]

It appears from this *hadith* that the essence of *riba* does not concern interest on loans, but only sales—that is, delay or excess in exchange of certain types of property such as currency and foodstuffs. The phrase "equal for equal" in this *hadith* establishes that certain goods of a single type can be exchanged only in equal amounts.[12] This is *riba al-fadl*. The phrase "hand to hand" refers to *riba al-nasi'a*, in which the exchange of certain goods may take place only in the present as instant barter.[13]

Based on an explication of *riba al-jahiliyya*, *riba al-fadl*, and *riba al-nasi'a*, many contemporary Muslim scholars have argued that all forms of interest are forbidden as *riba*.

Under *Shari'ah*, granting a loan is considered an act of charity.[14] If that is the case, it would be improper to make a profit on a loan by charging the borrower interest. This does not mean that making a profit itself is forbidden in Islam—quite the reverse. Islamic law encourages the circulation of wealth, investment, and profit.[15]

But profit must be made through trade and similar activities. A return on investment is justified only when the investor takes a commercial risk (i.e., shares in the risk of a venture before a return is sought). Lending money does not qualify as a commercial risk because the risk of nonrepayment (e.g., poor debtor creditworthiness) is deemed insufficient to warrant charging interest.[16] Profitability requires taking a real commercial risk.

---

[11] *Sahih Muslim*, book 10, no. 3853, University of Southern California's Center for Muslim-Jewish Engagement, www.usc.edu/schools/college/crcc/engagement/resources/texts/muslim/hadith/muslim/010.semt.html.

[12] Ibn Rushd, *Distinguished Jurist's Primer*, 2:158; Saleh, *Unlawful Gain*, 13; A. Saeed, *Islamic Banking and Interest: A Study of the Prohibition of Riba and Its Contemporary Interpretation* (Leiden, Netherlands: E. J. Brill 1996), 32.

[13] Ibn Rushd, *Distinguished Jurist's Primer*, 2:158; Saleh, *Unlawful Gain*, 13; Saeed, *Islamic Banking*, 32.

[14] U. F. Moghul and A. A. Ahmed, "Contractual Forms in Islamic Finance Law and *Islamic Investment Company of the Gulf (Bahamas) Ltd. v. Symphony Gems N.V. & Others*: A First Impression of Islamic Finance," *Fordham International Law Journal* 27, no. 1 (2003): 168.

[15] Quran 4:29, 2:275.

[16] A. Hanif, "Islamic Finance: An Overview," *International Energy Law Review* 1, (2008): 10.

Given the *riba* ban, the concept of sharing profit and loss is extremely important in Islamic finance.[17] Financiers generally do not receive interest on the funds they provide but instead participate in the project to the extent that they share in any profits or losses.[18] So unlike interest payments, charges for funding-based project participation can be justified, provided that the project yields a profit. Hence, Islamic debt instruments provide for profit-shared and risk-shared funding activities.

But the *riba* ban reaches much further. *Shari'ah*-compliant transactions preclude making money with money. Money itself may not be a source of profit because, many scholars of Islamic economics argue, money has no intrinsic value in Islam.[19] The ultimate purpose of money, from their point of view, is to help fulfill basic needs, such as food, clothing, and shelter. In this approach money must be seen (and used) as a means of exchange only, not as a basic need in itself.[20]

This position is at the heart of the *bay' al-dayn* doctrine (trade in debt claims).[21] Most *Shari'ah* scholars agree that the *riba* ban extends to this trade because trading in debt claims is similar to the forbidden use of money as a source of profit.[22] *Sukuk* must therefore be backed by tangible assets.

---

[17] D. Olson and T. A. Zoubi, "Using Accounting Ratios to Distinguish between Islamic and Conventional Banks in the GCC Region," *International Journal of Accounting* (2008): 47.

[18] This element is particularly noticeable in Islamic financial contracts, such as the *musharakah* and the *mudarabah*. For an account of Islamic financial contracts, see M. T. Usmani, *An Introduction to Islamic Finance* (The Hague, Netherlands: Kluwer Law International, 2002); El-Gamal, *Islamic Finance*; M. Ayub, *Understanding Islamic Finance* (Hoboken, NJ: John Wiley & Sons, 2008); and H. S. F. A. Jabbar, "Sharia-Compliant Financial Instruments: Principles and Practice," *Company Lawyer* 6 (2009): 176–88.

[19] This is not the same as denying the time value of money. On this distinction, see M. A. El-Gamal, *A Basic Guide to Contemporary Islamic Banking and Finance* (Plainfield, IN: Islamic Society of North America, 2000).

[20] Several *hadith* attest to this. On the interpretation of these *hadith*, see El-Gamal, *A Basic Guide*; H. S. F.A. Jabbar, "Islamic Finance: Fundamental Principles and Key Financial Institutions," *Company Lawyer* 1 (2009): 23–32.

[21] M. T. Usmani, "Principles of Shariah Governing Islamic Investment Funds," *Albalagh* www.albalagh.net/Islamic_economics/finance.shtml.

[22] Malaysia, which allows debt claims to be traded, is an exception. See A. H. Ismail, "A Malaysian View of Sharia," *American Journal of Islamic Finance*; A. Thomas, "Malaysia's Importance to the Sukuk Market," *American Journal of Islamic Finance* (March 2007); N. J. Adam and A. Thomas, *Islamic Bonds: Your Guide to Issuing, Structuring, and Investing in* Sukuk (London: Euromoney Books, 2004), 48–50; Securities Commission of Malaysia (SCM), *Resolutions of the Securities Commission Shariah Advisory Council*, 2nd ed. (Kuala Lumpur: SCM, 2006), 19.

Typically (and unlike in conventional forms of funding), *sukuk* certificate holders should have a claim to one or more tangible assets. These certificates can be traded on the international capital markets because their holders are entitled to the underlying tangible assets, and it is not only debt claims that are traded.

Although the equation of *riba* with interest has become common-place among Muslims, there are a significant number of scholars who do not believe that this equation is accurate. One such scholar, Mohammad Omar Farooq, notes that there are a number of problems with the orthodox understanding of *riba* as interest. He emphasizes the following points.

It is a misunderstanding that the prohibition on *riba* as interest is derived directly from the Quran.[23] There is no support from the foundational texts (the Quran and the *hadith*) for the notion that any conditions of an initial contract or agreement, including any stipulated excess over the principal, are covered by the Quran's prohibition of *riba*.[24]

Nor is there *ijma'*, or scholarly consensus, that *riba* equals interest, even though that view is widely held.[25] The prohibition on *riba*, specifically pre-Islamic *riba* (*riba al-jahiliyya*), in the Quran (2:275) is primary, referring to loans—presumably a particular type of loan that existed in pre-Islamic times.[26] Thus, the *hadith* concerning *riba* in the context of trade or credit sales cannot legitimately be used to broaden the scope of the prohibition on pre-Islamic *riba*.[27]

Moreover, the discussion of *riba* and loans in the Quran occurs in connection with transactions or contracts characterized by *zulm* (injustice and exploitation), with the broader context of the verse discussing spending and *sadaqa* (charity).[28] Thus, Farooq argues, it is a certain type of *riba*—one that renders a debtor financially vulnerable to poverty or need—that is specifically prohibited.[29] Although this view has been supported by several scholars from a wide range of perspectives, it is not accepted in Islamic finance as a whole.[30]

---

[23] M. O. Farooq, "Toward Defining and Understanding Riba: An Outline Essay," *Global Webpost*, 2007, www.globalwebpost.com/farooqm/writings/islamic/intro_riba.doc.

[24] Farooq 2007, p. 14.

[25] Ibid., p. 9.

[26] Ibid., p. 7.

[27] Ibid., p. 8.

[28] Ibid., p. 7–8.

[29] Ibid., p. 15.

[30] Some of the scholars who support this view are Muhammad Abduh, Rashid Rida, Abd al-Razzaq Sanshuri, Doualibi, Muhammad Asad, and Fazlur Rahman.

Gharar

The second ban in *Shari'ah* in relation to Islamic finance is that of *gharar*, or excessive uncertainty and risk. In contracts, *gharar* must be avoided as much as possible.[31]*Shari'ah* recognizes that ruling out uncertainty in financial transactions altogether is unrealistic.[32] For that reason, the *gharar* ban primarily concerns essential elements of contracts, such as price, deliverability, quality, and quantity.[33] That is, the essentials of a contract may not remain unspecified.

The *gharar* prohibition is also somewhat related to the Quran's ban on *qimar*.[34]*Qimar* pertains to yields that depend solely on luck or chance, such as gambling.[35] Many Islamic economists would argue that excessive speculation and gambling are prohibited because the profits achieved through them cannot be justified.[36] Yet ordinary entrepreneurial risks are not included in this ban. Conventional derivatives contracts are considered in this context to contain elements that are akin to speculation.[37]

THREE APPROACHES TO ISLAMIC FINANCE

The idealistic vision of Islamic banking and finance that existed in the literature before 1970 has changed significantly in practice. The 1950s and 1960s saw the development of models of Islamic banking and finance that adhered closely to ideas developed by the classical jurists. However, the reality of operating in contemporary financial markets, in a context very different from the classical period, has challenged modern scholars to reconsider these conceptions. Although the ideal models still exist, other more pragmatic approaches have been developed.

Overall, three approaches to Islamic banking and finance have emerged that can be placed on a continuum: from idealistic to pragmatic to liberal.

---

[31] Quran 2:90–91.

[32] M. Fadeel, "Legal Aspects of Islamic Finance," in *Islamic Finance: Innovation and Growth*, ed. S. Archer and R. A. A. Karim (London: Euromoney Books and AAOIFI, 2002), 91; (IOSCO), *Islamic Capital Market Fact-Finding Report* (Kuala Lumpur, Malaysia: Islamic Capital Market Task Force, 2004), 8.

[33] S. Archer and R. A. A. Karim, "Introduction to Islamic Finance," in *Islamic Finance: Innovation and Growth*, (London: Euromoney Books and AAOIFI, 2002), 3; IOSCO, *Islamic Capital Market*, 8.

[34] Quran 2:219, 5:90.

[35] Ayub, *Understanding Islamic Finance*, 112.

[36] IOSCO, *Islamic Capital Market*, 8.

[37] Hanif, *Islamic Finance*, 10.

The idealistic approach seeks to maintain the original vision of Islamic banking in the 1950s and 1960s and to remain faithful, as much as possible, to the instruments and contracts developed in classical *fiqh*.

At the opposite end of the continuum is the liberal approach, consisting of Muslim scholars who argue that interest is not inherently evil and that *riba* does not include modern bank interest. This approach even makes the case that there is no need for Islamic banks and financial products at all.

Between these two extremes lies the pragmatic approach. This is realistic enough to see that idealistic models of Islamic banking have significant problems in terms of practicality and feasibility, but at the same time it maintains the interpretation of *riba* as interest.

It is possible to argue that the majority of Islamic bankers can be classified as pragmatists, prepared to balance practical realities with traditional Islamic principles. These bankers and their *Shari'ah* advisors have opted for a more pragmatic form of Islamic banking, interpreting relevant texts using an eclectic approach to the sources of Islamic law and principles of Islamic jurisprudence. Here the practical and feasible is given priority over the idealistic and impractical, even though this has led to a somewhat questionable outcome in terms of moving toward a so-called Islamic banking and finance system.

The use of eclectic *ijtihad* in a pragmatic approach is discussed later in regard to *sukuk* structures, and this pragmatic approach is contrasted to the idealistic approach.

THE HISTORY OF *SUKUK*

The Arabic word *sukuk* is the plural of the word *sakk*, meaning "certificate" or "order of payment."[38] Documentary evidence confirms the use of the word *sakk* in the early Islamic caliphates.[39] The Muslim societies of the premodern period used *sukuk* as papers that represented financial obligations originating from trade and other commercial activities.[40] In the earlier theoretical legal works, written instruments of credit were present. Such written instruments are encountered frequently in *genizah*

---

[38] M. A. Khan, *Islamic Economics and Finance: A Glossary* (London: Routledge, 2003), 163; S. Cakir and F. Raei, *Sukuk vs. Eurobonds: Is There a Difference in Value-at-Risk?* (Washington, DC: International Monetary Fund, 2007), 3.

[39] Adam and Thomas, *Islamic Bonds*, 43.

[40] N. J. Adam and A. Thomas, "Islamic Fixed-Income Securities: *Sukuk*," in *Islamic Asset Management: Forming the Future for Shari'a-Compliant Investment Strategies*, ed. S. Jaffar (London: Euromoney Books, 2004), 73; A. Thomas, "What Are *Sukuk*?", *American Journal of Islamic Finance*, vol. 2; Khan, *Islamic Economics*, 163.

documents.[41] A *genizah* is a storage place in mosques and synagogues for documents that may not be put in the garbage because they have God's name written on them.

Documents in the Cairo Genizah contain fragments that indicate the existence of the *sakk* in the 12th century CE, and this money order was remarkably similar in form to a modern check.[42] It stated the sum to be paid, the name of the payee, the date, and the name of the issuer.[43]

During the Middle Ages, a *sakk* was a written vow to pay for goods when they were delivered, and it was used to avoid having to transport money across dangerous terrain.[44] As a result, these *sukuk* were transported across several countries and spread throughout the world.

Jewish merchants from the Muslim world transmitted the concept and the term *sakk* to Europe.[45] The outcome of the trade and transport of these *sukuk* is that they were a source of inspiration for the modern-day check, which has a British background.[46] Yet the modern

---

[41] A. L. Udovitch, "Bankers without Banks: Commerce, Banking, and Society in the Islamic World of the Middle Ages," in *The Dawn of Modern Banking*, ed. UCLA Center for Medieval and Renaissance Studies (New Haven, CT: Yale University Press, 1979), 268–74.

[42] A. Z. J. ben Josef, "Cheques," document T-S Ar. 30.184, Taylor Schechter Collection, Cambridge University Library, www.lib.cam.ac.uk/Taylor-Schechter/exhibition.html.

[43] Ibid. Some sources even suggest that the ancient Romans used an early form of check known as *praescriptiones* in the first century BCE. During the third century CE, banks in Persia and its territories also issued a letter of credit known as a *sakk*. Hence, it is believed that the Arabic word *sakk* comes from the Persian language. However, the first evidence of *sakk* dates from the Middle Ages. StateMaster, "Cheque," *Encyclopedia*, www.statemaster.com/encyclopedia/Cheque#_note-Vallely; A. Markels, "The Glory That Was Baghdad," *U.S. News*, April 7, 2008, www.usnews.com/articles/news/religion/2008/04/07/the-glory-that-was-baghdad .html; M. Wright, "Just Write Me a 'Sakk'," *Sunday Mirror*, February 22, 2009, www .mirror.co.uk/sunday-mirror/2009/02/22/just-write-me-a-sakk-115875--21142872/.

[44] P. Vallely, "How Islamic Inventors Changed the World," *Independent*, March 11, 2006, www.independent.co.uk/news/science/how-islamic-inventors-changed-the-world-469452.html.

[45] F. Braudel, *The Mediterranean and the Mediterranean World in the Age of Philip II*, vol. 2 (New York: William Collins Sons, 1973), 817.

[46] English banks started using checks in the 17th or 18th century in order to counteract the issuance monopoly of the Bank of England. P. de Vroede, *De cheque: De postcheque en de reischeque* (Antwerp, Belgium: Kluwer 1981), 3; J. A. F. Geisweit van der Netten, *De cheque* (Utrecht, Netherlands: Utrechtsche Stoomdrukkerij, 1892), 5; H. Cabrillac, *Le chèque et le virement*, nr. 2; J. van Ryn and J. Heenen, *Principes de droit commercial*, nr. 2976.

English word *check* appears to have been derived from the Arabic word *sakk*.[47]

Today, *sukuk* are known as instruments of the Islamic capital markets. In modern-day Islamic finance, *sukuk* refer to Islamic securities with rather distinctive features. One of the very first definitions of modern-day *sukuk* was given in February 1988 during the fourth session of the Council of the Islamic Fiqh Academy in Jeddah, Saudi Arabia. Resolution No. 30 of the council dealt with investment certificates and, more specifically, with *mudarabah* (partnership) *sukuk*.

The council defined these *sukuk* as "investment instruments which allocate the [*mudarabah*] capital by floating certificates, as an evidence of capital ownership, on the basis of shares of equal value, registered in the name of the owner, as joint owners of shares in the venture capital or whatever shape it may take, in proportion to . . . each one's share therein."[48]

This is arguably the first description of *sukuk* in present times. Shortly after this description, in 1990 one of the first *sukuk* was issued by Shell MDS in Malaysia.[49] After this, there were no more active issuances by other *sukuk* issuers until the beginning of the 21st century.[50] In 2000, a number of institutions started issuing *sukuk*, and the *sukuk* market took off from there.[51]

The immense growth of the market required certainty in regard to *Shari'ah*-related matters and standardization. Hence, the AAOIFI issued its *Shari'ah* standard number 17 on investment *sukuk* in May 2003, which

---

[47] G. W. Heck, *Charlemagne, Muhammad, and the Arab Roots of Capitalism* (Berlin: Walter de Gruyter, 2006), 217–218; Udovitch, "Bankers without Banks," 268–74; A. L. Udovitch, "Trade," in *The Dictionary of the Middle Ages*, ed. J. R. Strayer, vol. 12 (New York: Charles Scribner's Sons, 1989), 105–108; "1001 Inventions: Discover the Muslim Heritage in Our World," a British-based educational project and exhibition exploring the Muslim contributions to building the foundations of modern civilizsation, www.1001inventions.com; Vallely, "How Islamic Inventors Changed the World."

[48] International Islamic Fiqh Academy, *Resolutions and Recommendations of the Council of the Islamic Fiqh Academy, 1985–2000* (Jeddah, Saudi Arabia: Islamic Development Bank, 2000), 61–62.

[49] A. W. Dusuki, "Challenges of Realizing *Maqasid al-Shari'ah* (Objectives of Shari'ah) in the Islamic Capital Market: Special Focus on Equity-Based Sukuk," paper presented at the International Islamic Management Conference on the Islamic Capital Market, Penang, Malaysia, October 2009.

[50] Ibid.

[51] R. Haneef, "From 'Asset-Backed' to 'Asset-Light' Structures: The Intricate History of *Sukuk*," *International Journal of Islamic Finance* 1, no. 1 (2009): 103–126; Dusuki, "Challenges," 8–9.

became effective on January 1, 2004. This standard defines investment *sukuk* as "certificates of equal value representing undivided shares in ownership of tangible assets, usufruct, and services or (in the ownership of) the assets of particular projects or special investment activity."[52]

The AAOIFI standard on *sukuk* describes 14 different *sukuk* structures of Islamic financial contracts, such as *musharakah*, *mudarabah*, *ijarah*, and *murabahah*. In the first decade of the 21st century the market witnessed several *sukuk* issuances in different forms and structures. In 2007, the *sukuk* market reached its peak in terms of issuance volume.[53] The AAOIFI standard number 17 also provides specific rules to safeguard the *Shari'ah*-compliance of each *sukuk* structure.

SUKUK STRUCTURES: PRAGMATIC AND IDEALISTIC APPROACHES

In light of the prohibition of *riba* under *Shari'ah*, trading in pure debt instruments is forbidden. Hence, *sukuk* are structured to generate the same economic effects as conventional bonds, but in a *Shari'ah*-compliant manner.[54] Each *sakk* represents an undivided interest in an asset.[55] *Sukuk* reflect participation in the underlying tangible assets, so what is being traded is not merely a debt.[56] *Sukuk* are entitlements to rights in certain assets inclusive of some degree of ownership.[57] For a *sukuk* structure to comply with *Shari'ah*,

---

[52] Accounting and Auditing Organization for Islamic Financial Institutions, Bhahrain, Bahrain.

[53] The prevailing *sukuk* structures in 2007 were the equity-based ones. S. Mokhtar, "A Synthesis of *Shari'ah* Issues and Market Challenges in the Application of *Wa'd* in Equity-Based *Sukuk*," *International Journal of Islamic Finance* 1, no. 1 (2009):139–145; Dusuki, "Challenges," 8–10. In 2008 the *ijarah sukuk* started to dominate the *sukuk* market because of a drop in equity-based *sukuk* structures resulting from a resolution issued by the AAOIFI that year. O. Salah, "Islamic Finance: The Impact of the AAOIFI Resolution on Equity-Based *Sukuk* Structures," *Law and Financial Markets Review* 4, no. 5 (September 2010):507–517.

[54] M. Ainley, A. Mashayekhi, R. Hicks, A. Rahman, and A. Ravalia, *Islamic Finance in the UK: Regulation and Challenges* (London: Financial Services Authority, 2007), p. 24.

[55] Adam and Thomas, *Islamic Bonds*, 42.

[56] Z. Iqbal and A. Mirakhor, *An Introduction to Islamic Finance: Theory and Practice* (Singapore: John Wiley & Sons, 2006), 177; L. Saqqaf, "Middle East Debt: The New *Sukuk*; Innovative Structures Are Changing the Face of Islamic Bonds," *International Finance Law Review* 10, (2006), 19.

[57] Allen & Overy, "Allen & Overy Advises on Islamic First," press release, August 12, 2003.

the underlying assets must themselves also comply with *Shari'ah*, which means that they must be halal.[58]

In this section we will discuss *sukuk* structures and contextualize them in the broader discussion of the different approaches of Islamic finance. The *Shari'ah* requirements for a valid *sukuk* structure will be described. Once the *Shari'ah* framework is clarified, we will discuss how some *sukuk* structures were structured in practice. This will show that the *sukuk* practitioners developed several mechanisms that seemed necessary from a practical point of view. We will contrast this pragmatic approach to the idealistic approach.

Shari'ah Requirements for Sukuk Structures

The most important Islamic principle for *sukuk* transactions, and probably for Islamic finance as a whole, is the prohibition of *riba*. Two important aspects of the prohibition of *riba* are paying or receiving interest and *bay' al-dayn*, or trade in debt claims. As mentioned above, according to the majority of contemporary scholars, the prohibition of *riba* is a prohibition on all forms of interest. Since interest payments are forbidden under *Shari'ah*, the transaction must be structured so that no interest payments are present in the entire transaction. Contrary to conventional bonds, for which the periodic payments are interest payments, the source for the periodic payments of the *sukuk* must be the return on the underlying transaction.

In the AAOIFI definition of *sukuk* certificates, they must represent ownership rights in the underlying assets. This is the result of the prohibition of *riba* and indirectly leads to a prohibition on trading in debt receivables (*bay' al-dayn*). Therefore, pure debt instruments are forbidden. Money must be used to create real economic value, and trade in claims and receivables is not allowed. Consequently, the presence of underlying tangible assets in the transaction is required. This means that the special purpose vehicle (SPC) must hold underlying tangible assets in order to issue *sukuk*. In addition, the *sukuk* holders must hold some degree of ownership in the underlying tangible assets as a consequence of the prohibition on the *bay' al-dayn*.[59]

---

[58] T. Box and M. Asaria, "Islamic Finance Market Turns to Securitization," *International Finance Law Review* 7](2005): 22; M. J. T. McMillen, "Contractual Enforceability Issues: *Sukuk* and Capital Market Development," *Chicago Journal of International Law* 7, no. 2 (Winter 2007): 427–29.

[59] A. H. Abdel-Khaleq and C. F. Richardson, "New Horizons for Islamic Securities: Emerging Trends in *Sukuk* Offer Earnings," *Chicago Journal of International Law* 7, no. 2 (Winter 2007): 418–19.

This makes the *sukuk* tradable in secondary markets, because what is being traded is not merely a debt claim but is rather an ownership right in a tangible asset.

Sukuk Structures: A Pragmatic Approach

Now that the *Shari'ah* framework of *sukuk* transactions has been clarified, three *sukuk* structures will be discussed in further detail to illustrate how they are structured in practice.

Ijarah Sukuk

The *ijarah sukuk* structure is based on the contract of *ijarah*.[60] An *ijarah* contract allows the transfer of the usufruct of an asset in return for rental payment; as such, it is similar to a conventional lease contract.[61] Thus, the *sukuk* are based on the underlying tangible assets that the SPC has acquired rather than being debt securities, which is the case with the issuance of conventional bonds.[62] Instead, the *ijarah sukuk* structure uses the leasing contract as the basis for the returns paid to investors, who are the beneficial owners of the underlying asset and, as such, benefit from the lease rentals and share in the risk.[63] Figure 3.1 illustrates the *ijarah sukuk* structure.

The structure commences with a party who is in need of financing, here referred to as the originator. The originator establishes a special purpose company (SPC), a separate legal entity with the sole purpose of facilitating this transaction. Next, the SPC purchases certain tangible assets from the originator at a prenegotiated purchase price, which is equal to the principal amount of the *sukuk*. In order to finance the purchase of the assets, the SPC issues *sukuk* to *sukuk* holders, who are investors looking for *Shari'ah*-compliant securities. The SPC uses the *sukuk* proceeds to pay the originator the purchase price of the tangible assets. The SPC also declares a trust over the tangible assets and hold these assets as a trustee for the *sukuk* holders as the beneficiaries.

---

[60] Iqbal Mirakhor, *Introduction to Islamic Finance*, 182.

[61] HM Revenue and Customs, *Stamp Duty Land Tax: Commercial* Sukuk; *Consultation Document* (London: HM Revenue and Customs, 2008), 20; HM Treasury, *Government Sterling Sukuk Issuance: A Consultation* (London: United Kingdom Debt Management Office, 2007), 17.

[62] HM Revenue and Customs, *Stamp Duty Land Tax* 20; HM Treasury, *Government Sterling Sukuk Issuance*, 17.

[63] Ibid., 17.

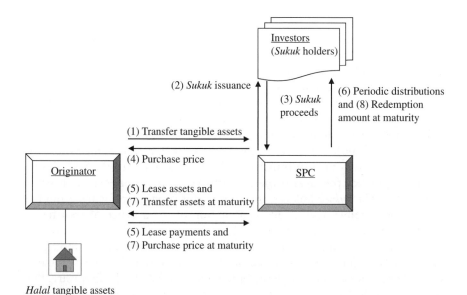

Halal tangible assets

FIGURE 3.1 Structure of *Ijarah Sukuk*

Next, the originator and the SPC contract a lease agreement for a fixed period. Under this agreement, the SPC (the lessor) leases the assets back to the originator (the lessee). Consequently, the SPC receives periodic rentals from the originator for the use of the underlying tangible assets. The SPC uses these amounts to pay the periodic return to the *sukuk* holders, since they are entitled to these payments as the beneficial owners of the tangible assets.

The lease payments from the originator to the SPC, and the periodic payments from the SPC to the *sukuk* holders, continue until the maturity date. At that time, the originator purchases the assets back from the SPC at a predetermined value pursuant to a purchase undertaking. The originator becomes the legal owner of the assets and pays a purchase price equal to the initial purchase price of the assets and thus also equal to the principal amount of the *sukuk*. Hence, the SPC can pay the *sukuk* holders the principal amount back, which allows the *sukuk* certificates to be redeemed.

Although, from a *Shari'ah* perspective, in an *ijarah sukuk* structure the *sukuk* holders must acquire the ownership rights over the tangible assets, from a practical perspective this is often not possible because of legal impediments in most jurisdictions, such as the inability to register the immovable assets in the name of thousands of *sukuk* holders. As a result, under the *ijarah sukuk* structure, the SPC holds the tangible assets in trust for the *sukuk* holders. This means that the legal ownership of the tangible assets will remain with the SPC, and the *sukuk* holders merely acquire the beneficial ownership of the underlying tangible assets.

In practice, however, more difficulties arose in meeting the ownership requirements of the *sukuk* holders. This is the first explication of the pragmatic approach of *sukuk* practitioners. Additional transfer taxes and restrictions on the disposal of governmental assets made it rather impossible for several originators to even transfer the title of the assets to the SPC.[64] As a result, in practice the legal ownership of the assets is not even transferred to the SPC. The *sukuk* holders are, consequently, one step further from the underlying tangible assets. The combination of the absence of transfer of legal ownership of the assets from the originator to the SPC, with purchase undertakings and other forms of guarantees given by the originator, provided the SPC and thus the *sukuk* holders with recourse to the originator instead of recourse to the underlying tangible assets.[65] In the literature, this development has been referred to as a move from asset-backed *sukuk* to asset-based *sukuk*.[66]

Hybrid *Sukuk*

Because of the significant growth of the market, *sukuk* issuance and trading have become important means of investment. However, the *ijarah sukuk* structure limits the originator, who cannot issue *sukuk* if it does not have sufficient tangible assets. Thus, to meet the demands of investors, the hybrid *sukuk* emerged in the market.[67]

In a hybrid *sukuk* structure, the underlying pool of assets can comprise an *istisna* (working capital) contract, a *murabahah* (markup) contract, and an *ijarah* contract, which allows for a greater mobilization of funds.[68] Hence, the hybrid *sukuk* makes it possible to use financing contracts for refinancing means. It even shows similarities to a securitization structure,

---

[64] Haneef, "From 'Asset-Backed' to 'Asset-Light' Structures," 2009, pp. 103–126.

[65] Ibid., pp. 103–126.

[66] Ibid., pp. 103–126.

[67] In the literature, hybrid *sukuk* are also referred to as "blended assets" *sukuk*. Ibid., pp. 103–126.

[68] A. A. Tariq and H. Dar, "Risks of *Sukuk* Structures: Implications for Resource Mobilization," *Thunderbird International Business Review* 2 (2007): 205; Dar Al Istithmar, Sukuk: *An Introduction to the Underlying Principles and Structure* (Oxford, UK: Dar Al Istithmar, 2006), 31.

whereby debt receivables are sold to an SPC over which the SPC issues conventional bonds.

The structure involves the following steps. First of all, the originator transfers tangible assets with underlying *ijarah* deals as well as *murabahah* and *istisna* deals to the SPC.[69] The SPC issues *sukuk* to the *sukuk* holders and receives *sukuk* proceeds from them, which are used to pay the originator.[70] The revenues realized with these three types of contracts are paid to the *sukuk* holders. At the maturity date, the originator purchases the assets back, consisting of tangible assets with all three contracts, from the SPC.[71] The *sukuk* holders receive fixed payment of return on the assets, and the *sukuk* is deredeemed.[72]

In essence, the hybrid *sukuk* involves the same transaction as the *ijarah sukuk*. However, in an *ijarah sukuk* transaction the SPC always owns the tangible assets, which are transferred from the originator to the SPC, whereas in a hybrid *sukuk* transaction there is a transfer not merely of tangible assets but also of *ijarah*, *murabahah*, and *istisna* deals from the originator to the SPC. Figure 3.2 illustrates the hybrid *sukuk*.

With this structure, we witness the second explication of the pragmatic approach. Because of the growth of the market and the demand of issuers and investors for the product, the *sukuk* market has seemed to deviate from the strict requirement of tangible assets in *sukuk* transactions.

As a result, at least 51 percent of the pool in a hybrid *sukuk* must comprise tangible assets. This refers to the presence of *ijarah* contracts, because *murabahah* and *istisna* contracts cannot be traded in the secondary market as securitized instruments.[73] These contracts cannot be traded in the secondary market, because they create debt as the result of the *istisna-* and *murabahah*-based sale. Since the prohibition of *riba* does not allow trade in debt receivables, at least 51 percent of the pool in a hybrid *sukuk* must consist of *ijarah*, because that means that there are underlying tangible assets in the transaction.

The *sukuk* market has witnessed an even further deviation over time. In some structures, even a minority of 30 percent of tangible assets included in the pool of assets has been accepted by the relevant *Shari'ah* scholars.[74] Once again, the pragmatic approach toward the *Shari'ah* framework is clearly evident in the mentality of the market.

---

[69] Dar Al Istithmar, *Sukuk*, 33.

[70] Ibid.

[71] Ibid.

[72] Ibid.

[73] Ibid., 31; Tariq and Dar, "Risks of *Sukuk* Structures," 205.

[74] Haneef, "From 'Asset-Backed' to 'Asset-Light' Structures," 2009, pp. 103–126.

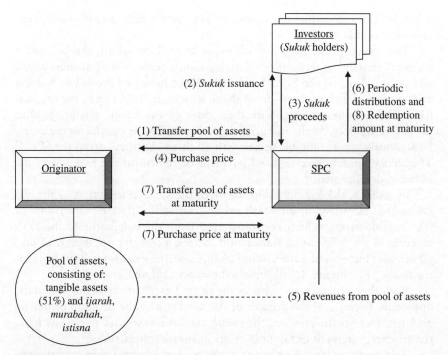

FIGURE 3.2   Structure of Hybrid *Sukuk*

Mudarabah Sukuk

Mudarabah sukuk is structured through the *mudarabah* contract, which is a form of partnership. The structure commences, once again, with a party looking for *Shari'ah*-compliant financing, the originator. The originator establishes an SPC and creates a *mudarabah* contract with this SPC. Both the originator and the SPC are the partners in the *mudarabah* contract. The originator acts as the managing partner, the entrepreneur of the *mudarabah* venture. As the *mudarib*, the managing partner contributes his or her labor, skills, and expertise. The SPC acts as the silent partner, the *rab-al-mal* of the *mudarabah* venture. As the *rab-al-mal*, the SPC contributes in the form of financial investment.

As the financing party of the *mudarabah*, the SPC issues *sukuk* certificates to *sukuk* holders. The *sukuk* proceeds are used to make the financial investment in the *mudarabah*. The SPC declares a trust over all the units it is holding in the *mudarabah* in favor of the *sukuk* holders. Thus, *mudarabah sukuk* allows the pooling of investors' funds with the *sukuk* holders having a common share of the *mudarabah* capital, so they are entitled to returns in

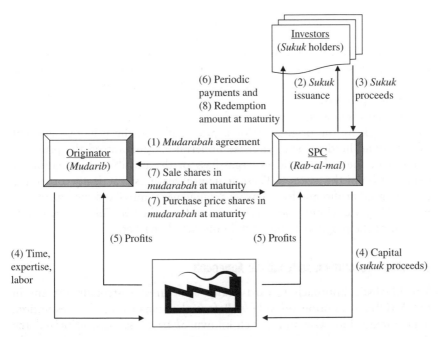

FIGURE 3.3 Structure of *Mudarabah Sukuk*

proportion to their investment.[75] The profits of the *mudarabah* agreement are paid to the *sukuk* holders according to an agreed-on percentage of the realized revenues.

Participation in the *mudarabah* continues until the maturity date. At that time the managing partner buys the units in the *mudarabah* from the *sukuk* holders through the SPC. The managing partner pays an amount to the SPC to purchase the units in the *mudarabah*. That amount is used by the SPC to pay the *sukuk* holders their capital back, so that the *sukuk* certificates can be redeemed.

Figure 3.3 gives a schematic overview of this structure.

The *mudarabah sukuk* is an equity-based *sukuk* structure in which profits and losses are shared by the partners. Therefore, the periodic payments to the *sukuk* holders cannot be fixed returns, nor can their principal amount be guaranteed at maturity. However, in practice, several instruments were used to fix the periodic returns over the *sukuk* and to guarantee the principal amount of the *sukuk* holders.[76] The periodic returns were often fixed

---

[75] HM Treasury, *Government Sterling Sukuk Issuance*, 19.
[76] Salah, "Islamic Finance," 2010, pp. 507–517.

returns; the actual profits realized were less than the promised returns the originator provided for funding. In case of excess profits, the surplus was an incentive fee for the originator.[77] This limited the equity character of these securities, since the losses were born by the originator and the periodic returns to the *sukuk* holders were fixed, regardless of the performance of the underlying projects.

At maturity, pursuant to a purchase undertaking, the assets were purchased back by the originator for a price equal to the principal amount of the *sukuk* holders. The purchase undertaking guaranteed the principal amount of the *sukuk* holders, regardless of the possible appreciation or depreciation of the assets.[78] These structural features practically turned the equity-based profit- and loss-sharing arrangements into fixed-income instruments. Here we witness the third deviation from the *Shari'ah* framework as a result of the pragmatic approach in the *sukuk* market.

The AAOIFI Resolution: An Idealistic Approach

The idealistic approach toward *sukuk* structures is strongly present in the AAOIFI resolution on *sukuk*. Before the issuance of this resolution, Muhammad Taqi Usmani, a well-known *Shari'ah* scholar, criticized the developments in the *sukuk* market in a paper on the contemporary application of *sukuk*.[79] Several finance publications reported his finding that 85 percent of all the *sukuk* outstanding at that time were not *Shari'ah*-compliant.[80] The main target of his criticism was the equity-based *sukuk* structures: the *sukuk* issues based on *musharakah*, *mudarabah*, and *wakalah*.[81] He also addressed some elements of *sukuk* issuances that were relevant to the *ijarah sukuk* structure and the hybrid *sukuk* structure.[82]

---

[77] Salah, "Islamic Finance," 2010, pp. 507–517.

[78] Ibid., pp. 507–517.

[79] M. T. Usmani, *Sukuk and Their Contemporary Applications* (Bahrain: AAOIFI, 2007), 14.

[80] W. McSheehy, "Islamic Bond Scholars Toughen Rules on *Sukuk* Sales," *Bloomberg* March 13, 2008; Arabian Business, "Most Sukuk 'Not Islamic,' Body Claims," Reuters, November 22, 2007, www.arabianbusiness.com/504577-most-sukuk-not-islamic-say-scholars; M. Abbas, "Sukuk Should Be Equity Instruments," Reuters, June 7, 2008, http://gulfnews.com/business/investment/sukuk-should-be-equity-instruments-1.110624.

[81] Usmani, *Sukuk and Their Contemporary Applications*, 4–13.

[82] Ibid., 3–4.

Usmani's Critique

Usmani addressed the issue of the ownership rights of *sukuk* holders. He noted that the presence of ownership rights in *sukuk* structures is the most distinguishing characteristic of *sukuk* compared to conventional bonds.[83] Usmani noticed that the *sukuk* market had witnessed several structures in which there was doubt regarding their representation of ownership rights, such as that the *sukuk* merely offered the *sukuk* holders rights to returns.[84] Usmani emphasized that such *sukuk* structures cannot be *Shari'ah*-compliant.[85] This point is relevant to the *ijarah sukuk* structure.

Usmani also addressed the occurrence of the hybrid *sukuk* structure in the *sukuk* market. He noticed that the hybrid *sukuk* raised questions of *Shari'ah* compliance and should be considered carefully because of the presence of debts in the pool of assets.[86] According to Usmani, the presence of debts and receivables in the hybrid *sukuk* structure raises issues in regard to the forbidden *bay' al-dayn*, or trade in debt claims, even if the percentage of the debts (as a result of the *murabahah* contracts) is considerably less than that of the tangible assets (linked to *ijarah* contracts).[87] Thus, he not only addressed the development of hybrid *sukuk* structures in which the tangible assets form a minority of 30 percent of the pool of assets, he even questioned the *Shari'ah* compliance of hybrid *sukuk* structures in which the pool of assets form a majority of 51 percent of tangible assets.

Usmani then criticized three elements in the contemporary application of equity-based *sukuk* structures. First, he mentioned that the payment of any surplus as an incentive fee to the originating partner in the transaction is a mechanism that comes from conventional financing transactions and does not adhere to the Islamic finance concept, in which the investor is taking more risks and thus must be rewarded for taking those risks.[88] The payment of any surplus to the originating partner is a form of fixing the return to the investors and limits the profit and loss sharing between them.[89]

Second, he criticized the payment of interest-free loans.[90] This mechanism is basically a form of fixing the periodic returns to the investors, and

---

[83] Usmani, *Sukuk and Their Contemporary Applications*, 2008, pp. 3–4.
[84] Ibid.
[85] Ibid.
[86] Ibid.
[87] Ibid.
[88] Ibid., pp. 5–7.
[89] Ibid.
[90] Ibid., pp. 7–8.

thus the investors are not taking the risk that entitles them to a reward.[91] The third point that Usmani condemned was the use of purchase undertakings at face value.[92] Through purchase undertakings, the originating party guarantees the principal amount of the *sukuk* holders, and this too is not in line with the concept of profit and loss sharing.[93]

An idealistic approach toward the issuance of *sukuk* clearly resonates in Usmani's critique. This is even more evident when he places his entire argument in the context of the higher purposes and objectives of Islamic economics.[94] Usmani emphasizes, for example, that the essence of equity-based transactions in Islamic finance is equitable profit distribution, because the financier does not transfer all the risks to the borrower. Meanwhile, the borrower does not acquire all the benefits of the investment of the financier because the profits are divided between them.[95]

The AAOIFI's Response

In February 2008, shortly after Usmani's critique, the AAOIFI resolution was issued.[96] This resolution responded to the developments in the *sukuk* market and to Usmani's critique with six rulings, of which four are relevant.

First, in regard to the ownership requirement, the AAOIFI resolution confirmed that in order to be tradable, *sukuk* must be owned by the holders with all rights and obligations of ownership in the underlying tangible assets.[97] The AAOIFI ruled that the manager issuing *sukuk* must certify the transfer of ownership of such assets in its books and must not keep them as his or her own assets, which means that there must be a real transfer of assets.[98]

As a result of this, the transfer of the beneficial ownership of the assets from the originator to the SPC is not sufficient anymore, and one might even question the extent to which the transfer of merely beneficial ownership from the SPC to the *sukuk* holders is sufficient. Above, however, we noted that the transfer of legal ownership from the SPC to the *sukuk* holders is almost impossible from a practical perspective.

---

[91] Usmani, *Sukuk and Their Contemporary Applications*, 2008, pp. 7–8.
[92] Ibid., pp. 8–13.
[93] Ibid.
[94] Ibid., pp. 13–14.
[95] Ibid., pp. 2–3.
[96] AAOIFI, *Resolutions on Sukuk* (Bahrain: AAOIFI, 2008), www.aaoifi.com/aaoifi_sb_sukuk_Feb2008_Eng.pdf.
[97] Ruling 1 AAOIFI Shari'ah Board, *Resolutions on Sukuk*, 2008.
[98] Ibid.

In its second ruling, the AAOIFI resolution stated that *sukuk*, in order to be tradable, must not represent receivables or debts at all.[99] Exceptions are made in cases in which a portfolio of the assets of a financial entity that are sold unintentionally includes some debts that are incidental to the tangible assets present therein.[100] Thus, in all other cases the pool of assets cannot represent debts or receivables, not even when the debts represent a minority of the pool of assets.

The third ruling related to equity-based structures. The AAOIFI stated that it is not permissible to offer interest-free loans to the *sukuk* holders in case of shortfalls.[101] However, it is permissible to establish a reserve account for the purpose of covering such shortfalls.[102] The AAOIFI also permitted account payments, as long as these payments are subject to final settlement at the maturity date.[103]

The fourth ruling clarified that purchase undertakings, according to which interests in the partnerships (i.e., in *mudarabah, musharakah,* or *wakalah*) are purchased back at nominal value, are not permissible.[104] It is, however, permissible to offer a purchase undertaking according to which the originator can purchase the interests back at their market value or at a price to be agreed on at the moment of the sale.[105]

The AAOIFI resolution clearly rules out several structural mechanisms that were developed in practice. Although an idealistic approach toward the *Shari'ah* framework was adopted in the resolution, practical considerations are also taken into account, and several mechanisms were therefore provided as alternatives, such as the reserve account and account payments in the equity-based structures. As a result, the idealistic approach in the AAOIFI resolution did not merely criticize contemporary practice by referring to the ideal structures from a *Shari'ah* perspective; it also provided some real alternatives to show the way forward to the market.

CONCLUSION

The history of *sukuk* and its development show that in the first decade of the 21st century, an imbalance was created in the *sukuk* market between an idealistic approach to *sukuk* structures and the pragmatic approach that *sukuk*

---

[99] Ruling 2 AAOIFI Shari'ah Board, *Resolutions on Sukuk,* 2008.
[100] Ibid.
[101] Ruling 3 AAOIFI Shari'ah Board, *Resolutions on Sukuk,* 2008.
[102] Ibid.
[103] Ibid.
[104] Ruling 4 AAOIFI Shari'ah Board, *Resolutions on Sukuk,* 2008.
[105] Ibid.

practitioners have actually adopted. The *Shari'ah* framework of *sukuk* contextualized this imbalance. It will be interesting to see how the market will react to the criticism by the idealists of the pragmatists' approach.

Most likely, a compromise of these two approaches will be the result. The difficulties associated with both the idealistic and pragmatic approaches, however, do not necessarily justify the liberal approach, which rejects *sukuk* entirely and argues that Islamic capital markets do not differ at all from the conventional capital markets. Even when the pragmatic approach is adopted, certain conventional financial products, such as credit default obligations or credit default swaps, would be difficult, if not impossible, to realize in Islamic capital markets.

One wonders if there is room in this debate for a more context-based *ijtihad*. Such *ijtihad*, being less concerned with the outward form of the structures, would shift the focus toward *maslahah*, the public interest, and the underlying objectives of *Shari'ah*, such as fairness, justice, and equity. In the future, this might provide a solution that will meet the needs of practitioners while adhering to the true spirit of *Shari'ah*.

CHAPTER 4

Contract Design and the Structure of Common *Sukuk* Securities Issued to Date

This chapter and the next two are connected. This chapter reviews the financial and legal structures of the six major types of existing *sukuk* securities: *mudarabah* (partnership), *musharakah* (profit sharing), *murabahah* (markup), *ijarah* (leasing), *salam* (futures), and *istisna* (working capital). The next chapter describes the structures of the contracts that are widely available in different markets.

The cash-flow pattern of each type of structure and its variations are discussed in this chapter. There are a variety of *sukuk* types, based on their funding purposes, contractual specifications, payback schemes, and issues such as conversion. The details, characteristics, and specifications of them are elaborated in the following sections. Chapter 6 describes those that have not yet been issued.

MUDARABAH (PARTNERSHIP)

A *mudarabah sukuk* is based on *mudarabah* contract terms. *Mudarabah*, or partnership in profit, is one of the premier financing methods, with roots going back to the pre-Islamic era. The Prophet Muhammad (570–632 CE) used *mudarabah* with Khadijah bint Khuwaylid (555–619), a rich woman from Mecca who became his first wife, about 15 years before he began his prophetic mission.

Mudarabah is defined in jurisprudence as a mode of financing through which a financier provides capital for the venture of an entrepreneur. The financier is known as the *rab-al-mal*, and the entrepreneur is called the *mudarib*. The *rab-al-mal* may be an individual investor, an investment company, or a bank.

At the maturity of the contract or at some predetermined time, the profits generated from the venture are shared by the contracting parties according to a prenegotiated ratio. In case of a loss, each party bears the loss of his or her contribution to the contract. In other words, the financier bears all financial losses and the entrepreneur bears the operating losses such as time and effort. In the case of negligence or misconduct by the entrepreneur, he or she alone is liable to cover it.

The *rab-al-mal* is not allowed to have a management role in the *mudarabah* venture contract. Thus, the *mudarib* becomes a trustee as well as an agent of the business. As a trustee, the *mudarib* is responsible for losses stemming from willful negligence. As an agent, the *mudarib* is required to use and manage the capital in ways that generate the maximum profit.

Furthermore, similar to equity holders in modern finance, *mudarabah* investors have a profit that is proportionate to the performance of the firm. Such a contract has features of both equity and debt. However, *mudarabah* investors do not benefit from all the aspects of shareholders, like capital gains, and they do not have rights such as attending or voting at the annual general meeting. In the case of bankruptcy, *sukuk* holders are in a higher position than equity shareholders with residual claims—a position akin to the modern conventional bond or loan contracts.

Although *mudarabah* may be applied in various economic activities, the majority of Islamic jurists and scholars hold the view that *mudarabah* contracts are most suitable for commercial activities. In practice, however, the nature of a *mudarabah* contract is limited because of operational difficulties and business ethics constraints. In Muslim countries, an inefficient tax system, a high rate of illiteracy, low accounting standards, and the practice of keeping a double set of accounts by the majority of small businesses are major issues hindering the practical implementation of a system of profit and loss sharing.

In order to issue a *mudarabah sukuk*, a special purpose company (SPC) is set up. This SPC acts as the *rab-al-mal*, and the originator acts as the *mudarib*. The proceeds of the issue collected by the SPC from the *sukuk* investors are applied as the capital of the *mudarabah*, which the *mudarib* manages for a fee and a share in the profits. The profit-sharing ratio is specified at the outset.

Although there should not be a predetermined rate of return in a *mudarabah* contract, the *sukuk* issued until early 2008 were designed to ensure that *sukuk* holders receive the so-called indicative rate of return announced at the inception of the issue. This was achieved by including clauses in the *mudarabah* agreement that specified a maximum rate of return. Any profit to be generated above that rate of return was directed to a reserve account, which could be used to cover any shortfall in future years.

In case of insufficient profits as well as insufficient funds in the reserve account, the issuing company is required to provide *Shari'ah*-compliant funding to meet the shortfall and make it up to the indicative rate of return, in effect guaranteeing the rate of return independent of the actual profit generated. Muhammad Taqi Usmani, the chairman of the AAOIFI *Shari'ah* council, ruled against the practice of guaranteeing the indicative rate of return.

As mentioned before, *mudarabah sukuk* are pure debt. They are mere cases of borrowing money; thus, they are not tradable. However, some scholars have pointed out that in practice the *mudarabah sukuk* are structured in a way to be tradable. *Mudarabah sukuk* are tradable and negotiable if the *mudarabah* assets are not entirely eomposed of the *sukuk* proceeds (in which case they would be liquid assets and could not be traded). In most *mudarabah sukuk*, there is a combination of tangible assets and *sukuk* proceeds, and the *mudarib* is allowed to mingle his or her own assets with those of the *mudarabah*. Such an arrangement mostly meets the *Shari'ah* requirement of having more than 51 percent of the assets in tangible form for tradability and negotiability.

The International Islamic Financial Market (IIFM) surveyed the *sukuk* market in 2010 and reported on international *mudarabah sukuk* contracts. Before 2011, there were more than US$8.7 billion international *mudarabah sukuk* issues in the market (excluding domestic issues), ranging from US$200 million to US$2.5 billion each. The UAE had issued most of the international *mudarabah sukuk* contracts. Moreover, the data show that all the international *mudarabah sukuk* were issued in 2007; there was no issuance before that.

MUSHARAKAH (PROFIT SHARING)

Musharakah is an arrangement in which two or more parties establish a joint commercial enterprise, and all generally contribute capital as well as labor and management. In contrast to the *mudarabah* contract, in *musharakah* the investors have the right to participate in the management of the business partnership. The *musharakah* contract may require the establishment of a new partnership or company in which the *musharakah* contract parties are the participants and the owners.

Musharakah sukuk securities can be issued based on such a financing concept. *Musharakah* equity finance demands that both the profit ratio and the length of the joint venture agreement be decided in advance. As in *mudarabah*, loss is shared in proportion to the capital contribution unless the loss is proved to be caused by the negligence of one party. Therefore, all profits and losses generated from the *musharakah* are shared by the parties on the basis of a prenegotiated participation ratio.

As a result, *musharakah* is suitable for financing private or public companies and projects. It is also used by Islamic banks, which typically issue it through joint ventures with business firms for certain operations.

Because of its nature and advantages in providing equal (but proportionate) benefits for all parties, *musharakah* has the support of all Islamic scholars and is valid under *Shari'ah* principles. However, the parties to *musharakah* usually need the help of a legal expert to ensure that any potential *riba* or *gharar* is carefully avoided. One scholar has concluded the following:

> *The only requirement of the* Shariah *would be justice, which would imply that the proportional shares of partners in profit must reflect the contribution made to the business by their capital, skill, time, management ability, goodwill, and contacts. Anything otherwise would not only shatter one of the most important pillars of the Islamic value system but also lead to dissatisfaction and conflict among the partners and destabilize the partnership. The losses must, however, be shared in proportion to capital contribution, and the stipulation of any other proportion would be ultra vires [beyond the scope of legal power] and unenforceable.*[1]

There are two ways to construct a *musharakah* contact. Both forms are based on the same general concept of *musharakah*, in which the contracting parties (the financier and the entrepreneur) are ensured equitable shares in the profit or loss on prenegotiated terms. The difference lies in the prenegotiated sharing ratio.

In the first method, the ratio is fixed for the whole period of the contract. In the second method, the ratio declines over the contract period. This diminishing, or declining, *musharakah* contract is preferred by some financiers since it allows them to release their capital from the investment by reducing its equity share each year and to receive more of the periodic profits based on the remaining share balance. In contrast, the equity share of the entrepreneur increases over time to the extent that he or she becomes the sole owner of the firm.

There are several varieties of *sukuk* based on *musharakah* contracts. *Sukuk* based on diminishing *musharakah* are gaining momentum since they enable Islamic banks or *Shari'ah*-compliant investment companies to provide upfront investment funding to the issuer. In this regard, both parties establish a SPC to administer the *sukuk*. In order to issue a diminishing *musharakah sukuk*, the issuer transfers the ownership of an asset to the SPC to enter the partnership agreement.

---

[1] U. M. Chapra, "The Major Modes of Islamic Finance," course in Islamic Economics, Banking, and Finance series, Islamic Foundation, Leicester, UK, 1998.

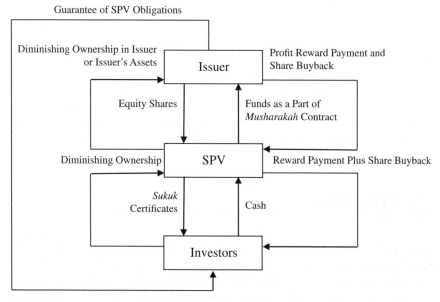

FIGURE 4.1　Diminishing *Musharakah Sukuk* Structure

In contrast, investors enter the agreement by paying cash. Therefore, both the investors and the issuer are equity partners in the SPC. However, the investment share in the SPC diminishes over time as the issuer pays installments to the investors to repurchase their respective shares in the asset. These installment payments, plus the issuer's rental payments for use of the asset (i.e., the asset's generated income) constitute the cash-flow stream for *sukuk* holders. In fixed-ratio *musharakah sukuk*, the cash-flow stream for the *sukuk* holder is only from the income generated from the asset and not from the installment part. The structure of diminishing *musharakah sukuk* is depicted in Figure 4.1.

Flexibility in the payment schedule and amount has made diminishing *musharakah sukuk* more convenient to use. However, all arrangements should be agreed upon in advance by all parties to the SPC. The payments are usually monthly or quarterly but are not necessarily in equal amounts. Smaller installments can be made during the initial period of the *sukuk*, with most of the asset value or SPC capital remaining with the investors, but the amount of the installment payments could increase in a linear fashion or according to some predetermined formula. As the issuer's share in the asset increases through the buyback process, the periodical rental might be expected to decrease because of the decline in the remaining share. However, this does not necessarily have to be the case, especially if there is capital appreciation in the value of the asset. In other words, when installment and rental payments are aggregated, they might be constant, diminishing, or increasing over time, provided both parties agree to the formula used and the documentation is transparent.

The IIFM surveyed the international *sukuk* market in 2010 and reported on international *musharakah sukuk* contracts. Before 2011, there were more than US$8.5 billion *musharakah sukuk* issues in the market (excluding domestic issues), ranging from US$100 million to US$3.5 billion each.

MURABAHAH (MARKUP)

Murabahah contracts govern the process of buying, purchasing, or importing an item by one party, mainly an Islamic bank, and then reselling it to another party. The markup is the bank's profit for funding this transaction. The Islamic bank's benefit is generated from the markup on the cost of purchase of the goods, which is agreed upon in advance.

Murabahah contracts, which are based on a cost-plus basis, are especially used for foreign trade and working capital financing in circumstances in which banks purchase raw materials, goods, or equipment and sell them to the customer. The ownership of the *murabahah* asset remains with the Islamic bank until all payments are settled, in contrast to the conventional system, in which the ownership of the assets is immediately transferred to the buyer. Therefore, from modern finance point of view, *murabahah* is equivalent to an asset-backed risky loan and is a popular substitute for interest-based conventional trade financing in Islamic banks.

To initiate a *murabahah*, the customer provides the bank with the detailed specification and prices of the goods to be purchased or imported. Having received the application documents, the Islamic bank analyzes and collects the necessary information from the vendors, especially on the price and payment conditions. Then the bank and the customer applying for the *murabahah* agree on the terms of the deal. Finally, the bank purchases the goods or commodities and resells them to the customer. In order to conduct a *murabahah* contract, the following requirements should be met:

- Goods and commodities mentioned in the contract must be classified—clearly identified according to commonly accepted standards—and must exist at the time of the sale.
- The Islamic financier must hold the ownership of the goods at the time of sale to the buyer.

- The cost in terms of net purchase price and the markup must be known at the time of the sale and be declared to the customer. If the bank succeeds in reducing the price by obtaining a discount from the vendor, this discount should be shared with the customer.
- The delivery schedule and the payments must be specified in the contract and cannot be changed during the life of the contract.
- The contract must be based on the sale of a commodity or tangible goods and cannot be based on the sale of money.

Murabahah contracts constituted the majority (54 percent) of the total financing and investment portfolios of the 10 largest Islamic banks in 2004–2006. However, *murabahah* was more popular in 1994–1996, when it made up 65 percent of the portfolios.

Murabahah contracts typically have short-term maturities. Hence, Islamic banks basically use *murabahah* for short-term investment and liquidity management, since Islamic banks are still not fully developed for long-term financing. However, *murabahah* contracts have low returns, leading to an inefficient use of funds and a lower rate of return for Islamic banks. The way *murabahah* contracts are conducted and practiced contradicts with *Shari'ah* principles, however, because Islamic banks transfer all costs of insuring *murabahah* goods against possible damage, destruction, and theft to the *murabahah* customer.

Islamic banks also perform some other actions that are not *Shari'ah*-compliant, such as benchmarking the interest rate to fix the returns on *murabahah*, assigning higher markups for *murabahah* contracts with longer periods, charging fines to customers who delay in making their installment payments, and recovering losses from customers who breach their promises to buy the *murabahah* goods.

The *murabahah* contract is only a contract of appointing the bank as an agent on behalf of the customer in the process of purchasing goods; it does not necessarily involve financing the purchase. In the basic *murabahah* contract, the customer should pay the cost of the goods and the profit margin immediately after the delivery of the goods. However, the customer can pay by deferred installments (*bai bithaman ajjal*) or a deferred lump sum without an increase over the original value (*bai muajjal*). In a *bai muajjal murabahah sukuk*, the issuer pays back the total amount borrowed at a certain time in a predetermined lump sum payment.

With a *murabahah sukuk*, an Islamic bank securitizes its trading transactions with a proportion of the fixed markup providing the return to the *sukuk* investor, and the bank uses the repayment from its trading client to repay the *sukuk* holder on termination of the contract.

The IIFM surveyed the international *sukuk* market in 2010 and reported on international *murabahah sukuk* contracts. Before 2011, there were almost US$440 million international *murabahah sukuk* issues in the market (excluding domestic issues), ranging from US$98 million to US$210 million each.

IJARAH (LEASING)

Ijarah, which means to rent something, is the recompense that proceeds from a rental contract between two parties in which the lessor (the owner of a capital asset) leases the asset to the lessee (the user of the asset). There is a tendency toward lease financing (*ijarah*) in the Islamic banking sector, since it promises higher yields than trade finance (*murabahah*) and also has longer financing horizons, which is an important feature for business investments.

In order to be permissible under *Shari'ah*, the *ijarah* contract must satisfy several conditions. The primary requirement is that the lessor be a real owner and in possession of the asset to be leased under contract, based on the principle that ownership is a prerequisite for a financial transaction. As a result, the lessor should solely bear all risks and uncertainties associated with the asset and be responsible for all damage, repair, insurance, and depreciation of the asset.

It could be inferred that charging a rental payment is not allowed until the lessee actually takes possession of the asset and that the lessee must pay the rental only as long as the asset is in usable condition. In case of manufacturing defects that are beyond the lessee's control, the lessor is responsible. However, the lessee is responsible for the proper upkeep and maintenance of the leased asset.

The intention of posing such restrictions in an *ijarah* contract by *Shari'ah* is to protect both parties to the contract by reducing the uncertainty and ambiguity from the agreement. In addition, both the lessor and the lessee should be clear on the purpose of the *ijarah* and the usage of assets. Finally, the *ijarah* purpose itself must comply with *Shari'ah*.

There are two forms of leasing contracts. *Ijarah*, the direct leasing contract, is the case in which the lessee uses the capital asset owned by the lessor, with his or her permission, for a specific period and pays a monthly or annual rental fee. The owner bears the ownership title for the whole contract period and must perform ownership responsibilities, such as getting insurance and maintaining the workability of the assets. Possession of the asset is transferred back to the owner when the contract expires. There is no option to transfer the ownership of the asset at this point.

Ijarah wa iqtina, or hire purchase, is a contract in which the basic intention is to transfer ownership of the asset after completing the leasing period.

Ijarah wa iqtina is popularly practiced when an Islamic bank purchases equipment or some other capital asset based on the request of a customer and then rents it to the customer for a fixed amount. The customer promises to purchase the equipment or asset within a specified period, and ownership is transferred from the bank to the customer. The lease contract is completely separate and independent from the contract of purchase of residuals, which must be valued on a market basis and cannot be fixed in advance.

The purchase contract should be an optional, nonbinding contract, because the quality and the market price of the asset at the end of the lease period are unclear. In some cases, ownership is gradually transferred to the customer, as in conventional capital leasing contracts. In addition to the regular rental payment, the customer pays installments for the value of the asset in order to reduce the ownership share of the lessor in the asset until the ownership is fully transferred to the lessee. *Ijarah wa iqtina* has strong support from *Shari'ah* scholars and is widely used in the real estate, retail, and manufacturing sectors.

Ijarah sukuk is based on the *ijarah* contract. In order to issue *ijarah sukuk*, the originator, who primarily owns the assets, sells the assets to an SPC, which is typically a company in an offshore tax-free site. The SPC leases the assets back to the issuer at a specific predetermined rental fee, and then the SPC securitizes the ownership in the assets by issuing *sukuk* certificates to the public investors.

These *sukuk* certificates represent an undividable share in the ownership of the assets, which entitles the *sukuk* holders to distribution of the rental payments on the underlying assets. However, the rental payment could be fixed or floating for the whole period, depending on the leasing contract between the SPC and the originator. Since these *sukuk* certificates represent ownership in real assets, they can be traded in a secondary market.

The role of the SPC in conducting *ijarah sukuk* is the management of the *sukuk* cash flow, particularly receiving periodical rentals and installments from the originator and disbursing them to the *sukuk* holders. After maturation of the *sukuk*, the SPC no longer has a role.

Ijarah sukuk is typically issued for periods longer than five years and can be considered as long-term debt certificates. This may raise the issue of the SPC's default risk, so the investors typically receive a direct guarantee from the issuer of the SPC obligations. This guarantee includes the obligation by the issuer to repurchase the asset from the SPC at the end of the *ijarah* contract at the original sale price.

Because of its nature, the SPC does not have any of the risks associated with banks—that is, it is bankruptcy remote. If the issuer faces bankruptcy, the creditors to the issuer cannot claim the assets held by the SPC or otherwise interfere with the rights of the *sukuk* holders on the assets in the SPC.

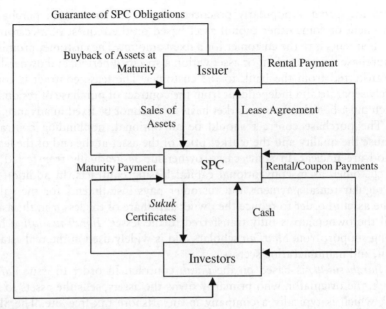

FIGURE 4.2   *Ijarah Sukuk* Structure

As a result, an SPC is attractive to both issuers and investors, and this may justify the relatively high legal establishment costs.

Figure 4.2 illustrates the *ijarah sukuk* structure.

Because of the fixed and predetermined nature of rental cash flow, *ijarah sukuk* holders receive steady income that is even more risk-averse than common stocks. General market conditions, price movements of real assets, the ability of the lessee to pay the rental or installments, maintenance, and insurance cost are sources of risks to *ijarah sukuk*. Because of these risk factors, the expected return on some *ijarah sukuk* may not be precisely predetermined and fixed. Thus, the fixed rental may only represent a maximum that is subject to some possible deductions.

The major criticism of *ijarah sukuk* is that the return is variable or floating in most cases. Moreover, for simplification this variable rate is sometimes benchmarked or pegged to an interest-based index such as the London Inter-Bank Offered Rate (LIBOR) for US$-based *sukuk* and local rates for other currencies.

AAOIFI *Shari'ah* council chairman Usmani criticized this practice by associating it with *riba* (excessive interest). *Shari'ah* scholars have suggested the use of other, noninterest benchmarks for pricing and valuation purposes. In order to overcome the *riba* issue, government or sovereign *sukuk* could be assessed by macroeconomic indicators, and corporate *sukuk* could be assessed based on company performance indicators.

Ijarah sukuk can have various types of payback structures. In the simplest form, payback could be fixed-promised regular payments and not a predetermined-promised maturity payment. The formal *ijarah* contract does not have the option for parties to transfer the ownership of the asset at the end of the period. Thus, at the end of an *ijarah* contract, the asset should be returned to the owner (i.e., the capital owner or the SPC).

In order to transfer the ownership back to the issuer at maturity, one should use an *ijarah wa iqtina* contract, in which ownership of the asset is transferred to the lessee (i.e., the issuer) at the maturity of the *sukuk*. The maturity payment is not determined at the issuance time. The valuation of the asset in *ijarah wa iqtina sukuk* is conducted at maturity, when the market value of the asset is recognized, and the maturity payment is set to be equal to that.

The IIFM surveyed the international *sukuk* market in 2010 and reported on international *ijarah sukuk* contracts. There were more than US$14 billion international *ijarah sukuk* issues in the market (excluding domestic issues), ranging from US$50 million to US$3.5 billion each.

SALAM (FUTURES)

Salam refers to a sale in which the seller promises to supply a specific commodity to the buyer at a future date in return for an advance price, paid in full on the spot. As mentioned before, *Shari'ah* prohibits the sale of goods that are not currently in the possession of the seller or that do not exist at the contract time, based on the principle of prohibition of *gharar*, or uncertainty.

However, *salam* and *istisna* (discussed in the next section) contracts are the exceptions to this general rule because they facilitate the financing process of agricultural and industrial projects under certain conditions. Because *salam* is a sales contract in which payment for purchased goods is made in advance of their delivery, in order to be *Shari'ah*-compliant the contract must meet the following requirements:

- The commodities and goods have not yet come into existence at the time of the contract.
- The quality and quantity of goods must be known at the time of the contract.
- The delivery schedule and venue must be determined at the time of the contract.
- The buyer must pay the entire price of the goods in advance to the seller at the time of the contract.

Salam originated in the pre-Islamic era and was widely used in agricultural business. *Salam* has the support of the *Sunnah*, the primary source of *Shari'ah*, which states the following:

> The Messenger of Allah came to Madinah and found its inhabitants entering Salam contracts (with the price paid in advance) in fruits for one, two, and three years. He said: Whoever enters into a Salam contract let him specify a known volume or weight, and a known term of deferment.[2]

In another narration the Prophet said, "Whoever enters into *Salaf* [the same as *salam*] should stipulate a determined weight and measurement and a determined date of delivery."[3]

A *salam* contract benefits both the buyer and the seller. The seller can finance working capital needs, and the buyer can benefit from the difference between the purchase price and the commodity price at the delivery time, which tends to be higher. In the meantime, the buyer can finance the advance payments by issuing certificates against the *salam* contract's goods, at purchase price; since these certificates represent real assets, they can be sold to the public or traded in the secondary market. The return for the buyers of these certificates is the difference between the commodity price at maturity and the discounted price he or she has paid.

In order to issue a *salam sukuk*, a nonprofit SPC should be created as a separate legal entity for the duration of the *sukuk* to administer the flow of payments between the issuer and the investors, as well as to hold the title of the underlying asset. To initiate the *sukuk*, the issuer transfers the title of the assets to the SPC, which, in turn, issues certificates of participation to the public investors. *Salam sukuk* represent an undivided right to an interest in the asset. In order to obtain a certificate of participation, an investor should make an advance payment, which entitles him or her to a future payback of the investment plus a fixed prenegotiated markup.

A well-known example of *salam sukuk* is the Bahrain *salam sukuk*, which is primarily designed to broaden the depth and liquidity of Bahrain's market. This short-term Treasury-bill type of *sukuk* has aluminum as its underlying asset. At maturity, the issuer, the Bahrain Monetary Agency, acts

---

[2] Quoted in M. A. El-Gamal, *A Basic Guide to Contemporary Islamic Banking and Finance* (Plainfield, IN: Islamic Society of North America, 2000).

[3] Quoted in R. Y. Al-Masri, "Market Price of *Salam* on the Date of Delivery: Is It Permissible?" *Journal of Islamic Economics* 16 (2003).

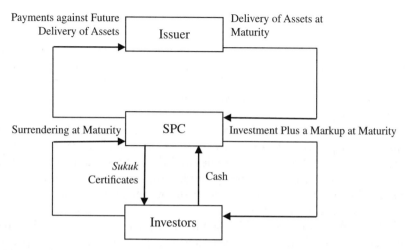

FIGURE 4.3 *Salam Sukuk* Structure

as a *sukuk* holder, selling the commodity at a prenegotiated price that guarantees a promised return rate to the *sukuk* holder.

Figure 4.3 illustrates the *salam sukuk* structure.

Because the capital owner in a *salam* contract pays in advance for a commodity to be delivered in the future, this capital owner (i.e., the *sukuk* holder) benefits from the difference between the amount paid in advance and the market price of the commodity at maturity. The promised maturity payment is therefore not predetermined at the time of issuance.

ISTISNA (WORKING CAPITAL)

Istisna, a contract to commission a manufactured product, is the proper method of financing working capital in the manufacturing and construction sectors. *Istisna* allows one party to obtain industrial goods with either advance cash payment and deferred delivery or deferred payment and delivery. The cost-reduction benefit for the issuer is in the term that all or part of the working capital is obtained from external resources; consequently, the final product is manufactured at a lower cost.

As mentioned before, even though *Shari'ah* prohibits the sale of goods that are not currently in the possession of the seller, *istisna* and *salam* are exceptions to this rule. *Istisna* is a contract in which the manufacturer-seller agrees to produce and deliver a prespecified, predesigned good in a specified quantity on a given future date at a fixed price.

In contrast to the terms of *salam*, there is no obligation in *istisna* for a lump-sum advance payment; however, it is not prohibited. Moreover, the price may be paid in accordance with the progress of production or partly in advance and the rest at delivery. Another distinction is that the delivery time may be unknown or unspecified at the time of the contract. Finally, the *istisna* contract usually involves a commodity or an item that requires manufacturing.

Istisna sukuk has also become the contractual form for financing construction projects. In order to issue *istisna sukuk*, a parallel *istisna* contract is used between the financier and the subcontractor of the project. The project commissioner provides the technical, financial, and project management specifications to the financier, who then finds the best subcontractor for the project.

The information required in the bid includes a proposal for selling the completed parts of the project over time and the amount of the expected installment payments. This stream of revenue, which is based on the expected installments income for a specific period, can be used for issuing the debt certificates.

However, since the *istisna* certificates are not based on any real asset and are solely representing debt obligation, they are not tradable in the secondary market at a discount. *Istisna sukuk* may only be exchanged at face value or be used to purchase goods or services whose price is equal to the face value of the certificate. Transference of the debt contract from the financier to a supplier of goods or service requires the permission of the debtor who commissioned the project.

As mentioned above, in *istisna* contracts, the capital owner pays in advance for a project to be completed in the future. The capital owner (i.e., the *sukuk* holder) benefits from the difference between the amount paid in advance and the market price of the project at maturity. The maturity-promised payment is not predetermined at the issuance time.

CONCLUSION

In this chapter, the reader has been introduced to the design, structure, and payoff modes for the six common securities. Although historical references indicate 12 different *sukuk* securities that have been traced back to the pre-Islamic era, only 6 of them are currently issued and/or traded in the markets. Of these, the *ijarah sukuk* contract dominates the Malaysian capital market, whereas the *musharakah sukuk* contract is familiar in most markets as a workable stocklike arrangement for financing ventures.

CHAPTER 5

Samples of *Sukuk* Issued

This chapter provides some real-world examples of already issued *sukuk* securities from different countries. *Sukuk* first came to the public exchange market in 1990, when Shell MDS offered an Islamic debt instrument and listed it for trading. Before this date, *sukuk* debt instruments were offered in over-the-counter markets and, in later years, in exchanges in countries other than Malaysia, which in 2014 accounts for four-fifths of the value of listing (see Table 5.1).

SUKUK SIMPANAN RAKYAT (MALAYSIA)

The Malaysian Ministry of Finance, on behalf of the government of Malaysia, is frequently issuing *Shari'ah*-based *sukuk* securities to public investors. One of the very well branded *sukuk* offers is the *sukuk simpanan rakyat* (SSR), which is offered to local investors. In 2009, a total amount of MYR5 billion (US$1.63 billion) was raised through the SSR instrument in two issues. The first, known as SSR2009/01, was issued on May 14, 2009. This offer was worth MYR2.5 billion with a maturity of three years. The government of Malaysia appointed the Bank Negara Malaysia, the country's central bank, to conduct the issuance process.

The SSR, with an average annual profit rate of 5 percent (paid quarterly) is offered to Malaysian citizens who are at least 21 years old. Returns on the issue are tax-exempt. In order to widen the spectrum of individual investors, the issuer has decided to impose a maximum investment limit of MYR50,000 per investor in addition to the usual minimum amount of MYR1,000. The SSR is nonnegotiable, nontransferable, and nonassignable.

TABLE 5.1 List of Notable *Sukuk* Issuances in Malaysia

Issuer	Amount	Year	Transaction Highlights
Shell MDS	RM125 million (US$33 million)	1990	World's first ringgit *sukuk* issuance by foreign-owned, non-Islamic company
Kumpulan Guthrie Bhd	US$150 million	2001	World's first global corporate *sukuk*
Government of Malaysia	US$600 million	2002	World's first global sovereign *sukuk*
International Finance Corporation (World Bank)	RM500 million (US$132 million)	2004	First ringgit *sukuk* issuance by supranational agency
Cagamas MBS Bhd	RM2.05 billion (US$540 million)	2005	World's first Islamic residential mortgage-backed securities
PLUS	RM9.17 billion (US$2.86 billion)	2006	Complex and innovative structure—conversion of existing debts of PLUS info Islamic financing
Khazanah Nasional (Rafflesia Capital Limited)	US$750 million	2006	World's first exchangeable *sukuk*
AEON Credit Services	RM400 million (US$125 billion)	2007	First Japanese-owned company issuing *sukuk*
Nucleus Avenue (Malakoff Corporation)	RM8 billion (US$2.5 billion)	2007	First hybrid *sukuk* in the world
Khazanah Nasional (Cherating Capital)	US$850 million	2007	Largest equity-linked *sukuk* issuance and record highest oversubscription
Maybank Berhad	US$300 million	2007	World's first international subordinated *sukuk*
Binariang GSM	RM15.35 billion (US$4.8 billion)	2007	Largest-ever *sukuk* issue in the world
Islamic Development Bank	RM1 billion	2008	First RM *sukuk*

TABLE 5.1 (*Continued*)

Issuer	Amount	Year	Transaction Highlights
Toyota Capital Services	RM1 billion	2008	First Japanese MNC issuing *sukuk*
Petronas	US$1.5 billion	2009	First Emas *sukuk*
Government of Malaysia	US$1.25 billion	2010	Second global sovereign Emas *sukuk*, the largest sovereign *sukuk* to date
Nomura	US$100 million	2010	First Japanese global Emas *sukuk*
Khazanah Nasional	SGD1.5 billion (RM3.6 billion)	2010	The largest and longest termed Singapore dollar denominated Emas *sukuk*
Islamic Development Bank	US$500 million	2010	First Emas *sukuk* by a multilateral development institution
Khazanah Nasional	RMB500 million (RM246 million)	2011	World's first Chinese renminbi-denominated Emas *sukuk*; World's first offshore RMB *sukuk*
PLUS	RM30.6 billion	2012	World's single largest *sukuk* issuance
Khazanah Nasional	US$357.8 million	2012	Exchangeable *sukuk* first to be priced at negative yield

Source: MIFC.com.

CENTRAL BANK OF BAHRAIN

Central Bank of Bahrain (CBB) uses *salam sukuk* securities as an instrument for short-term financing. CBB *salam* securities have a maturity of 91 days. *Salam* securities are very well accepted by investors and are mostly oversubscribed. CBB has used this method since 2001 and raised a total of BHD1.3 billion (US$3.87 billion) in 2003–2012. CBB planned to issue 12 tranches of *salam sukuk*, each worth BHD18 million (US$6.75 million), in 2013.

CBB *salam sukuk* uses aluminum as the underlying asset for the contract. The underlying asset is sold to the buyer (the government of Bahrain) at the end of the contract. Therefore, the contract is between the *sukuk* holders and CBB, and the *sukuk* proceeds are used as advance payment for the purchase of the underlying asset (aluminum). At the maturity of the contract, CBB sells the asset to the government and distributes the proceeds to the *sukuk* holders as the maturity payment. *Salam sukuk* securities are mostly purchased by local investment houses and banks as a mean of short-term liquidity management.

KHAZANAH NASIONAL BERHAD (MALAYSIA)

Khazanah Nasional Berhad (KNB), the sovereign wealth fund of Malaysia, is one of the innovative powerhouses in *sukuk* issuance. KNB has issued various types of *sukuk* securities, especially customized to the financing needs of its expansion policies. Some of the notable issues by KNB are listed in Table 5.1.

One of the well-cited issues is KNB's exchangeable (convertible) *sukuk*, which was the first one in the world. It was issued in October 2006 for US$750 million. This five-year-maturity *sukuk* had an option for *sukuk* holders to convert their *sukuk* certificates to ordinary shares of Tele-kom Malaysia (TM), Malaysia's telecommunication company, at a fixed exchangeable price of MYR1.00 per share. This *sukuk* was the first contract that used equity shares of a publicly listed company as the underlying asset, and hence it was tradable in the main secondary market.

One of the key features of this issue was that the periodic *sukuk* coupon payments were not guaranteed and were based on the dividend income generated from the underlying assets (TM shares). However, in order to reduce the cash-flow uncertainties of the periodic payments, a sinking fund was embedded in the structure of the *sukuk*. This *sukuk* was strongly favored by investors to the extent that it had recorded an oversubscription ratio of 6.6, that is 6.6 applications for each lot of shares.

QATAR CENTRAL BANK

Qatar Central Bank issued *sukuk* for the first time in 2003. The first issue was US$700 million, which was assigned an A+ rating by Standard and Poor's. The first issuance was made in the International Islamic Financial Market in Bahrain. This particular security had the feature of a floating periodical coupon payment rate because it was pegged to the London Inter-Bank Offer Rate (LIBOR). The coupon rate was set 40 basis points higher than the LIBOR rate. This feature was embedded in the contract to prevent the payment of a fixed rate to *sukuk* holders, which would have resembled *riba*.

Qatar Central Bank has issued a few more *sukuk* securities since then. As of 2013, there were a few outstanding *sukuk* issued by Qatar Central Bank, including a US$5 billion eight-year-maturity issuance in 2010, a US$33 billion three-year-maturity issuance in 2011, a US$500 million three-year-maturity issuance in 2013, and a US$500 million five-year-maturity issuance in 2013.

NAKHEEL SUKUK (UAE)

Dubai World, a real estate firm of the government of Dubai, issued three *sukuk* securities to finance the *nakheel* (palm tree) construction project on the shores of the Persian Gulf. The *nakheel sukuk* was structured based on the concept of an *ijarah* contract. This particular issue raised a total of US$3.52 billion for a term of three years and was supposed to mature on December 14, 2009.

However, the world financial crisis, and the subsequent Dubai financial crisis, resulted in the devaluation of the *nakheel sukuk*. On November 25, 2009, Dubai World approved a US$26 billion debt restructuring, and on November 30 it requested a suspension of trade on the *nakheel sukuk* until further clarification of its ability to pay it back. Although the *nakheel sukuk* was suspended from trade for few weeks, it was eventually redeemed. The US$10 billion bailout package from oil-rich neighbor Abu Dhabi helped the Dubai government to back the *nakheel sukuk*.

This episode shocked the *sukuk* markets around the world, because it was one of the first billion-dollar *sukuk* securities on the verge of default before it was saved by a government. The episode sparked a significant debate among practitioners and scholars about the issue of *sukuk* default and the missing legal framework to deal with this matter. The *nakheel sukuk* contract had a default clause; however, the clause was not enforceable under UAE jurisdiction, so the case was sent to a British court for resolution. Some Islamic jurisdictions (such as the UAE and other Gulf Cooperation Council countries) lack a clear resolution mechanism for default and solvency matters. This is in contrast to British law, which has a solid enforceable mechanism for such matters.

MAHAN AIRLINE COMPANY (IRAN)

The Iranian capital market has witnessed *Shari'ah*-compliant securities in the form of *musharakah* contracts since 1995. At that time, the authorities labeled them "participatory securities." Their issuances are mostly initiated by the government of Iran, government-linked-companies, or local munici-palities (with the guarantee of the central government). With few excep-tions, all the issuances are denominated in the local currency. A brief history of the development of Islamic banking and the capital market in Iran was published in 2012.[1]

The first *ijarah sukuk* in Iran was issued in 2011 by a private airline company, Mahan Airline Company, and it was worth IRR291.5 billion (US$30 million). The purpose was to finance the purchase of an airplane; hence, the underlying asset of this contract is the plane. The issue is a four-year contract that pays a 17.5 percent profit rate on a quarterly basis.

In 2013 the profit rate was increased to 20 percent, mainly because of an increase in the national interest rate. The issue is traded in Farabourse, Iran's over-the-counter market, because of a lack of trade infrastructure in the main market of the country.

CONCLUSION

These examples show the widespread use of this new form of debt financ-ing by private firms and government agencies. It shows that some issues are using the most common currency, the US dollar, as the issuing currency. Where foreign currencies are used as the issue currency, those markets are developing, as the Eurodollar financial markets did, in six major financial centers in the world.

Another notable feature is that the issues are aimed at the specific needs of the issuers (a distinct feature of Islamic debt structuring)—for example, the need of a real estate developer to fund a large project in the UAE, the need of a private firm to purchase an airline company in Iran, or the need of the government of Malaysia to provide a traded security as a savings instru-ment. These examples show the variety and specificity of project-based funding that is characteristic of the burgeoning Islamic debt markets.

---

[1] M. Karimzadeh, "Role of *Sukuk* in the Islamic Capital Market: Experience of Iran (1994–2011)," *Arabian Journal of Business and Management Review* 1, no. 7 (Feb-ruary 2012): 94–105.

CHAPTER 6

Contract Design and the Structure of *Sukuk* Securities Yet Issued

This chapter reviews the financial and legal structures of *sukuk* that have not yet been issued but have already been structured: *wakalah* (agency), *manfaah* (usufruct), *muzarah* (farmland leasing), *musaqa* (orchard leasing), and *muqarasah* (tree leasing).

WAKALAH (AGENCY)

Wakalah is an agency contract in which one party entrusts another party to act on his or her behalf. The principal (the investor) appoints the agent (the *wakeel*) to invest a certain amount of funds on behalf of the principal in a pool of investments or assets. The agent charges the principal a predetermined fee for his or her expertise and management skills. The *wakalah* agreement governs this relationship by setting the scope of services, responsibilities, and fees payable to the agent. This is for a specific purpose.

Wakalah sukuk are based on the *wakalah* contract and are of interest when there is no particular tangible underlying asset. *Wakalah sukuk* can be used when the underlying asset is a pool of investments or assets to be collected. Then, using his or her expertise, the agent selects and manages the portfolio of assets to ensure the generation of the principal's expected rate of return.

Wakalah sukuk may resemble some features of *mudarabah sukuk*; however, the main difference is that in *mudarabah*, the agent receives a portion of the profit, whereas in *wakalah*, the investors receive the prenegotiated profit share, while the balance of any profits is paid to the agent as a performance bonus.

Wakalah sukuk has some features that may be attractive to originators. The agent is free to choose the investment portfolio on the condition that the investment is made only in *Shari'ah*-compliant assets (e.g., equities, *sukuk*, derivatives). Hence, the portfolio can include a wide range of assets, unlike in conventional mutual funds. In addition, the originator may build his or her balance sheet by acquiring assets to be included in the portfolio and using them as the underlying assets of the *wakalah sukuk*.

Moreover, the originator may include some nontradable assets (such as *mudarabah sukuk*, which implies a debt) in the portfolio to the extent that they constitute only a portion of the underlying assets of the investment *wakalah sukuk* portfolio. (The maximum allowed is different under different *Shari'ah* jurisdictions.) In a sense, the fund is leveraged.

MANFAAH (USUFRUCT)

Manfaah, a usufruct contract, is used when a party sells its existing right, or usufruct, in some particular service or profit of a durable asset to another party. *Manfaah*'s use ranges widely, since the underlying services can differ case by case. However, since the right of usufruct is transferred to the other party, it can generate profit based on it. The *manfaah sukuk* may be structured based on different types of underlying rights and would be named accordingly. For instance, if the underlying asset is the right to use a lease property based on an *ijarah* contract, then the *sukuk* might be termed a *manfaah ijarah sukuk* or a *manfaah ijarah mowsufa bithimn sukuk*.

MUZARAH (FARMLAND LEASING)

Muzarah contracts govern the lease of a farm or arable land for agricultural purposes. Under such a contract, one party (the landlord) permits the other party (the farmer) to use the arable land for a certain period for agricultural purposes and, in return, receives a portion of the harvest.

Consequently, *muzarah sukuk* is the *sukuk* structure based on this form of contract. Similar to other structures, *muzarah* does not promise a fixed return to the investor, but only a predetermined portion of the profit (the harvest). The risks are borne by the *sukuk* holders unless there is proof of negligence.

Muzarah sukuk may be structured similar to the *ijarah* so that the agricultural company (the originator), which already owned the land, sells its ownership title to the *sukuk* holders through the SPC proxy. Then the originator uses the proceeds from the *sukuk* issuance and conducts agricultural activity on that particular land. At harvest time, the revenue is distributed between both parties based on the predetermined ratio. If the *sukuk* tenure is more than a cultivation year, then the same profit-sharing process repeats until maturity.

MUSAQAH (ORCHARD LEASING)

A *musaqah* contract is applied when an owner leases his or her orchard to a farmer for a period and, in return, receives part of the harvest. This contract is very similar to the *muzarah* contract, but in *muzarah* the leased property is a piece of land (mostly for the cultivation of grains), whereas in *musaqah* it is an orchard (for the cultivation of fruit-bearing trees).

Musaqah *sukuk* can be structured when the proceeds are used to purchase a garden. Hence, the *sukuk* holders collectively act as landlord, and the originator acts as a horticulturist who works in this particular orchard for a certain period. The harvested fruits from this garden are distributed proportionally, based on a predetermined agreement. The risks are borne by the *sukuk* holders unless there is proof of negligence.

MUQARASAH (TREE LEASING)

Muqarasah is a contract between a landlord and another party to plant and maintain trees. *Muqarasah sukuk* securities are based on this contract, which is similar to *muzarah* and *musaqah* except for the particular proceeds.

CONCLUSION

This chapter concludes the description of the *sukuk* contracts currently being used, as well as potential contracts that are likely to be issued as the market expands in the future. Some commentators have dubbed *sukuk* as project-funding arrangement. In a broad sense it is correct, because funding is sought for specific projects that are common production activities of humans.

It may also be called targeted funding, because *sukuk* contracts offer targeted financing that is tailored to the needs of a particular economic activity. Whereas working capital financing (*istisna*) provides cash for producing a clearly defined product before the product is made, three separate contracts provide financing to put agricultural land and crops (farmland, orchards, and trees) under a profit-sharing arrangement.

The latter three contracts have the attractive feature of avoiding the indebtedness of farming communities to a bank by cutting out the middleman. This is an attractive feature for economic activities that depend on seasonal features such as rain and that therefore risk recurrent crop failures. Rural indebtedness can be avoided if such instruments are used to allow tenant farmers to share the profits and the risk with the owners of the land.

In Pakistan, for example, and in many Latin American countries, the landowners live luxuriously and make the peasants bear the burden of crop failure. As a result, poverty prevails in the rural areas. Farming indebtedness is a major issue in both developed and developing economies. Putting profit- and loss-sharing contracts in place not only releases the farmer from penury in times of drought and crop failure but also spurs a mutual interest in increasing farming productivity.

CHAPTER 7

Sukuk Securities and Conventional Bonds

In order to investigate the possible existence of a difference between the yield to maturity (YTM) of *sukuk* securities and the YTM of conventional bonds for the same duration and same issuer, pair-sampled *t*-tests have been conducted. These tests were performed on maturities ranging from three months to 20 years from various types of issuers in Malaysia: (1) sovereign, or government (the government of Malaysia and Bank Negara Malaysia), (2) quasi-sovereign, or government agencies (Cagamas, a mortgage company, and Khazanah Nasional, the investment-holding arm of the government), (3) financial institutions (AAA rated), and (4) corporations (corporate-guaranteed AAA and corporate AAA). YTM data for the first working day of each month from August 2005 to January 2011 were collected from the BondStream database, a product of Malaysia's Bond Pricing Agency.

The tests found that the mean yield of *sukuk* securities for all types of issuers and all forms of maturities was 4.02 percent. However, the YTM varied from 2.83 percent (*sukuk* securities issued by BNM with three months' maturity) to 5.87 percent (*sukuk* securities issued by AAA-rated corporations with 20 years' maturity).

The mean yield of conventional bonds for all types of issuers and all forms of maturities was also 4.02 percent, and the range was from 2.82 percent (conventional bills issued by BNM with three months' maturity) to 5.76 percent (conventional bonds issued by AAA-rated corporations with 20 years' maturity).

The important policy issue examined in this chapter is testing whether the two forms of debt instruments yield the same rewards. A valid answer to this question is urgently needed for the industry to decide clearly how to classify the two forms of debt instruments. The market players (e.g., regulators, rating agencies, pricing agents) treat the two forms of debt as similar and even use the conventional benchmarks of one to describe the other to the extent that conventional valuation formulas are used to price the other.

We have shown in previous chapters that *sukuk* securities are structured differently, have the feature of profit sharing only after risk sharing, and are asset backed or sometimes asset based. Our purpose in this chapter is to find the dissimilarities between the two forms of debt. Such a finding has important implications for industry policy and practices, regulatory differentiation, and market advocacy practices.

COMPARISON OF THE YIELDS OF ISLAMIC SECURITIES AND BONDS

The results of the paired-sample t-tests are summarized in Table 7.1, which is divided into two panels: one for the test of means and the other for the

TABLE 7.1 Paired-Sample t-Test Results between Bonds and *Sukuk* with Similar Features of Issuer and Tenure

	Mean				Median			
	Sukuk	Conv.	$\Delta Y (s - c)$	t-Stat	*Sukuk*	Conv.	$\Delta Y (s - c)$	t-Stat
			Government-Issued Securities					
3M	2.9362	2.9148	0.0214	2.832***	3.1900	3.2050	−0.0150	−1.988*
6M	2.9764	2.9594	0.0170	2.489**	3.2250	3.2450	−0.0200	−2.934***
1Y	3.0567	3.0380	0.0186	2.445**	3.2800	3.3100	−0.0300	−3.936***
2Y	3.2497	3.2171	0.0326	3.482***	3.3700	3.3500	0.0200	2.138**
3Y	3.4553	3.3867	0.0686	5.011***	3.4400	3.3900	0.0500	3.651***
5Y	3.7205	3.6638	0.0567	5.278***	3.6900	3.6650	0.0250	2.329**
7Y	3.8762	3.8353	0.0409	5.219***	3.8500	3.8050	0.0450	5.741***
10Y	4.0876	4.0538	0.0338	3.843***	4.0950	4.1100	−0.0150	−1.706*
15Y	4.3085	4.2902	0.0183	2.530**	4.3250	4.3050	0.0200	2.760***
20Y	4.4715	4.4591	0.0124	1.600	4.5450	4.5050	0.0400	5.150***
			BNM-Issued Securities					
3M	2.8336	2.8212	0.0124	3.128***	2.9400	2.9400	0.0000	0.000
6M	2.8662	2.8522	0.0140	2.908***	2.9750	2.9750	0.0000	0.000
1Y	2.9440	2.9158	0.0282	4.691***	3.0200	3.0200	0.0000	0.000
2Y	3.1065	3.0535	0.0530	5.289***	3.0600	3.0600	0.0000	0.000

TABLE 7.1 (*Continued*)

	Mean				Median			
	Sukuk	Conv.	$\Delta Y\,(s-c)$	*t*-Stat	*Sukuk*	Conv.	$\Delta Y\,(s-c)$	*t*-Stat
Cagamas-Issued Securities								
3M	3.2056	3.1782	0.0274	2.574**	3.4200	3.4200	0.0000	0.000
6M	3.2791	3.2561	0.0230	2.549**	3.4450	3.4550	−0.0100	−1.107
1Y	3.3858	3.3721	0.0136	1.387	3.4900	3.4900	0.0000	0.000
2Y	3.6147	3.5968	0.0179	1.609	3.6100	3.6000	0.0100	0.900
3Y	3.8305	3.8058	0.0247	1.830*	3.7300	3.6850	0.0450	3.334***
5Y	4.1748	4.1545	0.0203	1.800*	4.1350	4.1150	0.0200	1.773*
7Y	4.4055	4.3721	0.0333	3.075***	4.3000	4.2800	0.0200	1.845*
10Y	4.7064	4.6692	0.0371	3.228***	4.6450	4.5550	0.0900	7.827***
15Y	5.0042	4.9452	0.0591	3.922***	5.0300	4.8500	0.1800	11.946***
20Y	5.2156	5.1512	0.0644	3.691***	5.2250	5.0650	0.1600	9.171***
Khazanah-Issued Securities								
3M	3.0256	3.0339	−0.0083	−1.121	3.2750	3.3250	−0.0500	−6.728***
6M	3.0776	3.0882	−0.0106	−1.877*	3.3200	3.3750	−0.0550	−9.734***
1Y	3.1600	3.1752	−0.0152	−1.785*	3.3700	3.4300	−0.0600	−7.069***
2Y	3.3706	3.3858	−0.0152	−2.311**	3.4600	3.5150	−0.0550	−8.388***
3Y	3.5676	3.5811	−0.0135	−1.984*	3.5300	3.5650	−0.0350	−5.151***
5Y	3.8798	3.8889	−0.0091	−1.260	3.8450	3.8800	−0.0350	−4.853***
7Y	4.0576	4.0682	−0.0106	−1.767*	4.0000	4.0100	−0.0100	−1.666*
10Y	4.2912	4.3014	−0.0102	−1.394	4.2700	4.3100	−0.0400	−5.493***
15Y	4.5539	4.5538	0.0002	0.018	4.6150	4.6100	0.0050	0.605
20Y	4.7380	4.7368	0.0012	0.124	4.7750	4.7600	0.0150	1.529
AAA-Rated Financial Institution–Issued Securities								
3M	3.4189	3.3948	−0.0241	1.486	3.5700	3.5950	−0.0250	−1.542
6M	3.5171	3.5044	0.0127	0.794	3.5950	3.6300	−0.0350	−2.183**
1Y	3.6811	3.6965	−0.0155	−1.142	3.6700	3.7000	−0.0300	−2.217**
2Y	3.9186	3.9335	−0.0148	−0.867	3.7900	3.8000	−0.0100	−0.584
3Y	4.1544	4.1724	−0.0180	−0.985	3.9600	4.0000	−0.0400	−2.185**

(*continued*)

TABLE 7.1 (*Continued*)

	Mean				Median			
	Sukuk	Conv.	$\Delta Y(s-c)$	*t*-Stat	*Sukuk*	Conv.	$\Delta Y(s-c)$	*t*-Stat
AAA-Rated Financial Institution–Issued Securities (*continued*)								
5Y	4.4968	4.5070	−0.0102	−0.606	4.4250	4.4500	−0.0250	−1.493
7Y	4.7712	4.7711	0.0002	0.010	4.7700	4.8100	−0.0400	−2.632**
10Y	5.1226	5.1071	0.0155	1.085	5.1600	5.2000	−0.0400	−2.808***
15Y	5.5162	5.4447	0.0715	2.895***	5.5850	5.5600	0.0250	1.012
20Y	5.7950	5.7191	0.0759	3.004***	5.9800	5.8600	0.1200	4.749***
AAA-Rated Corporate-Issued Securities								
3M	3.3312	3.3521	−0.0209	−3.602***	3.4900	3.5650	−0.0750	−12.921***
6M	3.4276	3.4576	−0.0300	−4.940***	3.5400	3.6100	−0.0700	−11.527***
1Y	3.6020	3.6770	−0.0750	−6.198***	3.6000	3.7200	−0.1200	−9.916***
2Y	3.8433	3.9302	−0.0868	−5.873***	3.7600	3.8850	−0.1250	−8.456***
3Y	4.1029	4.1785	−0.0756	−5.065***	4.0100	4.0500	−0.0400	−2.680***
5Y	4.4406	4.4945	−0.0539	−4.411***	4.4150	4.4600	−0.0450	−3.680***
7Y	4.7529	4.7988	−0.0459	−5.459***	4.7250	4.7650	−0.0400	−4.756***
10Y	5.1430	5.1408	0.0023	0.163	5.2000	5.0900	0.1100	7.913***
15Y	5.5789	5.4853	0.0936	3.010***	5.6550	5.4900	0.1650	5.305***
20Y	5.8724	5.7668	0.1056	3.136***	6.0500	5.7750	0.2750	8.166***
AAA-Rated Corporate Guaranteed–Issued Securities								
3M	3.2880	3.3009	−0.0129	−1.704*	3.4800	3.5150	−0.0350	−4.632***
6M	3.3774	3.3998	−0.0224	−3.676***	3.5150	3.5450	−0.0300	−4.918***
1Y	3.5365	3.6036	−0.0671	−6.279***	3.5550	3.6650	−0.1100	−10.291***
2Y	3.7698	3.8405	−0.0706	−6.130***	3.6900	3.7500	−0.0600	−5.209***
3Y	4.0170	4.0786	−0.0617	−5.436***	3.9400	3.9600	−0.0200	−1.763*
5Y	4.3347	4.3836	−0.0489	−5.977***	4.3150	4.3350	−0.0200	−2.443**
7Y	4.6282	4.6717	−0.0435	−5.730***	4.5600	4.6000	−0.0400	−5.271***
10Y	4.9574	5.0023	−0.0448	−3.815***	4.9000	4.9500	−0.0500	−4.253***
15Y	5.3580	5.3282	0.0298	1.505	5.3900	5.3600	0.0300	1.512
20Y	5.6259	5.5883	0.0376	1.802*	5.6400	5.6300	0.0100	0.480

Note: *, **, and *** indicate significance level at 0.10, 0.05, and 0.01, respectively.

tests of medians, since further calculations are based on both. We performed a test of medians to counter the criticism that a test of means is likely to have errors from the distribution of yields being leptokurtic (i.e., not normal). However, since the results of the two tests are not different, a discussion of the test of medians has been omitted.

Out of the 64 tested pairs of mean yields of *sukuk* and of conventional bonds, 46 cases (i.e., 72 percent) showed significant differences in their YTMs. In 32 cases, the null hypotheses were rejected at 1 percent levels. Thus, one can conclude that the YTM of *sukuk* securities differs from that of conventional bonds, even when the issuer and the issue tenure are the same. Although from a general perspective the yields of *sukuk* differ from the yields of conventional bonds, this is not exactly the same for all issuers.

This variation in the significance of difference between the mean yields of *sukuk* and of conventional bonds suggests that issuer type may have some effect on the yield of a *sukuk* security.

The mean yields of *sukuk* and conventional bonds are significantly different for all forms of securities issued by BNM. The difference between the means is a positive figure, indicating that Islamic securities tend to yield more than conventional bonds issued by BNM.

For securities issued by the government of Malaysia, the difference is significant for all cases except 20 years' maturity securities. The difference between the means is a positive figure, indicating that Islamic securities tend to yield more than conventional bonds issued by the government of Malaysia.

For securities issued by government agencies such as Cagamas, the mean yields of *sukuk* securities and conventional bonds are significantly different, except for securities with one or two years' maturity. The difference between the means is a positive figure, indicating that Islamic securities tend to yield more than conventional bonds issued by Cagamas.

However, the mean yields of *sukuk* and conventional bonds are significantly different for only five pairs of securities issued by Khazanah Nasional (six months; one, two, three, and seven years' maturity). The difference between the means is a positive number for securities with 10 years' maturity or less, whereas for securities with 15 years' maturity or more, the difference is negative. In other words, the yield of Islamic securities issued by Khazanah Nasional is higher than its conventional bonds only for issues with less than 10 years' maturity. For securities with 15 or 20 years' maturity, the mean yield is less than that of conventional bonds.

The mean yields of Islamic securities and conventional bonds issued by AAA-rated financial institutions are significantly different only for two pairs

(15 or 20 years' maturity). The difference between the means is a positive number for securities with six months' maturity or less or with seven years' or more. However, for securities with maturity between six months and seven years, the difference is negative. In other words, the mean yield of Islamic securities issued by AAA-rated financial institutions is higher than that of conventional bonds for issues with six months' or less maturity or with seven years' or more maturity. For the securities with maturities between six months and seven years, the mean yield of Islamic securities is less than that of conventional bonds.

For AAA-rated corporation-issued securities, the mean yields of Islamic securities and conventional bonds are significantly different for all cases except for 10 years' maturity. The difference between means is a negative number for securities with 7 years' maturity or less, whereas for securities with 10 years' maturity or more, the difference is positive. In other words, the mean yield of Islamic securities issued by AAA-rated corporate issuers is lower than that of conventional bonds for issues with 7 years' or less maturity. For the securities with 10 years' or more maturity, the mean yield of Islamic securities is more than that of conventional bonds.

For AAA-rated corporate guaranteed–securities, the yields of Islamic securities and conventional bonds are significantly different for all cases except in the case of 15 years' maturity. The difference between the means is a negative number for securities with 10 years' maturity or less, whereas for securities with 15 years' maturity or more, the difference is positive. In other words, the yield of Islamic securities issued by AAA-rated guaranteed corporate issuers is lower than that of conventional bonds for issues with 10 years' or less maturity. For the securities with maturities of 15 years or more, the mean yield of Islamic securities is more than that of conventional bonds.

YIELD CURVES

Yield curve is the relation between the cost of borrowing and the time to maturity of a security for a given issuer. Yield curves for Islamic securities and conventional bonds issued by various issuers are plotted here in four figures. As Figure 7.1 suggests, the yield of government Islamic issues (GII) is higher than that of conventional bonds issued by the same issuer (Malaysian government securities, or MGS). The difference between the *sukuk* yield and the conventional bond yield tends to be larger for maturities between 2 years and 15 years. The maximum difference between the

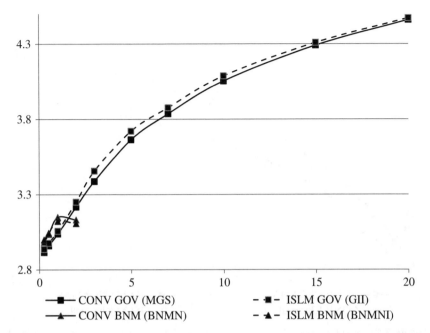

FIGURE 7.1 Yield Curve of Government-Issued Securities (Conventional Bonds versus *Sukuk*)

yields of *sukuk* securities and conventional bonds issued by the government occurs for securities with 3 years' maturity, and the difference is 6.86 basis points.

Figure 7.1 also depicts the yield curve of the BNM-issued *sukuk* securities and conventional bonds. These securities are issued only with up to two years' maturity. As the graph shows, the yield of *sukuk* is higher than that of conventional bonds, for all maturities. Moreover, the difference between these yields increases as the maturity of the pair of securities increases. The maximum difference between the yield of *sukuk* securities and that conventional bonds issued by BNM is 5.30 basis points for securities with two years' maturity.

Figure 7.2 shows the yield curves for securities issued by quasi-government firms, or government agencies: Cagamas and Khazanah Nasional. The yield of *sukuk* securities issued by Cagamas is higher than the yield of Cagamas's conventional bonds. This difference increases as the tenure period of the securities grows beyond five years. The maximum

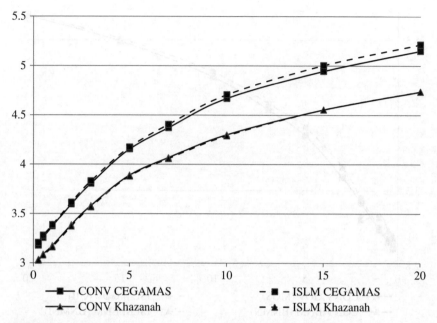

FIGURE 7.2 Yield Curve of Government Agency–Issued Securities (Conventional Bonds versus *Sukuk*)

difference between the yields issued by Cagamas occurs for securities with 20 years' maturity; it is 6.44 basis points. In contrast to Cagamas securities, Khazanah Nasional issued securities that show a very small difference in yield. The maximum difference between the yields of securities issued by Khazanah Nasional is for securities with one or two years' maturity; it is −1.52 basis points. The yield is lower for *sukuk*.

Figure 7.3 shows the yield curves for securities issued by AAA-rated financial institutions. The yield of Islamic securities tends to be very close to the yield of conventional bonds for securities with less than 10 years' maturity. However, for securities with longer maturity periods, the *sukuk* yield is higher than the conventional bond yield. The maximum difference between the yields of securities issued by AAA-rated financial institutions is for 20 years' maturity; it is 7.59 basis points.

Figure 7.4 shows the yield curves for securities issued by AAA-rated corporations. The yield curve is generated for both guaranteed securities and general forms of securities. For corporate issues, the yield of *sukuk* securities is less than the yield of conventional bonds with less

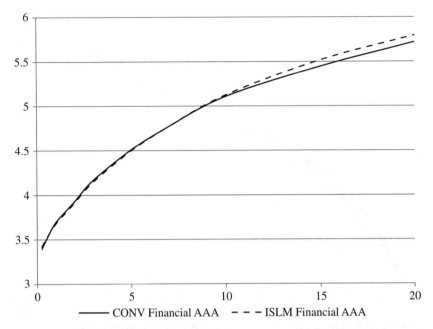

FIGURE 7.3 Yield Curve of AAA-Rated Financial Institution–Issued Securities (Conventional Bonds versus *Sukuk*)

than 10 years' maturity. However, the yield of *sukuk* securities is more than the yield of conventional bonds with more than 10 years' maturity. The maximum difference between the yields of Islamic securities and conventional bonds issued by corporate issuers with less than 10 years' maturity is for securities with 2 years' maturity; it is −8.69 basis points. However, the maximum amount of this figure for securities with longer than 10 years' maturity is 10.56 basis points for securities with 20 years' maturity.

For corporate-guaranteed issues, the yield appears to be less than the yield of conventional bonds with less than 15 years' maturity. However, the yield of *sukuk* securities is more than the yield of conventional bonds with 15 years' maturity or more. The maximum difference between the yields of guaranteed *sukuk* securities and conventional guaranteed bonds issued by corporate issuers with less than 15 years' maturity is observed for securities with 2 years' maturity; it is −7.07 basis points. However, the maximum amount of this figure for securities with longer than 10 years' maturity is 3.76 basis points for securities with 20 years' maturity.

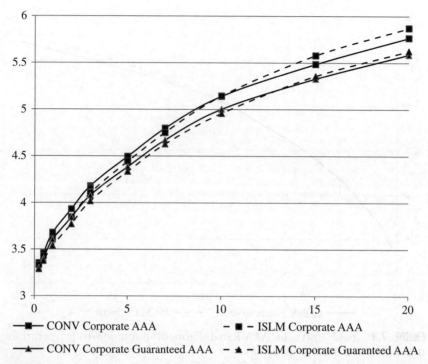

--- CONV Corporate AAA   - ■ - ISLM Corporate AAA
--- CONV Corporate Guaranteed AAA   - ▲ - ISLM Corporate Guaranteed AAA

FIGURE 7.4   Yield Curve of AAA-Rated Corporate-Issued Securities (Conventional Bonds versus *Sukuk*)

THE GRANGER CAUSALITY TEST FOR THE YIELDS OF *SUKUK* AND CONVENTIONAL BONDS

The previous section showed that the mean yield of *sukuk* bonds is statistically different from the mean yield of conventional bonds. Thus, one may conclude that *sukuk* securities and conventional bonds are two different types of securities. However, since each pair of securities is issued by the same issuer for same amount of time, it is expected that the correlation between the yields of these securities will be high. This may be a basis for a hypothetical argument that they have causal relations. As a result, one may want to know whether changes in one can cause changes in the other. In other words, one may want to use the Granger causality test on the yields of *sukuk* securities and conventional bonds.

In order to test for a causal relationship between the yields of *sukuk* and conventional bonds, two Granger causality tests were conducted on each pair of securities. First, it was tested to verify whether a change in the yield of *sukuk* caused a change in the yield of conventional bonds. Second, each pair was tested to verify whether a change in the yield of conventional bonds caused a change in the yield of *sukuk*. The results of the pairwise Granger causality tests are presented in Table 7.2.

In the first test, the null hypothesis was that the yield of *sukuk* does not cause the yield of conventional bonds. As the test results in Table 7.2

TABLE 7.2 Results of Pairwise Granger Causality Tests

Hypothesis Tested	Islamic Security Does Not Cause Change in Conventional Bond		Conventional Bond Does Not Cause Change in Islamic Security	
Maturity	F-Statistic	Probability	F-Statistic	Probability
Government of Malaysia				
3M	0.345	0.709	0.797	0.455
6M	1.140	0.326	0.921	0.403
1Y	2.017	0.142	1.629	0.204
2Y	2.467*	0.093*	1.746	0.183
3Y	2.032	0.140	3.003*	0.057*
5Y	2.336	0.105	0.182	0.833
7Y	1.487	0.234	0.420	0.658
10Y	0.490	0.615	0.003	0.996
15Y	0.592	0.556	0.634	0.533
20Y	0.721	0.490	0.847	0.433
BNM				
3M	3.197*	0.050*	1.104	0.340
6M	3.877**	0.028**	1.277	0.289
1Y	3.875**	0.028**	1.282	0.287
2Y	6.694***	0.003***	0.047	0.953
Cagamas				
3M	0.605	0.549	1.043	0.358
6M	0.758	0.472	1.342	0.269
1Y	0.336	0.715	1.401	0.254
2Y	0.185	0.831	1.459	0.240

(continued)

TABLE 7.2 *(Continued)*

Hypothesis Tested	Islamic Security Does Not Cause Change in Conventional Bond		Conventional Bond Does Not Cause Change in Islamic Security	
Maturity	*F*-Statistic	Probability	*F*-Statistic	Probability
Cagamas *(continued)*				
3Y	0.020	0.979	1.718	0.188
5Y	0.252	0.777	0.949	0.392
7Y	0.480	0.620	0.643	0.529
10Y	1.264	0.29	0.318	0.728
15Y	0.721	0.490	0.552	0.578
20Y	0.778	0.463	0.997	0.375
Khazanah Nasional				
3M	1.031	0.362	0.425	0.655
6M	0.535	0.587	1.414	0.251
1Y	1.201	0.307	4.199**	0.019**
2Y	3.538**	0.035**	6.865***	0.002***
3Y	1.868	0.163	2.743*	0.072*
5Y	1.372	0.261	0.842	0.435
7Y	1.174	0.316	1.714	0.188
10Y	0.832	0.44	0.521	0.596
15Y	0.905	0.41	0.664	0.518
20Y	1.758	0.181	0.979	0.381
Financial Institutions				
3M	3.543**	0.035**	7.481***	0.001***
6M	4.083**	0.021**	10.292***	0.000***
1Y	1.152	0.322	6.367***	0.003***
2Y	0.312	0.732	0.084	0.918
3Y	0.595	0.554	0.467	0.629
5Y	1.558	0.219	1.291	0.282
7Y	1.376	0.260	0.424	0.656
10Y	3.926**	0.025**	2.425*	0.097*
15Y	5.223***	0.008***	1.925	0.154
20Y	2.594*	0.083*	1.789	0.176

TABLE 7.2 (*Continued*)

Hypothesis Tested	Islamic Security Does Not Cause Change in Conventional Bond		Conventional Bond Does Not Cause Change in Islamic Security	
Maturity	F-Statistic	Probability	F-Statistic	Probability
		Corporate Guaranteed		
3M	0.373	0.689	2.139	0.126
6M	0.951	0.392	5.018***	0.009***
1Y	2.813*	0.068*	4.578**	0.014**
2Y	3.175**	0.049**	3.340**	0.042**
3Y	0.713	0.494	0.556	0.576
5Y	1.335	0.270	0.077	0.925
7Y	2.103	0.131	2.726*	0.073*
10Y	0.447	0.641	1.769	0.179
15Y	0.763	0.470	3.269**	0.045**
20Y	0.572	0.567	4.898**	0.010**
		Corporate		
3M	1.289	0.283	5.093***	0.009***
6M	1.903	0.158	6.903***	0.002***
1Y	2.724*	0.073*	5.369***	0.007***
2Y	4.782**	0.011**	3.330**	0.042**
3Y	0.919	0.404	1.072	0.348
5Y	0.193	0.824	0.246	0.782
7Y	1.358	0.265	1.324	0.273
10Y	0.521	0.596	1.058	0.353
15Y	0.649	0.525	1.602	0.210
20Y	0.559	0.574	1.283	0.284

Note: *, **, and *** indicate significance level at 0.10, 0.05, and 0.01, respectively.

suggest, out of 64 pairs of securities tested, only in 10 pairs (15 percent) was the null hypothesis rejected at a 5 percent significance level. This indicates that one may not generally conclude that the yield of *sukuk* securities causes the yield of conventional bonds.

The results also show that the yields of the *sukuk* issued by BNM (six months, 1 year, and 2 years), Khazanah (2 years), AAA-rated financial institutions (three months, six months, 10 years, and 15 years), AAA-rated guaranteed corporations (2 years), and AAA-rated corporations (2 years) caused the yields of conventional bonds.

The results do not show a concrete pattern of causality related to the issuer or the maturity of the security. However, 8 out of 10 pairs of securities with up to three years' maturity showed causal relations. A causal relation between *sukuk* and conventional bonds was more common among the securities issued by BNM (3 out of 4 pairs) and by financial institutions (4 out of 10 pairs). However, these patterns are not conclusive.

In the second test, the null hypothesis was that the yield of conventional bonds does not cause the yield of *sukuk* securities. Out of 64 pairs of securities tested, only in 13 pairs (20 percent) was the null hypothesis was rejected at a 5 percent significance level. This indicates that one may not generally conclude that the yield of conventional bonds causes the yield of *sukuk*.

The results also show that the yield of conventional bonds issued by Khazanah (1 and 2 years), AAA-rated financial institutions (three months, six months, and 1 year), AAA-rated guaranteed corporations (six months, 1 year, 2 years, and 20 years), and AAA-rated corporations (three months, six months, 1 year, and 2 years) caused the yield of *sukuk*.

The results do not show a definite pattern of causality related to the issuer or the maturity of the security. However, 12 out of 13 pairs of securities with up to two years' maturity showed causal relations. A causal relation between conventional bonds and *sukuk* was more common among the securities issued by AAA-rated guaranteed corporations (4 out of 10 pairs), AAA-rated corporations (4 out of 10 pairs), and financial institutions (3 out of 10 pairs). However, these patterns are not conclusive.

Finally, the statistics in Table 7.2 suggest a bidirectional causality between the yields of *sukuk* and conventional bonds in 5 out of 64 pairs (7 percent). Thus, both null hypotheses were significantly rejected.

This finding could also indicate that both of these variables are caused by a third variable yet to be identified. The results show that the yields of *sukuk* and conventional bonds have a bidirectional causal relation in securities issued by Khazanah (two years), AAA-rated financial institutions (three months and six months), AAA-rated guaranteed corporations (two years), and AAA-rated corporations (two years).

CONCLUSION

The main message of this chapter is that the two forms of debt are not the same. This means that the *sukuk* industry has to evolve policies and practices that are tailored to the differences incorporated in *sukuk* designs. Obviously, the design features introduce higher risk, particularly given the sharing of loss in a case of failure as well as the general risk-sharing nature of these instruments.

This finding is very important. This infant industry must align its practices with the specific character of this market. No longer is it feasible to merely follow the advocacy services in the conventional bond markets, as has been done for centuries. We will call attention to this again at the conclusion of this book.

Sukuk Securities
in Practice

Two

Sukuk Securities in Practice

CHAPTER 8

Regulations with a Difference

S*ukuk* securities, similar to their conventional counterparts, are regulated—in fact, extra regulated. In addition to having to comply with the common financial regulations, they are required to follow *Shari'ah* regulations. This chapter discusses three major international *Shari'ah* regulatory bodies.

REGULATING *SUKUK*

In order to be recognized as an Islamic, or participation, transactions, *sukuk* products must comply with Islamic moral and ethical codes in financial contracting. The *Shari'ah* regulations governing *sukuk*, which are similar to those governing other Islamic finance and banking practices, are dictated by three sources: international organizations, local authorities, and *Shari'ah* supervisory boards and advisory councils.

Some major Islamic financial institutions have their own in-house *Shari'ah* supervisory boards. This is mostly the case among investment companies and banks. In the process of issuing *sukuk*, according to the Liquidity Management Center of Bahrain, *Shari'ah* advisors should study the proposed *sukuk* structure and suggest a structure that fulfills the economic aims of the issuance of the *sukuk*. In addition, the *Shari'ah* advisors should work closely with the legal counsel of the issuer and the arranger (the investment banker) to ensure that the legal documents are in line with *Shari'ah* requirements. Finally, the *Shari'ah* advisors should issue a fatwa, a legal opinion on the compliance of the *sukuk* products with basic Islamic principles—similar to the opinion that tax authorities provide on a tax question—so that a *sukuk* deal can be put into circulation.

Islamic financial institutions are subject to the rules and regulations of the local *Shari'ah* authority as well. Some countries such as Malaysia have set up their own *Shari'ah* advisory councils at a national level, which oversee and determine the proper way of conducting Islamic financial transactions. These councils are part of the Securities Commission or of the central bank of the country. At the international level (i.e., the Organization of Islamic Countries) there is a *Shari'ah* council based in Saudi Arabia.

There are few international organizations that attempt to regulate and screen the conduct of *sukuk* issuance and trades. The most influential are the Accounting and Auditing Organization for Islamic Financial Institutions (AAOIFI), the Islamic Financial Services Board (ISFB), and the International Islamic Financial Market (IIFM). Although these organizations try to base their rulings on *Shari'ah* principles, there are occasions when the *sukuk* based on their guidelines have variations in practice. Therefore, increased communication among these organizations is necessary to bridge the differences in *sukuk* contracts.

The decisions on the permissibility of each *sukuk* contract is made by expert scholars of Islam who are appointed to the *Shari'ah* board. Currently, the number of these experts is estimated to be between 100 and 200 worldwide. This indicates an urgent need to train more expert scholars to sit on *Shari'ah* boards in Islamic financial institutions. In order to address this shortfall, some Islamic institutions, such as the International Shari'ah Research Academy for Islamic Finance and the International Centre for Education in Islamic France (both based in Kuala Lumpur, Malaysia), plan long-term training programs as certified *Shari'ah* scholars. However, some other institutions (e.g., the Dr. Kahf Institute, REDmoney Islamic Finance, and the UK Islamic Finance Council) are currently providing short-term courses on this topic.

The Accounting and Auditing Organization for Islamic Financial Institutions

On its website, the AAOIFI introduces itself as an Islamic international, autonomous, nonprofit corporate body that prepares accounting, auditing, governance, ethical, and *Shari'ah* standards for the Islamic financial industry. The AAOIFI was established in 1990 by Islamic financial institutions in Algiers. In 1991 it was registered in Bahrain. As an independent international organization, the AAOIFI is supported by more than 200 members from 45 countries. Members include central banks, Islamic financial institutions, and other participants from the international Islamic banking and finance industry. Compliance is voluntary; there is no mechanism to enforce the standards.

The AAOIFI has gained solid support for the implementation of its standards, which have been adopted in Bahrain, Dubai, Jordan, Lebanon, Qatar, Sudan, and Syria. The relevant authorities in Australia, Indonesia,

Malaysia, Pakistan, Saudi Arabia, and South Africa have issued guidelines that are based on the AAOIFI's standards and pronouncements. The establishment of the AAOIFI represented a shift from the authority of independent *Shari'ah* supervisory boards in individual Islamic banking and finance operations to a centralized model for the dissemination of standards, procedures, and best practices.

The AAOIFI is governed through a board of trustees that appoints the members of two other boards: the accounting and auditing standards board and the *Shari'ah* board. The primary role of the former is to study and develop standards, mainly from the practitioners' points of view, and the main task of the latter is to analyze the drafts from a *Shari'ah* perspective. The *Shari'ah* board members are *fiqh* (Islamic jurisprudence) scholars who represent *Shari'ah* supervisory boards in the Islamic financial institutions or central banks that are members of the AAOIFI. An influential scholar, Shaikh Muhammad Taqi Usmani, is the chairman of the body.

As an international standard setter, the AAOIFI develops, prepares, and issues financial accounting standards, *Shari'ah* standards, and their relevant exposure drafts through a system of due process and industry practitioner consultations. By the end of August 2010, there were 26 accounting standards, 5 auditing standards, 7 governance standards, 2 ethics standards, and 35 *Shari'ah* standards developed and issued by the AAOIFI.

In May 2003, the AAOIFI issued *Shari'ah* financial accounting standard (FAS) 17, Investment *Sukuk*. In this standard, the AAOIFI issued criteria for 14 different types of *sukuk* in which some of the *sukuk* are classified as tradable and others are classified as nontradable based on their type and characteristics. The *sukuk* mentioned in FAS 17 are *murabahah, istisna, salam, ijarah, mudarabah,* and *musharakah.* Other types of *sukuk* that are defined in this AAOIFI standard but not widely used are *wakalah, muzarah, musaqa, muqarasah, ijarah mowsufa bithimn, manfaah ijarah, manfaah ijarah mowsufa bithimn,* and *milkiyat al-khadamat.*

The AAOIFI and its *Shari'ah* board chairman, Usmani, have paid special attention to *sukuk* because it is one of the most favored Islamic financing instruments and there is a possibility of variation in contract formation by the practitioners. Usmani has made some comments on the practice of *sukuk* over time. For instance, he has highlighted the following:

> *Since* Ijarah sukuk *represent the pro rata ownership of their holders in the tangible assets of the fund, and not the liquid amounts*

*or debts, they are fully negotiable and can be sold and purchased
in the secondary market. Anyone who purchases these* sukuk
*replaces the sellers in the pro rata ownership of the relevant assets
and all the rights and obligations of the original subscriber are
passed on to him. The price of these* sukuk *will be determined on
the basis of market forces, and are normally based on their profitability.*[1]

However, his most cited and debated comment regarding *sukuk* is his
statement in November 2007 that as much as 85 percent of the outstanding *sukuk* had failed the test of *Shari'ah* compliance on the basis that they
were asset based rather than asset backed, with the guaranteed return of
the face value of the *sukuk* on maturity and in the absence of a transfer
in asset ownership to *sukuk* holders. After that, the juridical validity of
sukuk became suspect. Usmani's reasons for such a declaration were as
follows:

- There have been cases in which the assets in the *sukuk* were the shares
  of companies that do not confer true ownership but that merely offer
  sukuk holders a right to returns.
- Most *sukuk* issued are identical to conventional bonds in terms of the
  distribution of profits from their enterprises at fixed-percentage benchmarked on interest rates. The legal presumption regarding *sukuk* is that
  no fixed rate of profit or the refund of capital can be guaranteed.
- Virtually all *sukuk* issues guarantee the return of the principal to the
  holder at maturity (just as in conventional bonds) through a binding
  promise from either the issuer or the manager to repurchase the assets
  at the stated price regardless of their true or market value at maturity.

In February 2008, the AAOIFI issued a guidance statement on accounting for investments and an amendment to FAS 17. The important issues
raised in this guideline may be summarized as follows:

- *Sukuk* issuances have to be backed by real assets, the ownership of
  which has to be legally transferred to the *sukuk* holders to be tradable.
- *Sukuk* must not represent receivables or debts, except in the case of
  a trading or financial entity selling all its assets or a portfolio with a
  standing financial obligation in which some debts, owed by a third

---

[1] M. Usmani, *Principles of* Shari'ah *Governing Islamic Investment Funds* (Bahrain:
AAOIFI, 2001).

party and incidental to physical assets or usufruct, are unintentionally included.

- The manager of the *sukuk* is prohibited from extending loans to make up for the shortfall in the return on the assets, whether acting as a *mudarib* (investment manager), *sharik* (partner), or *wakil* (agent);
- Guarantees to repurchase the assets at nominal value upon maturity are prohibited, except in *ijarah sukuk* structures.
- Closer scrutiny of documentation and subsequent execution of the transaction are required by *Shari'ah* supervisory boards.

Some scholars who investigated this controversial issue concluded that for some, Usmani's salvo was a long overdue and much needed corrective to what they saw as the excesses of *sukuk* issuances and structured financing vehicles, which came very close to mimicking conventional bonds. To others, it was an overreaction, born of impatience with the pace of development of Islamic financial institutions and markets, and an unrealistic appraisal of what Islamic finance can actually accomplish in a globally interdependent world.

The Islamic Financial Services Board

The IFSB, which is based in Kuala Lumpur, was established in 2002 and funded by 45 central banks. It serves as an international standard-setting body of regulatory and supervisory agencies that have a vested interest in ensuring the soundness and stability of the Islamic financial services industry (banking, the capital market, and insurance). The IFSB promotes the development of a prudent and transparent Islamic financial services industry through introducing new, or adapting existing international standards consistent with *Shari'ah* principles and recommending them for adoption. The work of the IFSB complements that of the Basel Committee on Banking Supervision, the International Organization of Securities Commissions, and the International Association of Insurance Supervisors.

As of August 2010, the 195 members of the IFSB comprised 52 regulatory and supervisory authorities; 6 international intergovernmental organizations; and 137 market players, professional firms, and industry associations operating in 40 jurisdictions.

Drafting of standards in IFSB is done by a task force or working group. The IFSB council appoints members of a technical committee who are responsible for advising the council on the technical issues within scope. The Islamic Development Bank's *Shari'ah* supervisory board is responsible for the *Shari'ah* supervision of IFSB's standards. There are currently six *Shari'ah* scholars on this committee.

The following three standards of the IFSB affect *sukuk*'s issuance, trading, and investing:

1. **IFSB-1.** Guiding principles of risk management for institutions (other than insurance institutions) offering only Islamic financial services, issued in December 2005. This guideline includes the various risk elements affecting institutions offering investment certificates such as *sukuk* and the operational consideration regarding them. This guideline offers a general perspective on risk sources and risk management and is not specific for *sukuk*.

2. **IFSB-2.** Capital adequacy standard for institutions (other than insurance institutions) offering only Islamic financial services, issued in December 2005. This standard is an overview of the various Islamic contracts (some of which are underlying contracts of *sukuk*) and provides capital requirement for each.

3. **IFSB-7.** Capital adequacy requirements for *sukuk*, securitizations, and real estate investment, issued in January 2009. The first part of this guideline investigates the *sukuk* and its securitization; *sukuk* structures; the operational requirements pertaining to *sukuk*; the treatment, for regulatory capital purposes, of *sukuk* and securitization exposures; and the treatment of credit risk exposures of *sukuk*.

The International Islamic Financial Market

The IIFM, located in Bahrain, is a global standardization body for the Islamic capital and money market segment of the Islamic financial services industry. Its primary focus is the standardization of Islamic products, documentation, and related processes. The IIFM was founded with the collective efforts of Central Bank of Bahrain, Bank Indonesia, Central Bank of Sudan, the Labuan Financial Services Authority (Malaysia), the Ministry of Finance of Brunei, and the Islamic Development Bank (a multilateral institution based in Saudi Arabia).

The IIFM is also supported by its permanent members: State Bank of Pakistan and the Dubai International Financial Centre Authority (UAE). The IIFM is further supported by a number of regional and international financial institutions and other market participants as its members. IIFM activities are under supervision of its *Shari'ah* advisory panel, which currently has 10 members.

The focus of the IIFM's work is Islamic capital and money markets. Currently, the IIFM has no specific standard or guideline pertaining to *sukuk*. However, it released a report on *sukuk* in 2010 in which it investigated the current *sukuk* market from an international and a domestic perspective. It investigated various *sukuk* structures for international issues and studied some *sukuk* issues as case studies.

CONCLUSION

The scrutiny of the regulatory process applied to cases examined in this chapter provides additional information to the conclusions in Chapter 4. The *sukuk* markets are remarkably different in design, contracting, and practice. No wonder their yields are significantly different as well. Although securitization may share features with conventional bond issuance, there are significant differences in the initial public offering process of this whole new form of debt contracting. This chapter expanded this theme to show that the regulatory process also differs from that applied to conventional bonds.

Conventional bond issues are general-purpose funding contracts (despite the prospectus indicating the intended use of the proceeds). The regulatory process is much simpler for this huge market for funds. The *sukuk* bond market is no more than 1 percent of the world market for bonds. As emphasized in an earlier chapter, *sukuk* funding is targeted funding for specific aspects of the producer's funding needs. This introduces complexity in the design of *sukuk* products. By necessity the regulatory process is much more onerous than is the case for conventional bond design, issue, sale, and listing. This fundamental difference makes *sukuk* bonds very different from conventional bonds for regulatory purposes.

CHAPTER 9

Securitization, Trading, and Rating

This chapter provides an introduction to the market-making process used by the players in the Islamic debt securities marketplace. The process of structuring a *sukuk* contract is vastly different from its conventional counterpart in two respects: *Sukuk* funding is targeted funding, compared to general-purpose lending in conventional debt, and the mode of pricing is based on the sharing of profit and loss. Both aspects, along with the asset-backing principle, make for a unique securitization process, very different from that of conventional banking practices.

SUKUK TRADING

Sukuk, like other financial securities, can be offered only after meeting all the requirements of the relevant rules and regulations of the countries where they are structured for issue. Its initial public offering (IPO), disclosure requirements, and structure of a special purpose company (SPC) are discussed in the following subsections.

Sukuk Securitization as IPO

The essence of *sukuk*, from a modern perspective, lies in the concept of asset monetization (i.e., securitization), which is achieved through the process of *sukuk* issuance, known as *taskeek*. Its great potential is in transforming an asset's future cash flow into present cash flow. *Taskeek* usually takes place in the primary market where the issuing company will sell debt certificates (*sukuk*) to investors. The Liquidity Management Center of Bahrain listed the following steps in the issuance of *sukuk*:

- Preparing a detailed feasibility study stating clearly the objectives of the proposed *Shari'ah*-compliant business.

- Setting up a general framework and an organizational structure through the investor and an institutional relationship to support the issuance process.
- Working out an appropriate *Shari'ah*-compliant structure to achieve the objectives.
- Arranging for the lead manager (the investment bank) to underwrite the *sukuk* issue.
- Arranging legal documentation for the agreed-upon structure, from both the issuer's and the arranger's perspectives.
- Setting up the SPC to represent the investors (*sukuk* holders).
- Putting the *sukuk* into circulation.

Most *sukuk* securities issued to date have been privately placed. *Sukuk* securities are mostly offered to institutional investors (i.e., wholesale investors), who invest in large denominations, rather than to the general public (i.e., retail investors), which tends to subscribe to securities on a smaller scale. Moreover, many of the *sukuk* securities are not traded on a stock exchange but are traded by investors over the counter in the secondary market. It has been estimated that only a quarter of *sukuk* securities are listed and that the remainder are traded over-the-counter. Although the stock exchange does not function as a primary trading platform for *sukuk*, many issuers endeavor to list *sukuk* for the following reasons:

- **Regulatory oversight.** The fact that the offering document must be reviewed and approved by the relevant stock exchange assures investors that the issuer, the offer, and the disclosure contained in the offering document complies with certain minimum standards, which thereby makes the offer more attractive to investors.
- **Investor requirements.** Certain investors may be permitted to invest in only listed *sukuk* (e.g., in order to benefit from favorable tax treatment of cash flow from *sukuk*).
- **Public profile.** The listing enhances the public profile of the issuer and thereby attracts more interest from investors in the secondary market.

Any issuer wishing to list a *sukuk* for trading on a secondary exchange market is required to apply to the respective listing authorities—namely, the Securities Commission and the stock exchange. The listing procedures, prospectus, transparency regimen, and classification of *sukuk* instruments are based on the governing listing rules of that specific market. For instance, *sukuk* issuers are required to apply to the UK Listing Authority, a division of the Financial Services Authority (the functions of which were taken over in 2013 by the Bank of England) before being listed on the London Stock Exchange.

Disclosure

Authorities of financial markets always require market participants to disclose some information to the public. This is to prevent the exploitation of individual, less informed, minority investors by the issuing firms. In Islamic capital markets, and especially in *sukuk* markets, in order to accomplish the principle of avoiding excessive uncertainty and to reduce information asymmetry among the various parties in a *sukuk* contract, disclosure of certain information is required by the *Shari'ah* authorities, which is an additional layer for investor and consumer protection. The disclosure of information regarding *sukuk* investment is done not only at the issuance time but also after that. This is a special aspect of *sukuk* market making.

One of the key documents in the process of *sukuk* issuance, as in conventional funding, is the prospectus. The contents of a prospectus must be in compliance with the authority's efforts to promote greater disclosure of information vital to investment decisions. A prospectus must include all information that investors and their advisors would reasonably require and expect to find in a prospectus for the purpose of making informed investment decisions.

The guidelines on a prospectus issued by a local authority in an Islamic financial market set out the minimum level of information that must be disclosed as an initial guide to the market. Common disclosures that are required under these guidelines include information pertaining to the issuer, the terms and conditions of the funding, financial information, risk analysis, ratings, recourse in the event of default, the intended utilization of the proceeds, and details on related-party transactions.

For instance, the Securities Commission of Malaysia adopted a disclosure-based approach for the issue, offer, or invitation of a conventional bond or *sukuk* issue for domestic issuers. The Securities Commission grants its approval upon fulfillment of the following requirements:

- Submission of a full set of documents and relevant information, as clearly outlined in the private debt security guidelines, the asset-backed securities guidelines, or the Islamic securities guidelines, which allow investors to make informed decisions.
- Compliance with a set of transparent criteria required of an issuer and a principal advisor under these guidelines.
- Compliance with any additional requirements that may be imposed by the Securities Commission to protect the interests of private debt security or *sukuk* holders.

The Securities Commission imposed some additional requirements for a *sukuk* issuance. An issuer must appoint an independent *Shari'ah* advisor who possesses the relevant qualifications and expertise, particularly in *fiqh al-mu'amalat* (Islamic principles of trade), and who has a minimum of three years' working experience or exposure to Islamic finance. Alternatively, the issuer may appoint the *Shari'ah* committee of an Islamic bank or a licensed institution approved by Bank Negara Malaysia, the central bank. The main duty of such a *Shari'ah* advisor is to advise on all aspects of Islamic securities, including documentation, structuring, investment, and other administrative and operational matters pertaining to Islamic securities.

The information disclosure of the *sukuk* issuer is not limited to the issuance period. After listing a *sukuk* on a market, the respective authority will demand that the issuer disclose some information on a periodic or continual basis. For instance, the Dubai International Financial Center's *sukuk* guidebook mentions once a *sukuk* is listed on NASDAQ Dubai, the relevant reporting entity is obliged to comply with the continuing obligations under the Listing Rules and the Offered Securities Rules (OSRs) until the *sukuk* matures or is redeemed.[1]

The purpose of the continuing obligations is to "give investors in securities proper information to assess the current value of the securities [and] to evaluate [whether] the NASDAQ Dubai market is well-regulated."[2] The continuing obligations are broadly divided into two categories: obligations that apply continuously and obligations that apply only on a periodic basis. The continuing obligations imposed by the OSRs and the Listing Rules for *sukuk* are substantially similar to the continuing obligations imposed for corporate bonds, with some additions and variations.

The first category of obligations relates primarily to the disclosure of price-sensitive information to the market.[3] Price-sensitive information is information that is liable to lead to a substantial movement in the price of securities or information that significantly affects the ability of the issuer to meet its commitments. The reporting entity is required to consider whether any material development is likely to constitute price-sensitive information. Any price-sensitive information must be disclosed to the market in a timely manner through NASDAQ Dubai's company announcement platform (CAP).[4]

The second category of obligations requires the reporting entity to file specific types of information periodically, and these obligations apply regardless of the occurrence of any material events. For example, the reporting entity is required to disseminate its annual report and year-end

---

[1] Listing Rule 28 and Appendix F, parts 1 and 2; OSR, chapter 8.
[2] Listing Rule 27.
[3] Listing Rule 28 and Appendix F, part 1.
[4] Listing Rule 28, part 2.

audited accounts through the CAP system within four months of the end of the relevant financial period.[5]

Whereas these continuing obligations apply to all reporting entities, certain additional obligations apply to reporting entities of listed *sukuk* (or other *Shari'ah*-compliant securities). For example, a reporting entity is required to disclose, through an announcement to NASDAQ Dubai, any changes to the composition and membership of the relevant *Shari'ah* board that issued the fatwa, or legal opinion.[6]

However, in a majority of *sukuk* issuances, the *fatwa* will have been issued by the *Shari'ah* board of one of the arranging banks because the reporting entity might not have its own *Shari'ah* board. It will therefore not be possible for the reporting entity to monitor changes to the composition of the *Shari'ah* board on an ongoing basis. In such cases, the reporting entity may apply to the Dubai Financial Services Authority for an exemption from this rule.

The Listing Rules also contain a technical requirement for a reporting entity to provide an annual certificate from the relevant *Shari'ah* board certifying that the *sukuk* continues to meet standards.[7] This is an additional layer of supervision that makes *sukuk* issues subject to continual vetting. However, because of the concerns raised by issuers about the feasibility of complying with this rule, NASDAQ Dubai has not insisted on compliance with this requirement, according to market players.

Special Purpose Company (SPC)

Structuring *sukuk* is, in many respects, similar to structuring conventional securitization—but with asset backing as a novel idea based on historical precedence. The design of the security is derived from the conventional securitization process, in which an SPC is set up to acquire the assets of the borrower and to issue financial claims by investors on the assets. Such financial claims represent a proportionate beneficial ownership for a defined period, when the risk and the return associated with the cash flow generated by an underlying asset is passed to the *sukuk* holders.

The core contract utilized in the process of *sukuk* securitization is a *mudarabah* (partnership) contract. This contract is used to create a special-purpose *mudarabah* (SPM) entity, similar to the conventional SPC, to play a well-defined role in acquiring certain assets and issuing certificates against the assets. The underlying assets acquired by the SPM must be *Shari'ah*-compliant and can vary in nature. Depending on the nature of the

---

[5] OSR Appendix 2.1.1, rule 13.
[6] Ibid., rule 5.
[7] Listing Rules, Appendix F, part 2, paragraph 15.

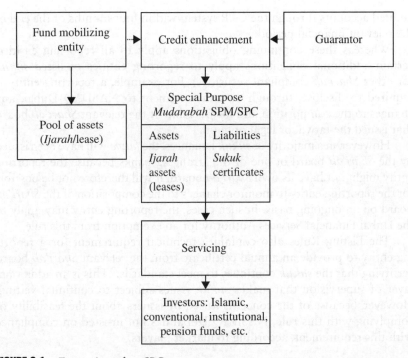

FIGURE 9.1 Formation of an SPC
Source: Z. Iqbal, "Financial Engineering in Islamic Finance," *Thunderbird International Business Review* 41 (1999).

underlying assets and the slight differences in interpretation by the various schools of thought, the tradability and negotiability of the issued certificates is determined. The process of formation of an SPC is depicted in Figure 9.1.

The SPC is subject to the rulings and regulations of the local authority that governs the financial market in which the SPC is intended to be adjudicated. For instance, under the 2009 regulations of the Dubai International Financial Center (DIFC), an SPC is a company limited by shares that is established under standard articles of association published by the DIFC Authority. Each SPC is registered in the General Register of Companies and Recognized Companies as well as in a new separate register maintained by the DIFC Authority called the Special Purpose Companies Register.

Activities that an SPC can undertake include the following activities, whether conducted in a conventional or a *Shari'ah*-compliant manner:

- The acquisition (e.g., through leasing, title transfer, or risk transfer), holding, and disposal of any asset (tangible or intangible, including but not limited to receivables and shares).

- The obtaining of any type of financing (banking or capital market), the granting of any type of security interest over its assets, the providing of any indemnity or similar support for the benefit of its shareholders or any of its subsidiaries, or the entering of any type of hedging arrangements.
- The financing of the entity for whose transaction the SPC has been established, or another SPC.
- The acting trustee or agent.

SPCs are often intended to be insolvency or bankruptcy remote, which means that circumstances that could lead to a declaration of their insolvency are minimized to the greatest extent possible. This prevents investors from rushing to secure all the assets of a borrower when a borrower is experiencing temporary cash-flow problem. Under an SPC arrangement, the decision involves only the SPC, not the parent firm.

Therefore, an SPC is not expected to have any employees of its own; instead, the SPC appoints a corporate service provider. The corporate management services typically provided by to an SPC include corporate officers such as directors and a secretary, a registered office, and other day-to-day administration and accounting services.

Sukuk and other structured financial transactions have often utilized companies established in offshore jurisdictions. This has been partly for tax purposes but is also because of uncertainties in the legal framework and enforcement process in the courts about structured finance.

SUKUK RATING METHODOLOGIES

A rating is an evaluation of a corporate (or municipal) bond's relative safety, from an investment standpoint. In the conventional sense, it scrutinizes the issuer's ability to repay the principal and make interest payments. Then a grade (the most controversial part of the rating process) is given to the bond that indicates its credit quality. Private independent international rating companies such as Standard & Poor's (S&P) and Moody's, or domestic rating agencies such as the Rating Agency Malaysia (RAM) and the Malaysian Rating Corporation (MARC), provide these evaluations of an issuer's financial strength. As a result, bonds are rated in a range from AAA or Aaa (the highest), to C or D, which represents a company that has already defaulted. Each rating company has its own definition and methodology for rating and its own set of rating ranges. Fitch has become the dominant rating agency for these instruments across the world as of 2014.

The introduction of *sukuk* rating in 1994 represented another critical milestone in the development of the *sukuk* market. Bond ratings are principally designed to arrive at a reasoned judgment on credit risk through a careful analysis of the critical issues surrounding the specific debt of an issuer to service the obligations.

From the global capital market point of view, *sukuk* can be rated just like any conventional bond and can be traded as such. In general, rating agencies have broadly the same criteria for corporate bond rating. The criteria incorporate issue structure (e.g., repayment schedule and debt types), business risk analysis, financial risk analysis, management, ownership, and other qualitative factors. However, because of the uniqueness and types of *sukuk*, the rating methodology should be different from conventional bonds rating methodology

Sukuk structures fall into two categories:

1. **Asset-backed** *sukuk*. For this, the ratings are dependent on a risk analysis of the asset. However, the investors hold rights to the underlying assets through the SPC and not directly; hence, *sukuk* performance is driven by assets and not linked to the originator.
2. **Unsecured** *sukuk*. For this, the ratings are primarily dependent on the riskiness of the sponsor, the originator, or the borrower.

Therefore, as with conventional bonds, the risk elements affecting *sukuk* should be thoroughly investigated by the rating agencies. Of all the risk elements, credit risk is the most critical. Other factors are currency risk (for international issues), tax risk, and reserve funds.

In contrast to highly sensitive conventional bonds, *sukuk* are less sensitive to interest rate. The Zurich-based investment bank Credit Suisse believes that investment in Islamic finance and banking products does not expose the investor to interest-rate risk, since Islam prohibits charging interest and *sukuk* securities are unaffected by the credit crisis in the international finance and banking industry. The risk characteristics of each type of *sukuk* structures are depicted in Table 9.1.

Standard & Poor's

S&P uses three analytical approaches for rating *sukuk*. First, it determines the extent of any credit enhancement (such as an irrevocable purchase undertaking), and the nature of any collateral security. Second, it analyzes the source of repayment of the *sukuk* (periodic reward distributions versus rental payments). Third, it determines the extent of any government support.

S&P's credit analysts have explained their rating methodology of *sukuk*. S&P's ratings are an opinion of the issuer's ability and willingness to meet its financial obligations in a timely manner, without commenting on *Shari'ah* compliance. The rating of an Islamic debt instrument varies, depending on

TABLE 9.1 Summary of Risk Characteristics of *Sukuk* Structures

Type of *Sukuk*	Description of *Sukuk* Structure	Credit Risk	Rate of Return (Interest Rate Risk)	Foreign-Exchange (FX) Risk	Price Risk	Other Risks
Zero coupon *sukuk*	*Istisna, murabahah* debt certificates; nontradable.	Unique basis of credit risks exists.	Very high because of fixed rate; remains for the entire maturity of the issue.	If all other conditions are similar, FX risk will be the same for all cases of *sukuk*. However, those *sukuk* that are liquid or that are relatively short-term in nature will be less exposed. The composition of assets in the pool will also contribute to the FX risk in different ways. Hence, this can be a very useful tool for overcoming the FX risk by diversifying the pool in different currencies.	Related to the underlying commodities prices and assets in relation to the market prices. *Ijarah sukuk* is most exposed to this because the values of the underlying assets may depreciate faster compared to market prices. Maintenance of the assets will play an important part in this process. Liquidity of the *sukuk* will also play an important part in the risk. *Salam* is also exposed to price risks. However, through parallel contracts these risks can be overcome.	Liquidity risk is serious as far as the nontradable *sukuk* are concerned.
Fixed-rate *ijarah sukuk*	Securitized *ijarah*; certificate holder owns part of asset or usufructs and earns fixed rent; tradable.	Default on rent payment with a fixed rate makes credit risk more serious.	Very high because of fixed rate; remains for the entire maturity of the issue.			Business risk of the issuer is a risk underlying *sukuk* compared to traditional fixed incomes.
Floating-rate *ijarah sukuk*	Certificate holder owns part of asset or usufructs and earns floating rent indexed to market benchmark such as LIBOR; tradable.	Default on rent payment with a floating rate makes default risk less serious than previous case.	Exists only within the time of the floating period, normally six months.			*Shari'ab*-compliance risk is also unique in the case of *sukuk*.
Fixed-rate hybrid or pooled *sukuk*	Securitized pool of assets; debts must not be more than 49%; floating-rate possibility exists; tradable.	Credit risk of debt part of pool; default on rent with fixed rate makes credit risk serious.	Very high because of fixed rate; remains for the entire maturity of the issue.			Infrastructure rigidities (i.e., lack of efficient institutional support) increases the risk of *sukuk* compared to traditional fixed incomes.
Musharakah term-finance *sukuk* (MTFS)	Medium-term redeemable *musharakah* certificate based on diminishing *musharakah*; tradable as well as redeemable.	*Musharakah* has high default risk; however, MTFS could be based on the strength of the entire balance sheet.	Similar to floating rate but unique because the rate is not indexed with a benchmark like LIBOR; hence least exposed to this risk.			
Salam sukuk	Securitized *salam*; fixed rate and nontradable.	Unique credit risk.	Very high because of fixed rate.			

Source: (Tariq, 2004)

the degree of performance risk of the asset backing the transaction. In a 2008 report on *sukuk* rating, Islamic Finance Asia mentioned that beside the issuer's ability and willingness to meet its financial obligations in a timely manner, the rating also depends on the type of collateral and transaction structure. S&P has categorized this matter into three groups:

1. **Sukuk with full credit-enhancement mechanisms.** This sort of *sukuk* receives an irrevocable third-party guarantee, usually by a parent or the original owner of the underlying collateral. The guarantor provides *Shari'ah*-compliant shortfall amounts in case the issuer (i.e., the SPC) cannot make payment. The ratings of this type of *sukuk* largely depend on the creditworthiness of the guarantor or the entity providing the credit enhancement mechanisms, as well as the ranking of the *sukuk* (usually senior unsecured), among other financial obligations of the guarantor.
2. **Sukuk with no credit-enhancement mechanisms.** This structure resembles asset-backed securities in a securitization. The pool of underlying assets is the sole basis for reward and principal payment. The ratings of these *sukuk* are largely based on the ability of the underlying assets to generate sufficient cash in a timely manner to meet the SPC's obligations. For this type of *sukuk*, S&P's ratings are based on the performance of the underlying assets under different stress scenarios, along with the expected value of these assets at maturity.
3. **Sukuk with partial credit-enhancement mechanisms.** This structure combines the first two categories with a third-party guarantee absorbing limited shortfalls from an otherwise asset-backed transaction. S&P's ratings approach depends on its estimate of the capacity of the underlying assets to meet the SPC's financial obligations, the terms of the guarantee, and the creditworthiness of the guarantor.

S&P credit analysts Mohamed Damak and colleagues said the following:

We came to the conclusion that our existing stability ratings, used since 1999 to rate income funds in Canada, are applicable to IFIs [Islamic financial institutions] that offer PSIAs [participation security Islamic Assets], with only a few adjustments. We assign ratings of SR-1 to IFIs that we believe have the highest level of expected stability of distributable cash flow. Conversely, IFIs rated SR-7 have, in our opinion, the lowest degree of expected stability.[8]

They added that stability ratings range from SR-1 to SR-7.

---

[8] M., Damak, E. Volland, and K. Nassif, "Standard & Poor's Approach to Rating *Sukuk*," *S&P's Islamic Finance Outlook 2008*, 2007.

In 2005, Richard King investigated S&P's *ijarah sukuk* rating and reported that in most cases, S&P has assigned *ijarah sukuk* the same ratings it assigns to the originator. This practice reflects the unconditional and irrevocable nature of the lease, any third-party lease guarantees, sale and purchase agreements, and/or financial hedges that are found in the transaction. Ratings lower than those given to the lessee are assigned when there are diminished recovery prospects, greater risks associated with lease payments, or other factors supporting such a distinction. Higher ratings are unlikely without additional risk-mitigating features in the case of sovereigns, although corporate *ijarah sukuk* may resemble certain characteristics of secured loans and be notched up accordingly.

King highlighted that S&P bases its credit rating opinion on the compliance of an *ijarah sukuk* transaction with applicable commercial law, and the rating therefore does not reflect the compliance of the transaction with *Shari'ah*. S&P believes that a transaction governed solely by *Shari'ah* might be difficult to rate because of the lack of predictability of outcomes in a *Shari'ah* court, with the possibility of *Shari'ah* principles overriding otherwise valid commercial contractual obligations. Indeed, certain *Shari'ah*-compliant transactions have specifically disavowed *Shari'ah* jurisdiction as a matter of substance, although they may satisfy *Shari'ah* requirements as a matter of form.

Moody's

Moody's normally resorts to conservative assumptions in new markets such as the Middle East and Asia, where the provision of wider statistical data on the overall market cannot be obtained. A key element is the default rate of the assets and the corresponding recovery levels following a default. Moody uses either a statistical loss distribution approach (for highly granular portfolios) or a correlation structure model approach (for nongranular portfolios). This allows the rating agency to model the cash flow generated by the asset pool and to provide the primary quantitative input into the rating, but such analysis becomes irrelevant if the legal structure does not support the *sukuk* holder's rights to the underlying assets and their cash flow. Any other material factors such as currency risk, hedge agreements, and taxes are also modeled. The final result is a complete set of asset-pool loss scenarios accompanied by the probability of their occurrence.

Moody's then processes the cash flow through a model that replicates the succession of payments and any structural enhancements (e.g., interest coverage triggers or reserve funds) specified in the documentation. In some scenarios, a high default rate on the underlying assets results in impairment of the *sukuk* and a loss of the amount due to its holders. Each scenario will have a loss rate (0–100%); Moody's then takes the loss and multiplies it by the probability of its likelihood. When all these probability-weighted losses are summed up, the expected loss is obtained for the *sukuk*, which is then assigned a Moody's rating.

Similar to S&P, Moody's does not work directly with *Shari'ah* scholars when rating *sukuk* and Islamic banks. Ideally, given the influence the *Shari'ah* board members have over an institution, the decision would be considered more from the corporate governance perspective than from the accounting perspective.

Fitch

Fitch analyzes the structure of a proposed *sukuk* contract to understand and evaluate the cash flow. Fitch follows the general *Shari'ah* requirement that financial assets should not be based on *riba* (interest). When the rating quality of the instrument is tied to the rating quality of the issuer (such as in the case of asset-backed *sukuk* securities) the instrument's rating follows the issuer's rating. Hence, Fitch assumes originator-backed *sukuk* securities as senior unsecured and rates them accordingly by benchmarking to the issuer default rating.

Fitch distinguishes between asset-backed and asset-based securities and rates them differently. In the case of asset-backed securities, in which the underlying asset is collateral and the only credit support, Fitch uses the standard criteria of structured finance instruments. These include the *sukuk* holders having access to the assets in the case of insolvency or default. However, if the title of the asset is not officially transferred to the SPC (for reasons such as cost reduction or obstacles to foreign ownership) the effectiveness of the contract should be scrutinized under the jurisdiction in which the security is issued. In case of asset-based *sukuk* contracts, the ownership transfer is not legally recognized.

Maturity repayment is a debated issue in *sukuk* securities. Currently, there is a tendency toward fixing the repurchase price at issuance time. However, some *Shari'ah* scholars recommend contracts in which the maturity repurchase price is market based. Fitch cautiously approaches such a form of securities and has concluded in its *sukuk* rating guidelines that "if the repurchase price on maturity were to be subject to market risk and therefore have an impact on the repayment amount to *sukuk* holders, this would make the *sukuk* unratable under these criteria."[9]

---

[9] Fitch Rating Agency, *Rating Sukuk: Cross-Sector Criteria Report* (New York: Fitch, 2012).

Another debated issue of *sukuk* structures is the guarantee offered by the originator as a means of reinforcing the contract. Fitch does not always assume this to be a positive feature; it states that "in Fitch's opinion, an explicit guarantee may not necessarily be enforceable in all applicable jurisdictions, but Fitch considers in its review whether it believes that the originator will, nevertheless, perform its obligations under the guarantee."[10]

A majority of the *sukuk* currently issued are issued under English common law, but they are subject to the local legal restrictions on enforceability. Variation in jurisdiction-based laws as well as differences in *Shari'ah* schools of thoughts in different countries adds to the complexity of the legal risks associated with *sukuk* structures. Hence, Fitch investigates this form of risk thoroughly. Fitch incorporates the country risks (such as enforceability of court orders and default or insolvency procedures) in the issuer's risk rating.

However, in the case of *sukuk* securities, the prospectus and other documents are first reviewed. In addition to these documents (which are standard procedures for bonds), *Shari'ah* board decisions are studied exclusively for *sukuk*. Fitch may also review the legal opinions of the lawyers representing both parties of the contract.

RAM

RAM's credit opinions on *sukuk* are issue-specific; they essentially reflect RAM's view of the obligor's willingness and capacity to meet its financial commitments to a particular *sukuk* issue, a certain class of financial obligation, or a specific funding program promptly and in accordance with the terms of that specific commitment.

Thus, it is possible for different *sukuk* issues from the same obligor to carry different ratings because issue-specific ratings by nature depend on the intrinsic risk profile of the respective *sukuk* issue, the legal partiality of the obligation in the event of restructuring, reorganization, bankruptcy or other laws relating to creditors' rights, and any credit enhancement or support for the *sukuk* obligation, including the creditworthiness of guarantors and terms of the guarantees.

RAM's *sukuk* ratings are based on both qualitative and quantitative factors and are premised on the expectations of the obligor's future credit profile rather than on its absolute level of past or current financial measures. In terms of priority ranking of obligations, the contractual commitments

---

[10] Fitch Rating Agency, *Rating Sukuk: Cross-Sector Criteria Report* (New York: Fitch, 2012).

stipulated in the *sukuk* structure firmly render the transaction a financial obligation. It requires the obligor to treat the *sukuk* as it would its other direct, unsecured financial commitments, thus making it indistinguishable in terms of payment priority. In this instance, RAM ratings equalize the *sukuk* rating with the obligor's general credit rating, also referred to as a corporate credit rating (CCR) or senior unsecured debt rating.

However, if the *sukuk* transaction contains terms akin to those of a secured debt structure, with priority of claim over the obligor's assets, the *sukuk* rating may be notched up and rated above the obligor's CCR, depending on the type, nature, and characteristics of the security and its value relative to the *sukuk* obligation. Conversely, if the recovery prospects of the *sukuk* are notably inferior to those of the obligor's other debts, the *sukuk* rating is likely to be notched down from the obligor's CCR. The concept of notching is only meant to differentiate recovery prospects, since a default is likely to interrupt payments on all the issuer's financial obligations.

RAM's approach to *sukuk* transactions may be classified into the following framework:

- An asset-backed or structured-finance rating methodology is used if the *sukuk* transaction encompasses essential securitization elements establishing that the credit risk profile is determined solely by the underlying asset and that *sukuk* investors have ownership and realizable security over the assets.
- If the *sukuk* investors do not possess realizable security over the assets, then the credit risk assessment will be directed toward the entity with the obligation to redeem the *sukuk*; typically, this will be the issuer. In this instance, RAM applies the corporate rating methodology. The credit quality of the corporate obligor is the key driver affecting the credit risk of the *sukuk*, with the final rating assigned depending on the ranking of the *sukuk* vis-à-vis other existing senior unsecured obligations of the issuer.

Despite the responsibility given to *Shari'ah* scholars on the Islamic aspects, RAM's *sukuk* rating methodology still takes into account the distinguishing features of the Islamic securities. RAM's chief operating officer (Islamic ratings), Liza Mohd Noor, has explained as follows:

> *In this regard, our analytical task includes an examination of Shari'ah-related issues, to the extent that it is necessary to appreciate the contractual terms, operations, and mechanism of the underlying contract(s) supporting the Sukuk transaction to be rated, and*

TABLE 9.2 Main Risk Factors Pertaining to *Musharakah* and *Mudarabah Sukuk*

Performance Risks	Cash-Flow Risks	Structural Risks or Enhancements
Intrinsic risk of underlying business (asset)	Stability and adequacy of cash flow	M&A of issuer
Industry and business growth prospects	Cash-flow robustness	Other credit exposures
Cash-flow profile	Delinquency and cash-flow impairment	Conflict of interest
Management's ability	Shortfall coverage	Level of dependence on senior or key personnel
		Preemptive measures to ensure ongoing business

Source: M. I. Ismail, "Rating of *Sukuk,*" workshop at Conference on Structuring Innovative *Sukuk*, Jakarta, Indonesia, June 19, 2007.

also to identify Shari'ah-*related matters that may have a credit impact or a bearing on the risk profile of the* Sukuk.[11]

RAM's assessment of *Shari'ah* forms an added assessment factor to its analytical framework of *sukuk*. As a matter of practice, a declaration from *Shari'ah* scholars ascertaining the *Shari'ah*-compliant nature of the transaction is normally obtained before the final rating.

The common features of RAM's ratings of *mudarabah* and *musharakah sukuk* include business activity, defined maturity, structured finance techniques, and defined events of default (i.e., dissolution events). The critical risk factors in *musharakah* and *mudarabah sukuk* are performance, cash flow, and structure. Items pertaining to these factors are listed in Table 9.2.

MARC

Islamic Finance Asia claimed that at MARC, *sukuk* ratings were not fundamentally different from the conventional ratings before AAOIFI's pronouncement on *sukuk* in February 2008. The *sukuk* issuances that MARC rated before then were all rated by applying conventional credit rating methodology.

---

[11] Islamic Finance Asia, *Islamic Finance Asia Ratings: How Do They Do It?* (Kuala Lumpur, Malaysia: REDmoney Group, 2008).

The main difference is that *sukuk* issuances have to be *Shari'ah*-compliant. The transaction structure of a *sukuk* has to be reviewed by authorities on *Shari'ah* matters preissuance and usually before the rating engagement. MARC has an in-house *Shari'ah* panel to provide consultation on *Shari'ah*-related matters. MARC also has a different set of rating definitions for *sukuk* and non-*sukuk* Islamic debt instruments. This contrasts with the approach of the global credit rating agencies, which employ the same set of rating definitions for both conventional and Islamic financial instruments despite the prohibition of *riba*-based financing.

Since AAOIFI's pronouncement on *sukuk* in February 2008, MARC has believed that there will eventually be a need to differentiate fixed-income from variable-income Islamic financial instruments from a rating perspective, particularly in the light of the differences in the degree of security of principal and the predictability of financial returns. The rating opinion that MARC provides on fixed-income *sukuk* issues focuses on timely payment. In the case of variable-income financial instruments, MARC believes that the investment quality should take precedence over the likelihood of full and timely payment, given the predominant equity characteristics of such instruments.

According to MARC's 2008 report on *sukuk* rating, the key components of the rating of a *sukuk* transaction are as follows:

- **Analysis of the basic structure of the *sukuk*.** MARC's evaluation of a *sukuk* structure revolves around its structuring intent—that is, whether an issue is structured as an asset-backed transaction (in which case it would reflect the performance of the securitized assets) or to achieve a flow-through of the rating of the originator or third-party guarantor to the *sukuk*. The structure of the *sukuk* has a significant effect on the risk profile of the *sukuk* and determines the rating methodology to be used (i.e., the conventional corporate and project finance rating methodology or an asset-backed methodology).
- **Assessment of the key transaction parties.** MARC considers the roles of the key participants in the transaction—the originator, lessee or obligor, guarantor, contractor, and servicer—as well as their individual credit quality, their ability to perform their roles, and the corresponding implications of these for the risk profile of the *sukuk*. A shadow rating may be performed on key participants when MARC believes their credit quality to be an important driver of the rating of the *sukuk* issued.
- **Analysis of assets and cash flow.** This analysis is the most important driver of the ratings assigned to asset-backed and nonrecourse or limited-recourse project-finance *sukuk*. Some *sukuk* are structured with external liquidity support and/or reserve accounts to mitigate interim deficiencies in the returns from the assets. Alternatively, a deficiency

may be a direct and irrevocable obligation of the originator as manager of the *sukuk*. The valuation of the assets forms an important part of MARC's review when the redemption of the *sukuk* is to be partly or wholly derived from refinancing or disposal of the assets to third parties.

- **Assessment of credit enhancement and structural protections.** MARC assesses internal credit enhancements such as reserve accounts, payment succession, and collateral value in addition to external credit support that may be provided by the originator or third-party guarantors.
- **Legal analysis.** The perfection of legal interest in the underlying assets and the insulation of the assets from insolvency or reorganization of the originator or seller are important not only in the context of any securitization but also from the perspective of any secured financing.

The terms under which the *sukuk* are issued may specify certain trigger events that, if they occur, would cause the transaction to be canceled. These include the failure of the lessee to make the required lease payments under an *ijarah sukuk* structure and certain events of insolvency and default connected with the lessee. In *sukuk* structures involving an SPC issuer, MARC considers the bankruptcy remoteness of the SPC and the limitations on the business activities of the SPC.

CONCLUSION

The critical differences in the securitization of assets into a *sukuk* security (privately traded over-the-counter or publicly traded in exchanges) have been carefully examined in this chapter. We noted that the bulk of the *sukuk* issuance is still in institutions, whereas one-third of the issues are traded in exchanges. The process by which a *sukuk* is issued is identified as broadly similar to the process by which a conventional bond is issued. However, there are key differences, given the key differentiating characteristics of a *sukuk* security. The investment banking practices may be similar, but the design features and rating criteria are quite specific to this Islamic (participation) debt instrument.

CHAPTER 10

Worldwide *Sukuk* Markets

Contemporary practices in the *sukuk* trade developed relatively recently, in the last two decades. Hence, the practices and markets are in the making and are not finished products. This chapter reviews the existing modern *sukuk* market and the developments made since its inception in the 1990s.

Sukuk securities are a subset of broader Islamic banking, investment, and finance products. According to Ernst & Young's 2013 *World Islamic Banking Competitiveness Report*, a potential scenario showed that global Islamic banking assets within commercial banks would reach US$1.8 trillion in 2013 (from US$1.3 trillion in 2011), representing an average annual growth of 17 percent.

The Islamic banking growth outlook continues to be positive; Islamic banking is growing twice as fast as the much older modern banking sector in several core markets. In Saudi Arabia, the market share of Islamic banking assets is now over 50 percent, which is the highest rate of growth. Based on the current growth forecast, by 2015 Islamic financial institutions will require at least US$400 billion of short-term, credible, liquid securities to build liquidity for capital management purposes.

The demand for *sukuk* instruments will thus continue to grow, outpacing global supply and providing opportunities for banks to establish and expand their Islamic fixed-income advisory platforms. Including other investor classes, global *sukuk* demand could be in excess of US$600 billion by 2015; 2012 saw a demand in excess of US$110 billion in new issuances—a record year but still short of industry demand.

One source estimates that the market size in 2011 was about US$840 billion. There have been several large issues in 2012 onward, adding more to the outstanding value. The market value is estimated to be US$1,200 billion in 2014. *Sukuk* issues are found in 12 markets, and 3 more have announced their intention to start offering *sukuk*: Hong Kong, Seoul, and Cairo. Kuwait Finance House's 2012 report listed the following as the top countries in *sukuk* issuance: Malaysia, Saudi Arabia, the UAE, and Indonesia. It also noted that the demand for Islamic tradable securities, *sukuk*, is expected to jump from $300 billion in 2011 to $950 billion by 2017.

The *sukuk* market has thus grown rapidly in recent years. The emergence of more than 250 *takaful* (Islamic insurance) companies, 350 Islamic equity funds, and 370 Islamic banks worldwide has led to an enhanced demand for *sukuk*. *Sukuk* constitute about 85 percent of the Middle Eastern capital market, of which US$13 billion had an average growth rate of more than 45 percent in 2002–2007. The Middle East and Asia will primarily rely on *sukuk* to meet their US$1.5 trillion infrastructure needs in the next 10 years, according to various commentaries.

Whereas sovereign *sukuk* issues by Bahrain and Malaysia played an initial role in establishing the market, about 80 percent of the issues between 2001 and 2006 were corporate issues. However, in 2009—after the global financial crisis had begun—most *sukuk* issuers were government or quasi-government organizations.

In addition, the most important market for corporate *sukuk* issues, totaling US$44 billion during 2001–2006, was for infrastructure finance, with an issuance of US$17 billion, 39 percent of the total. The next largest markets

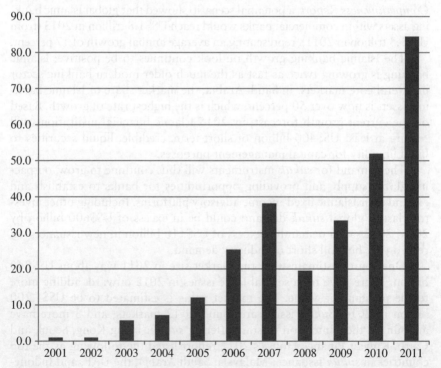

FIGURE 10.1 Number of Worldwide *Sukuk* Issues
Source: IFSL, Zawya *Sukuk* Monitor

were for financial services (18 percent) and energy (6 percent). There is a growing demand for investment in *sukuk*, going well beyond Islamic investors, among investors wishing to gain exposure to diverse but high-quality assets. The International Financial Services London reported that the *sukuk* issuance has increased significantly in the past three years, to the level of US$84.4 billion. The amount of new *sukuk* issues in the last 10 years is shown in Figure 10.1.

According to the 2010 report of the International Islamic Financial Market, the *sukuk* market size grew to more than US$136 billion in mid-2009. By the end of 2010, the total asset value of publicly listed *sukuk* was more than US$197 billion in 13 markets. Mass media reports suggest a much higher asset value by including privately issued *sukuk* in a number of major financial centers such as Switzerland, London, Frankfurt, and Singapore. Hence, the true figure may be closer to US$840 billion.

Currently, *sukuk* are offered in specialized exchanges such as the Labuan Exchange in Malaysia, the Third Market in Vienna, the Dubai International Finance Exchange, and the London Stock Exchange. Governments and regulators in a variety of countries have recognized the important role that *sukuk* can play in capital markets and have been giving priority to developing their countries as *sukuk* centers. Figure 10.2 shows *sukuk* issuance by country.

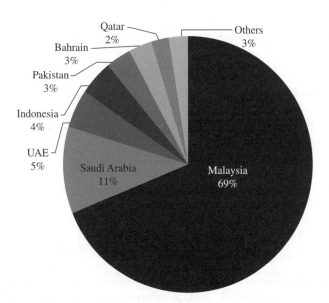

FIGURE 10.2 *Sukuk* Issuance by Country, 2011
Source: IFSL, Zawya *Sukuk* Monitor

THE GEOGRAPHICAL LOCATION OF *SUKUK* SECURITIES

The first *sukuk* security in a public market was issued by a Malaysian firm, in Malaysia, in 1990. Since then, many other firms and governments have issued such securities. These *sukuk* securities were issued either in their local markets or in a country other than the originating country. This section examines the geographical spread of the markets.

Country of Domicile

Sukuk securities have been issued in 11 markets and in five different currencies, including the US dollar. Table 10.1 presents the dispersion of *sukuk* issues based on country of domicile. Malaysia has been the most favored country for issuing *sukuk* securities, with a total of 224 (out of a total of 920 around the world). Malaysia is followed by the UAE with 20, the Cayman Islands with 18, Indonesia with 13, and Bahrain with 4.

TABLE 10.1   *Sukuk* Securities Issued Based on Country of Domicile

Country	Number of Issues	Value (in millions)	Currency
Bahrain	4	2,000	US$
Bermuda	1	500	US$
Cayman Islands	17	10,310	US$
	1	7,500	AED
Indonesia	13	35,307,560	IDR
Jersey (Channel Island)	4	4,230	US$
Malaysia	218	84,237	MYR
	6	6,150	US$
Pakistan	1	600	US$
Qatar	3	1,270	US$
Saudi Arabia	1	7,000	SAR
Singapore	1	29	SGD
UAE	6	15,150	AED
	12	13,320	US$
	2	1,000	MYR

The aggregate number of *sukuk* issued in different currencies was not converted to a base currency like the US dollar in order to highlight the variety and dispersion of different currencies used in market.

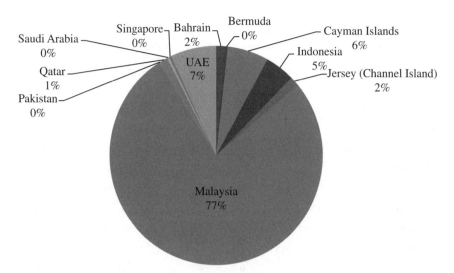

FIGURE 10.3   *Sukuk* Securities Issued Based on the Country of Domicile

As the table suggests, the Cayman Islands, Malaysia, and the UAE have allowed the US dollar as the issuing currency as has also others.

Figure 10.3 illustrates the distribution of various *sukuk* contracts based on country of domicile. As the figure shows, 77 percent of *sukuk* securities have been issued in Malaysia; hence, that country is the dominant market for the issuance of *sukuk* securities in terms of number.

Ijarah sukuk securities are issued in 10 markets around the world and are the most practiced form of contract in terms of wider acceptance in different markets. Table 10.2 is a summary of the securities issued in different markets and the aggregate value of the issuances at the end of 2011. Malaysia is the dominant market, with 31 issues, followed by the UAE with 14 and Indonesia with 13. Figure 10.4 illustrates this in percentage format.

Istisna sukuk securities are less popular around the globe, with only 21 issuances, of which 20 are in Malaysia. Table 10.3 presents the aggregate value of the sample issues in Malaysia as well as in Saudi Arabia.

There are 14 samples of *mudarabah sukuk* securities in the collected data. These are issued in Malaysia, the Cayman Islands, Jersey (an island in the English Channel), and the UAE, as shown in Table 10.4. *Mudarabah sukuk* securities are issued in the US dollar or the Malaysian ringgit.

Figure 10.5 illustrates the dispersion of *mudarabah sukuk* securities across markets. As it shows, Malaysia is the dominant market, with 43 percent of the securities.

TABLE 10.2   *Ijarah Sukuk* Securities Issued Based on Country of Domicile

Country	Number of Issues	Value (million)	Currency
Bahrain	4	2,000	US$
Bermuda	1	500	US$
Cayman Islands	8	3,625	US$
Indonesia	13	35,307,560	IDR
Jersey (Channel Island)	1	500	US$
Malaysia	27	12,200	MYR
	4	3,150	US$
Pakistan	1	600	US$
Qatar	1	700	US$
Singapore	1	29	SGD
UAE	6	15,150	AED
	8	7,820	US$

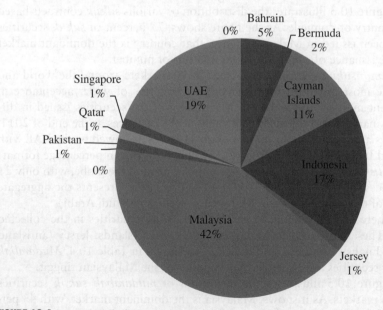

FIGURE 10.4   *Ijarah Sukuk* Securities Issued Based on the Country of Domicile

TABLE 10.3 *Istisna Sukuk* Securities Issued Based on Country of Domicile

Country	Number of Issues	Value (million)	Currency
Malaysia	20	1,437	MYR
Saudi Arabia	1	7,000	SAR

TABLE 10.4 *Mudarabah Sukuk* Securities Issued Based on Country of Domicile

Country	Number of Issues	Value (million)	Currency
Cayman Islands	4	3,935	US$
Jersey	3	3,730	US$
Malaysia	4	955	MYR
	2	3,000	US$
UAE	1	1,250	US$

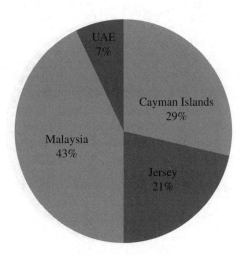

FIGURE 10.5 *Mudarabah Sukuk* Securities Issued Based on the Country of Domicile

TABLE 10.5   *Murabahah Sukuk* Securities Issued Based on Country of Domicile

Country	Number of Issues	Value (million)	Currency
Malaysia	64	16,650	MYR
UAE	2	1,000	MYR

Murabahah sukuk securities, which include *bai bithaman ajjal* structures, have been issued mostly in Malaysia. Table 10.5 shows that out of 66 securities issued, only 2 were issued outside Malaysia. The aggregated value of *murabahah sukuk* securities was MYR17.65 billion.

The *musharakah sukuk* security is the most practiced form, with 113 issues worldwide. Figure 10.6 illustrates that the dominant market is Malaysia, with almost 90 percent. Table 10.6 presents the number of issuances in different markets and the aggregate value in each market based on the currency used.

Issuing-Country Risk

Sukuk securities have been issued in 11 countries. Table 10.7 presents the dispersion of *sukuk* issues based on the country. Issuing-country risk is the

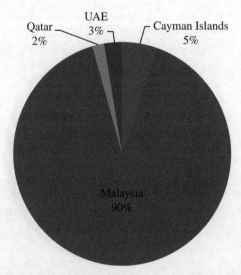

FIGURE 10.6   *Musharakah Sukuk* Securities Issued Based on the Country of Domicile

TABLE 10.6 *Musharakah Sukuk* Securities Issued Based on Country of Domicile

Country	Number of Issues	Value (million)	Currency
Cayman Islands	5	2,750	US$
	1	7,500	AED
Malaysia	102	52,995	MYR
Qatar	2	570	US$
UAE	3	4,250	US$

risk of the country in which the issuer is incorporated and active. This is in contrast to domicile-country risk, which is the risk of the country in which the security is issued. For instance, if a Kuwaiti company issues a security in a Cayman Islands market, the issuing-country risk is the risk associated with Kuwait, whereas the domicile-country risk is for the Cayman Islands.

As the statistics in Table 10.7 suggest, Malaysia is the most active issuing location for *sukuk* securities, with 220 issues present in the sample (out

TABLE 10.7 *Sukuk* Securities Issued Based on Issuing-Country Risk

Country	Number of Issues	Value (million)	Currency
Bahrain	4	2,000	US$
Bermuda	1	500	US$
Indonesia	13	35,307,560	IDR
Kuwait	4	875	US$
Malaysia	214	83,422	MYR
	6	6,150	US$
Pakistan	1	600	US$
Qatar	3	1,270	US$
Saudi Arabia	4	1,925	US$
	1	7,000	SAR
Singapore	1	29	SGD
UAE	7	22,650	AED
	23	24,460	US$
	2	1,000	MYR
United Kingdom	4	865	MYR

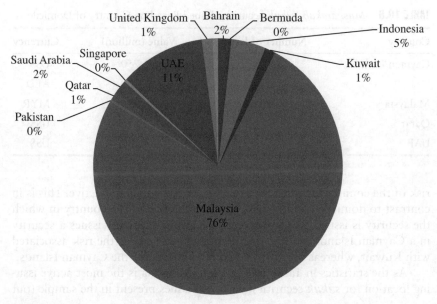

FIGURE 10.7 *Sukuk* Securities Issued Based on the Issuing-Country Risk

of a world total of 909). It is followed by UAE with 32, Indonesia with 13, Saudi Arabia with 5, and Bahrain with 4. *Sukuk* securities have been issued in the US dollar, the Malaysian ringgit, the UAE dirham, the Singaporean dollar, the Saudi riyal, and the Indonesian rupiah. Figure 10.7 illustrates the distribution of various *sukuk* contracts based on the issuing-country risk.

Ijarah sukuk have been issued in 10 countries. A summary of the number of issues as well as the aggregate values of the sample are presented in Table 10.8. Malaysia, the forerunner, accounts for 31 issues, followed by the UAE with 16 and Indonesia with 13. As Figure 10.8 indicates, 43 percent of *ijarah sukuk* securities are issued by Malaysian issuers, making them the dominant issuer of this type of securities in the world.

Istisna sukuk securities are issued only by either Malaysian or Saudi issuers. Table 10.9 shows that Malaysian issuers are the dominant players of this market in terms of number of issues.

Mudarabah sukuk are a less practiced form of *sukuk* securities, with only 14 issues. Malaysia and the UAE each has 43 percent of the issuances, as shown in Figure 10.9. Table 10.10 presents the number of issuers by country and the aggregate value. The table suggests that the aggregate value of securities issued in the UAE is larger than the Malaysian counterparts.

TABLE 10.8 *Ijarah Sukuk* Securities Issued Based on Issuing-Country Risk

Country	Number of Issues	Value (million)	Currency
Bahrain	4	2,000	US$
Bermuda	1	500	US$
Indonesia	13	35,307,560	IDR
Kuwait	1	100	US$
Malaysia	27	12,200	MYR
	4	3,150	US$
Pakistan	1	600	US$
Qatar	1	700	US$
Saudi Arabia	4	1,925	US$
Singapore	1	29	SGD
UAE	6	15,150	AED
	10	9,320	US$

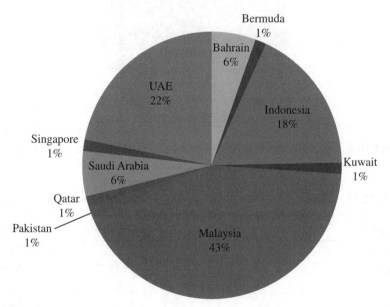

FIGURE 10.8 *Ijarah Sukuk* Securities Based on the Issuing-Country Risk

TABLE 10.9   *Istisna Sukuk* Securities Issued Based on Issuing-Country Risk

Country	Number of Issues	Value (million)	Currency
Malaysia	20	1,437	MYR
Saudi Arabia	1	7,000	SAR

Malaysians are the dominant issuers of *murabahah sukuk*, as shown in Table 10.11. Malaysians made 60 out of the 66 sample issues. Moreover, all *murabahah sukuk* issued were denominated in Malaysian ringgit.

Malaysians have issued 90 percent of *musharakah sukuk* securities. This has made Malaysia the dominant issuers of this type of security. Table 10.12 presents the number of issues based on the country of risk and the aggregate value of the issues for each country.

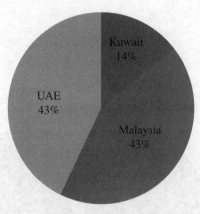

FIGURE 10.9   *Mudarabah Sukuk* Securities Based on the Issuing-Country Risk

TABLE 10.10   *Mudarabah Sukuk* Securities Issued Based on Issuing-Country Risk

Country	Number of Issues	Value (million)	Currency
Kuwait	2	675	US$
Malaysia	4	955	MYR
	2	3,000	US$
UAE	6	8,240	US$

TABLE 10.11   *Murabahah Sukuk* Securities Based on Issuing-Country Risk

Country	Number of Issues	Value (million)	Currency
Malaysia	60	15,835	MYR
UAE	2	1,000	MYR
United Kingdom	4	865	MYR

TABLE 10.12   *Musharakah Sukuk* Securities Based on Issuing-Country Risk

Country	Number of Issues	Value (million)	Currency
Kuwait	1	100	US$
Malaysia	102	52,995	MYR
Qatar	2	570	US$
UAE	1	7,500	AED
	7	6,900	US$

THE EFFECT OF GEOGRAPHICAL LOCATION ON CONTRACT SPECIFICATIONS

The country of domicile or the country of risk of a security may produce some effects on the security specification or pricing behavior. Some trivial statistical tests in the form of regression analysis were conducted to investigate such effects. The findings are presented in this section.

Promised regular-payment rate, similar to coupon rate, is an outcome of the security's risk, which in turn is affected by the country where the security is issued for trade or the nationality of the issuer. *Sukuk* securities issued in Indonesia pay the highest average promised regular-payment rate, 9.84 percent. It is followed by Malaysia, where, on average, a *sukuk* security has a payment rate of 4.82 percent. The lowest average coupon rates are paid by issuers from Qatar, which on average pay only a 1.13 percent payment rate.

The promised regular-payment rates of *sukuk* securities issued in Malaysia were analyzed based on the contract type. The results, which are statistically significant, show that the highest average payment rate is for *mudarabah sukuk* securities, at 5.35 percent. This is followed by *musharakah* at 4.96 percent, *istisna* at 4.84 percent, and *murabahah* at 4.83 percent. The lowest average promised regular-payment rate is for *ijarah sukuk* securities, at 4.28 percent. This sequence is similar to the risk order of securities, in which *mudarabah* has the highest contractual risk, and *ijarah* provides for the transfer of the ownership title of the assets.

Many *sukuk* securities pay promised regular payments to the *sukuk* holders. The number of payments in a given year (i.e., payment frequency, or coupon frequency, in conventional terms) and the exact dates of the possible promised payments are explicitly mentioned in the *sukuk* contract and are determined before issuance of the security.

Different markets may prefer a different number of promised regular payments for a given security. The maximum average payment frequency is practiced in Indonesia, where on average a *sukuk* security pays 4.30 promised regular payments per year. In contrast, *sukuk* issued in Malaysia pay the least frequent promised regular payments, 2.06 times per year.

Different contracts are structured with different numbers of promised regular payments per year. In Malaysia, *musharakah sukuk* have an average of 2.25 promised regular payments per year, but *murabahah*, *mudarabah*, and *ijarah sukuk* securities have an average of 2.00 promised regular payments per annum. *Istisna sukuk* securities have only 1.58 promised regular payments per year, on average.

Tenure, the duration from issuance to maturity in terms of years, indicates the length of time in which the issuing firm is in need of the fund. This is basically dependent on the specific reasons the issuer requires funding. In practice, it is based on more than the issuer's preferences. The issuer should also consider the financial market's preferences on the duration of the security. Market preferences might be revealed as charging excessive premiums for long-term securities or being less traded (i.e., illiquid).

Thus, there is a hypothetical effect from the market in which the security is issued, or where the issuer is coming from, on the length of the security. Such hypotheses could be tested by conducting regression analysis on the maturity length. The results of such tests have indicated that the longest average maturity of *sukuk* securities is 9.33 years, from Saudi Arabian issuers. *Sukuk* issued by Malaysians have an average maturity time of 8.04 years.

Different structures are used for financing projects of different lengths. The longest average tenure of a *sukuk* security in Malaysia is for *istisna* contracts, at 11.31 years. This is followed by *musharakah* at 8.57 years, *murabahah* at 7.34 years, and *mudarabah* at 7.17 years. The shortest *sukuk* securities are *ijarah*, at an average maturity of 6.03 years. This may be a result of the purpose and nature of funding by each contract. *Istisna* contracts are used to finance long-term projects, whereas *ijarah* is used for leasing purposes, which might be of shorter length.

The liquidity of a security, as a postissuance criterion, is affected by the country in which the *sukuk* is issued. Different markets may show different behavior in trading *sukuk* securities in terms of the number or the frequency of trades. Liquidity is measured by the ratio of the number of trade days since issuance to the total number of days since issuance. Thus, liquidity is between a minimum of zero (i.e., never been traded since issuance) to a maximum of one (i.e., has been traded on all days since issuance).

For the purpose of this study, securities with liquidity equal to zero have been excluded from the sample. Hence, liquidity is always greater than zero. *Sukuk* issued in Singapore are the most liquid, with a liquidity rate of 60 percent trade days.

The lowest average liquidity pertains to Malaysian *sukuk* securities, which on average have a liquidity rate of 4.4 percent traded days. In the Malaysian *sukuk* market, the most liquid securities are *mudarabah*, which have an average liquidity rate of 21.9 percent trade days. This is followed by *ijarah* at 11 percent, *musharakah* at 3 percent, and *murabahah* at 2 percent liquidity rates. The least average liquidity belongs to *istisna sukuk* securities, which have an average liquidity rate of 0.4 percent traded days.

CONCLUSION

The worldwide market size of *sukuk* securities was estimated in 2013 to be close to US$1.2 trillion in outstanding value. There are 12 active financial centers where investors buy and sell *sukuk* securities, which provide higher returns of 25–50 basis points compared with the equivalent conventional bonds. Besides this advantage, the structuring of *sukuk* in all these markets has a certain degree of similarity, although some important differences exist. The growth rate of this market is the highest of all the Islamic (participation) instruments.

The much older Islamic banks held total assets of about US$1,800 billion in 2013, after 50 years of developing this new banking market in 76 countries. It is the nature of new markets to grow fast, and it appears that *sukuk* as a market that started two decades ago has grown about 45 percent in the last three years. Perhaps the World Bank's participation in this market as an issuer, as well as its advocacy of this form of financing as suitable for infrastructural projects in developing countries, has something to do with the recent spurt in growth.

CHAPTER 11

Regulatory Issues for *Sukuk* Financial Products*

This chapter considers the regulatory issues for *sukuk* securities from the point of view of essentially secular financial services regulation. That is, it does not consider the question of what is or is not compliant with *Shari'ah*, although it necessarily considers issues of *Shari'ah* governance. This partly reflects my [original chapter author Peter Casey; see footnote] own background, but it also reflects the fact that the *sukuk* market is an international one, despite my location in Dubai as the regulator. *Sukuk* are originated, bought, and listed in many countries, including some (like the United States) where Muslims are a relatively a small percentage of the population.

In many such countries, for constitutional, political, or practical reasons, regulators must approach *sukuk* from an essentially secular standpoint, and this chapter sets out some of the issues they will face. Questions relating to *Shari'ah* permissibility are considered in other chapters. In dealing with the regulatory issues, we will consider *sukuk* as capital market instruments that raise market conduct issues that bear on investor protection. We will also consider them as instruments that may be held (or issued) by financial institutions, which raises issues of their treatment for capital adequacy purposes.

First we will consider the *sukuk* market as it currently exists, and then we will examine possible developments of it. We will concentrate on the corporate rather than the sovereign market, since that is where the main regulatory issues lie, but included within this analysis are the various government-related (but nonsovereign) issuers. We will deal only minimally

---

* This chapter was previously published in M. Ariff, M. Iqbal, and S. Mohamad, eds., Sukuk *Islamic Debt Securities: Theory, Practice, and Issues* (Cheltenham, UK: Edward Elgar, 2012). Permission of the copyright holder and the author (Peter Casey) has been obtained to reproduce this chapter in this book.

with the short-term (bill-like) *sukuk* issued by governments such as those of
Bahrain and Gambia.

THE CURRENT *SUKUK* MARKET

The *sukuk* market is primarily an institutional market. This is true of bond
markets generally; in the United States, for example, only 10 percent of debt
issues are held by individual investors, although the figures are higher for
certain types, such as municipal bonds. There are also exceptions such as
Italy, which has a strong and actively traded retail bond market. But these
are indeed exceptions.

None of the countries where *sukuk* are issued or listed have an active
retail debt market, and the issues themselves clearly target institutional
investors.[1] For example, the *nakheel sukuk* debt issued in 2006 had a minimum investment of $100,000, as did the issues from IIG (2007), the Saad
Group (also 2007), the government of Indonesia (2009), and the International Finance Corporation (2009). This clearly indicates that institutional
investors are the targets, and this is borne out in those cases for which it has
been possible to review lists of the initial subscribers.

The nature of the market has an important effect on the typical regulatory approach. In an institutional market, a regulator expects the primary
regulatory tool for the protection of investors to be disclosure. Furthermore,
a regulator expects that the investors in question are both able and willing
to analyze relatively complex documentation, either in-house or with the
aid of professional advisors. Disclosures may therefore be relatively long
and technical as long as they are accurate and complete. In a retail market,
much more attention is given to the clarity and comprehensibility of disclosures, especially disclosures of the associated risks. There might also be some
element of product control, such as a requirement for the issue to have an
external rating.

In the current market, *sukuk* are traded to only a very limited extent;
partly because demand exceeds supply, there is a general pattern of their
being held to maturity. Where they are traded, trading usually takes place
over-the-counter (OTC), even when the *sukuk* are listed on an exchange.
This means that the issues of clearing, settlement, and market manipulation
are less prominent in regulators' minds than they are in, for instance, the
equities market.

---

[1] There are a few exceptions issued by governments and aimed at their own citizens.
However, these are generally structured so as to pose minimal investor protection
risks.

REGULATION AND *SHARI'AH* ISSUES IN THE CURRENT *SUKUK* MARKET

We will discuss regulation in the current *sukuk* market before turning to the ways in which that market may develop and the consequent regulatory implications. At the end of the chapter we will examine prudential issues when *sukuk* are held, or occasionally issued, by financial institutions.

Let us begin with the issue of *Shari'ah* regulation, since it is a feature that distinguishes *sukuk* from any conventional instrument. Even a secular regulator will need to consider this issue to some extent, because any claim that an instrument is Islamic, even if only signaled through the use of terms like *sukuk*, is a representation to investors about something that may be important to them. Regulators should at least consider whether such a representation falls within their area of interest and, if so, what their attitude toward it should be.

Globally, different regulators have different views on this, ranging from an active avoidance of a religious issue to full control, typically through some form of *Shari'ah* council.[2]

The first position is typified by many Western regulators. In some instances they consider it unlawful for them to be involved in any way with religious matters, either because they have been given no express power to do so or because it would contravene a more general principle of the separation of secular and religious authority.

An example of an authority taking such a position would be the Autorité des Marchés Financiers in France. In other cases, although the regulator might be able to claim the necessary authority, it may conclude that for political or regulatory reasons it does not wish to become involved. The UK Financial Services Authority (FSA; the Bank of England since 2013) is an example.

Some regulators that decline to become involved in *Shari'ah* issues may consider that general principles relating, for example, to market disclosure nevertheless oblige *sukuk* issuers to make disclosures about *Shari'ah* compliance when these are material to an investment decision. For example, in 2007 the FSA said, "The FSA is in no position to assess the suitability of the scholars consulted by Islamic firms. It does, however, want to see [that] the basis on which an Islamic firm claims to be Sharia-compliant is communicated appropriately to the consumer."[3] Others would not go so far, at least

---

[2] See, for example, International Organization of Securities Commissions, *Analysis of the Application of IOSCO's Objectives and Principles of Securities Regulation for Islamic Securities Products*, September 2008, paragraph 2.3.

[3] M. Ainley, A. Mashayekhi, R. Hicks, A. Rahman, and A. Ravalia. *Islamic Finance in the UK: Regulation and Challenges*. London: Financial Services Authority, 2007.

in the sense of being willing to take action against a firm that failed to make such disclosures.

At the other end of the spectrum are those jurisdictions in which the regulator effectively takes full control of *Shari'ah* matters by setting up a *Shari'ah* council as the ultimate authority on what is or is not permissible in that jurisdiction. Examples are Malaysia or Sudan. A council may work directly or by overseeing the work of *Shari'ah* advisors or boards in individual institutions; for practical reasons, the latter model is more common in jurisdictions with a significant Islamic finance industry.

If such a council has authority over both capital markets and other Islamic financial institutions, such as banks, it may be able to ensure consistency between the views taken by issuers and by at least some major investors. Inevitably, however, its authority is confined to the jurisdiction in which it is established; its rulings cannot bind investors in other jurisdictions. Thus, there is a risk that it may approve *sukuk* structures that are shunned by investors in other markets with different traditions of jurisprudence.

The *Shari'ah* council approach may be difficult to apply in Muslim-minority countries for political or practical reasons or both. For example, although India has the third largest Muslim population in the world, its politics are dominated at different times by either a resolutely secular party or a clearly Hindu one. It is difficult to imagine either being content to see a regulator establish a *Shari'ah* council. In some other cases, such as in Europe, even if there are no ideological objections, it can be difficult to find enough credible scholars within the jurisdiction.

Another approach, which has been taken by the Dubai Financial Services Authority, is that of *Shari'ah* systems regulation. The regulator requires any firm that defines itself as Islamic to have a properly constituted *Shari'ah* supervisory board (SSB), systems to implement the SSB's rulings, and arrangements for *Shari'ah* reviews and audits. It may also require disclosure about the SSB and associated matters.

These arrangements are supervised in a way similar to other systems and controls requirements, but the regulator itself does not intervene in the substance of *Shari'ah* decisions. For a *sukuk* issuer, the requirements are more limited, but in this approach there is typically a requirement for a fatwa (a legal opinion formed after serious discussion) from a properly constituted SSB and for some relevant disclosures. This approach to *Shari'ah* governance allows greater diversity, which may be more appropriate for an international center, and it is capable of being monitored by competent supervisors of any religion. It may eventually prove acceptable in Muslim-minority jurisdictions that would have difficulty establishing a *Shari'ah* council within the regulator.

It is beyond the scope of this chapter to discuss in detail the advantages and disadvantages of these approaches, which may depend on the circumstances of the particular jurisdiction and will almost certainly not be driven dominantly by the *sukuk* market. Other markets—whether banking, insurance, or collective investment funds—typically require a higher frequency of *Shari'ah* decisions, and their needs are likely to drive the regimen, except in jurisdictions that see themselves only as capital market intermediaries.

The consequence of the diversity of approaches is that in the country of issue and/or listing, a *sukuk* issuer may face any one of a wide range of *Shari'ah* governance requirements, ranging from none at all to sign-off by an SSB overseen by a national *Shari'ah* council. The difference may be less important than it appears at first sight, since in practical terms investors are likely to require some form of *Shari'ah*-based approval, and market demand is thus likely to force the issuer to obtain a fatwa from an SSB or at least a respected *Shari'ah* advisor. Even non-Muslim investors might require such an approval to mitigate the risk that aspects of the structure may be challenged in a court on *Shari'ah* grounds, with unpredictable consequences for the interests of all investors.

CURRENT *SUKUK* STRUCTURES

At present, most issues in the *sukuk* market, whatever their form, are structured to have an economic effect similar to that of conventional bonds. That is, assuming that the instrument proceeds to term as planned, investors will receive their principal plus a return that is either fixed or determined by an external benchmark (e.g., LIBOR). None of the cash flow depends in any meaningful way on the performance of the underlying asset or business.

Guarantees of one kind or another are put in place to secure these returns. Typically, these guarantees can be called in the event of any default, offering the investors at least the option of exchanging their claim over the underlying assets for a claim against an obligor, usually the originator of the *sukuk*. They may also be callable in the event of certain external developments, such as a change in the relevant tax regime.

In addition, there are typically arrangements for a predictable stream of payments during the lifetime of the *sukuk*. These may, for example, be regarded as payments on account of the expected profits, in principle subject to a final reconciliation at the end of the *sukuk* period.

With both the ultimate guarantee and the interim payment arrangements in place, the *sukuk* become very close in economic effect to fixed- or floating-rate bonds, with the return dependent in practice only on the credit risk of one or more obligors. Published guidelines on *sukuk* structuring typically involve how to secure this economic effect in different situations and within the limits of *Shari'ah*.

For example, under a *mudarabah* contract, the *rab-al-mal* (silent partner) and the *mudarib* (managing partner) share the profits, but, unless there is negligence or misconduct on the part of the *mudarib*, losses are borne by the *rab-al-mal* alone.[4] In practice, the risk of loss is often mitigated by a purchase undertaking granted by the originator in favor of the special purpose vehicle (SPC), which acts as the issuer. This undertaking may be triggered if the proceeds of the enterprise are insufficient to meet the promised payments to investors.

Similarly, if the proceeds exceed the amount promised, the *mudarib* may receive most or all of the excess through a performance fee. Arrangements are put in place for predictable payments during the life of the *sukuk* so that investors are not subject to any timing risk.

Before 2008, it was also possible for the originator to grant an undertaking to repurchase the *mudarabah* assets at a price determined by a formula effectively ensuring that investors were all but certain to receive their principal *sukuk* investment and profit, subject only to the continuing solvency of the originator. Such a *sukuk* structure thus approximated a conventional bond very closely in its economic effects.

In February 2008, however, a statement by the *Shari'ah* council of the AAOIFI indicated that any repurchase undertaking must be referenced to the market value of the *mudarabah* assets at the time of the repurchase. It is interesting that the effect of this has been to substantially reduce the use of *mudarabah* as a basis for *sukuk*, mainly in favor of *ijarah*, for which no such restriction exists. There has also been an exploration in the literature, though relatively little practice, of alternative structures such as *wakalah* (agency) contracting with, sometimes, the explicit aim of being able to delink the payments to investors from the actual performance of the underlying assets.

Thus, it appears that those involved in the structuring of *sukuk* transactions are keen to replicate the economic effect of conventional bonds, in which a predetermined return to investors is effectively subject only to the credit risk of an ultimate obligor. They will use contractual structures that allow them to achieve this aim, choosing an appropriate primary contract and adding further structural elements typically based on *wa'd* (verbal or written promised terms).

---

[4] See, for example, AAOIFI, *Shari'ah* standard 13, May 2002.

Disclosures in the Current *Sukuk* Market

When *sukuk* are structured to be economically similar to conventional bonds, the normal response of the regulator, subject to points made below, is to require substantively similar disclosures, both initial and continuing. The disclosures must reflect the fact that the actual issuer of the *sukuk* will normally be an SPC, whereas *sukuk* holders actually depend for their return on an ultimate obligor, normally the originator of the transaction. Most of the business and financial disclosures therefore relate to that obligor and its group, rather than the issuer itself.

At the initial offer stage, the key features that distinguish *sukuk* disclosures are concern the nature of the securities on offer and the rights attached to them. A regulator is likely to take the view that this requires full disclosure of the *sukuk* structure, including at least the substantive provisions of each of the relevant contracts. It is likely that regulators will give more attention to these disclosures in the future, since there have been several high-profile defaults or renegotiations of *sukuk*. Some aspects of these failures or near-failures are discussed below.

When the market regulator accepts some responsibility for *Shari'ah* issues, some form of disclosure will generally be required about the basis on which the claim of *Shari'ah* compliance is made. Typically, this involves disclosing the details of the SSB or other body that has issued a fatwa. This is necessary even when there is an overarching *Shari'ah* council, at least when there is an international market, because the investors to whom compliance is important will want to continue evaluating the quality of the *Shari'ah* approval. Often the opinion itself is included in the public documentation, though usually only in summary form.

There has been some discussion about whether *sukuk* issuers should be obliged to go further and publish the reasoning leading to the fatwa for each issue. There are two arguments for this. The more straightforward argument sees disclosure as the means by which the SSB of a potential investor can satisfy itself on the relevant *Shari'ah* issues, thus reducing the risk that it will find unacceptable a novel structure that actually has good *Shari'ah* foundations. If this were the case, however, one might expect some issuers to be making such disclosures voluntarily, because it would help their marketing. Furthermore, substantial institutional investors would in practice be able to require this information, either publicly or privately.

The second, often unspoken, argument for disclosure is that it would force scholars to reason carefully before approving a structure and would expose some of the allegedly weaker structures in the market to external criticism. In principle, such an approach should be possible. It would have some effect on cost, but this would be limited in relation to the other costs involved in structuring and marketing a *sukuk* issue. It would add to the length of the prospectus and would be irrelevant to some readers, but again the effect of this would be limited. However, regulators are a little reluctant to force disclosures that do not appear to be wanted by investors.

Turning from initial disclosures to subsequent disclosures to the market, whether regular (like an annual report) or event driven (like a major change in management), in the conventional bond market these would naturally relate to the bond issuer. In a typical *sukuk* structure, it will be an SPC that acts as the issuer, but it is the creditworthiness of an ultimate obligor, normally the originator, on which the investors depend for both principal and the offered return on it.

In these circumstances, the obligor should make continuous disclosures to the market. This is relatively straightforward. Note, however, that when there is a guarantee from another party, such as another group company, it may be appropriate to seek disclosures in relation to that company, too. (An example of such a guarantee would be that given by Dubai World for one of the *sukuk* issues made by its *nakheel* subsidiary in Dubai.)

Having analyzed most current *sukuk* as economically equivalent to conventional bonds (see Chapters 4–6), I need to qualify this somewhat. The underlying assets are not wholly irrelevant because, as I have suggested, the *sukuk* holders may have at least the option of exercising a claim over them as an alternative to making a claim against an obligor. The problems or potential problems of several *sukuk* issues, including East Cameron, the Investment Dar, the SAAD Group, and *nakheel* have focused attention on the role of the underlying assets. There are fundamentally three questions about underlying assets considered as security: Can the investors take effective control of them? Do they want to? Do they understand the position?

Recent commentary has focused on the first question, including the difficulty of securing and registering good title to assets in jurisdictions where foreign ownership may be restricted or where the court system may be inadequate or inexperienced in these issues.[5]

The first of the three related *nakheel sukuk* issues, made in 2006 and subsequently redeemed with full payment to the investors, illustrates some of the issues that might arise. The offering circular for this *sukuk* states, "The *Sukuk* Assets shall comprise the leasehold rights for a term of 50 years over certain land, buildings, and other property at Dubai Waterfront (the *Property*) (as more particularly described in *Sukuk Assets*)." The description referred to, and the associated valuation report, makes clear that at

---

[5] See, for example, "*Sukuk* It Up," *Economist*, April 15, 2010, www.economist.com/businessfinance/displaystory.cfm?story_id=15908503.

least part of the land in question consists of man-made islands yet to be constructed.

One *nakheel*-related company, Nakheel Holdings-1, granted the issuing SPC a 50-year lease on these assets, and the SPC then leased them to another *nakheel*-related company, Nakheel Holdings-2. It is clear that had Nakheel Holdings-2 failed to meet its obligations under the lease, the ability of the SPC to take possession of the assets and lease them to another user would have been severely limited by the legal uncertainty of leasehold title to land that does not yet exist. This point did not, however, form part of the risk disclosures (and in practice has not been tested in court).

It is likely that regulators will, in the future, pay more attention to disclosures about the assets, the quality of any title to them, and the associated risks. However, the importance of this should not be overstated. Even if investors can take effective title to the assets, those assets may have limited use outside the business of the obligor, which, in a default situation, is hardly likely to be enjoying great success.

Even when the assets have an alternative use, which may be the case for land and buildings, it is unlikely that the investors will be in a good position to realize value from this when the original obligor could not. The *nakheel* case is again a good illustration. The assets formed (or were about to form) part of a very large development by Nakheel Holdings, and it is hard to imagine circumstances in which another user could derive much better economic value from them than a Nakheel-group company.

Thus, where the structure of an issue allows investors the opportunity to trigger a purchase obligation, even if this leads to their becoming unsecured creditors of the obligor, this may well be economically better for them than trying to take possession of the assets. If a purchase obligation is triggered, and the obligor lacks the liquidity to satisfy the obligation immediately, the investors may have the ability to bring insolvency proceedings against the obligor. This could be a very potent legal threat. Hence, a number of *sukuk* that were considered in danger of default have been either redeemed in full or restructured.

There are exceptions. In the case of the East Cameron *sukuk*, whose assets were a stream of royalty payments from oil and gas wells, the *sukuk* holders asserted a right to this stream of royalties ahead of any other creditors of the failed company. The judge hearing the case has so far appeared to back their claim.

The reasonable conclusion for a regulator, therefore, is that the assets, and the legal ability to assert a claim to them, are significant but probably not the dominant issue for investors; given the way current *sukuk* are structured, it is reasonable to suppose that investors acting rationally would be primarily interested in the counterparty risk of the obligor. Furthermore, in a mainly institutional market with substantial minimum investments, it is reasonable to assume that most investors will have made this analysis for themselves and, given adequate disclosure, will be able to assess how much weight to put on the supporting assets.

Do Regulators Have a Role in *Sukuk* Structures?

The question is sometimes raised whether regulators should intervene in the market to force or to discourage the use of particular structures. When the arguments for involvement are based on *Shari'ah* permissibility, this is equivalent to the question already discussed about the regulator's role in *Shari'ah* matters. But arguments are sometimes advanced based on either investor protection or the development of the market through standardization.

As far as investor protection is concerned, it is difficult to argue that there are any structures so inherently flawed that in an institutional market the interests of investors cannot be protected by disclosure. An institutional investor contributing in excess of $100,000 can be expected to devote time and legal resource to understanding the structure, and in any realistic situation, the success of the issue will almost certainly depend on there being some investors contributing large multiples of this sum. Their diligence on the structure will to some extent act as a proxy for other investors. In a retail market the arguments are more complex; they are discussed later.

As far as market development is concerned, the arguments depend in part on how the role of the regulator is viewed in more general terms. Some regulators would consider, perhaps based on an explicit mandate given to them by the legislature, that market development is no part of their role and should be left to other agencies or to the market itself. Others would see it as a proper role, which, often in the specific circumstances of the jurisdiction, only the regulator can play effectively.

If the regulator has a legitimate role, the standardization of structures may help in several ways. It may reduce transaction costs by allowing originators to work from more or less standard templates. It may increase investor acceptance of *sukuk*, effectively lowering the transaction costs by reducing the effort required to analyze structures and documentation. These gains, however, will be greater in the domestic than the international market, since major international investors will faced with products from many different markets. Forced standardization may also stifle innovation in what is currently a dynamic market.

Perhaps the best thing a regulator can do, when it has an appropriate mandate, is to facilitate standardization in areas where there is an emerging consensus but not force it, either positively or negatively. Standardization might then be achieved either through informal market practice or through the efforts of trade bodies whose standard documentation becomes widely but voluntarily adopted. This view is, however, subject to the remarks made below on retail markets.

Market Supervision

It is one thing to have regulation, in the sense of an appropriate legal regimen and structures; it is another to ensure, through supervision, that the regimen is observed and the structures work effectively.

In the current *sukuk* market, the issues of market supervision are relatively straightforward. Even when *sukuk* are listed, most trading takes place OTC, so as already noted, issues of clearing and settlement are minimal and there is little opportunity for market manipulation. The practical issues that arise are mainly concerned with ensuring adequate continuing disclosure. This is to some extent a position similar to that in the conventional bond market.

Because bonds are rather less sensitive than equities to commercial developments in the issuer entity, they are less traded, and their originators are perhaps less aware of the need for continuing disclosures. In addition, businesses may raise money through the bond (or *sukuk*) markets rather than the equity markets precisely because they do not want the dilution of control, and the corporate governance disciplines, that come from an equity issue. But those disciplines will normally include the institution of processes to assess what information should be released to the market and when. In a bond or *sukuk* issuer, those processes may well be less developed.

A further factor is that instruments that are listed but not traded usually produce little revenue for the exchange in question. The incentive for the exchange to enforce market disclosure requirements is therefore limited. Yet these so-called compliance listings have value for issuers precisely because they are a signal to the market that certain regulatory standards are being met. It is difficult to see how any listing authority can allow its name and reputation to be used to give such a signal without taking reasonable steps to ensure that it is well-founded.

All these factors lead to a position in which the regulator may need to take a more active role in ensuring that proper disclosures are made to the market for *sukuk* than for an equity listing.

POSSIBLE DEVELOPMENTS AND IMPLICATIONS

This section deals with four possible changes in the *sukuk* market and their regulatory implications: the extension of *sukuk* to the retail market, the possibility of new *sukuk* structures, longer-dated *sukuk*, and pressure for more investments to be traded on exchanges or at least centrally cleared.

There are other possible developments in the market, such as increased governmental issuance of short-dated *sukuk* and the use of different structures to continue to replicate conventional bonds. These, however, have minimal regulatory implications.

The Extension of *Sukuk* to the Retail Market

Some countries, such as Italy, have established retail bond markets.[6] Regarding *sukuk*, there have been some government issues aimed at retail investors, such as the 1Malaysia 2010 issue in May of that year. That issue was based on commodity *murabahah* and can be resold only through agent banks at fixed prices. It was also a government issue in the national currency and aimed at its own citizens. These factors mean that the issue carries minimal risks to investors and (like similar issues by other governments) raises minimal regulatory questions.

The situation would be very different for a commercial issue (posing real counterparty risks), especially of a traded instrument whose market value might therefore vary. The French securities regulator Autorité des Marchés Financiers called attention to the risks of conventional retail bonds in a press release in May 2010.[7] It drew attention particularly to the counterparty risks and to the risk that liquidity might be low or nonexistent throughout the life of the bond. Its best-practices guide for issuers pointed out the need to address market risks, liquidity risks, and counterparty risks in a clear, precise, and nonmisleading client document.[8]

If these disclosures are challenging for a conventional bond, they are still more challenging for *sukuk*. In addition to the risks noted, there

---

[6] The term *retail* is used somewhat loosely here to include investors, whether individual or corporate, who have neither great investable assets nor sophisticated knowledge of the markets. It is not intended to be a specific dividing line in any jurisdiction's regimen, but it would certainly cover those often referred to as "mass affluent." References to a retail market are to direct investment by such people; indirect investment, such as through collective investment funds, would generally rank as institutional.

[7] Autorité des Marchés Financiers, press release, May 28, 2010, www.amf-france .org/documents/general/9445_1.pdf.

[8] Autorité des Marchés Financiers, *Guide de bonnes pratiques pour la commercialisation des emprunts obligataires auprès des clients non professionnels*, October 2009, www.amf-france.org/documents/general/9120_1.pdf.

would surely need to be clear disclosures of the structure, the extent of any asset backing, and the basis on which *Shari'ah* compliance is claimed. The assumption, reasonable in an institutional market, that investors can and will analyze a lengthy prospectus and draw their own conclusions from the material presented, provided that it is complete and accurate, will not hold in a retail market.

It is not clear that there are straightforward answers to these disclosure issues. When disclosure does not work, the normal regulatory alternatives are either product regulation, restricting by one means or another the *sukuk* that can be sold to retail investors, or suitability, requiring any purchase or sale to be on the basis of advice from a regulated intermediary who is held responsible for the advice given.

It would be possible for a regulator to limit *sukuk* in the retail market to a limited number of structures. This would be more attractive than requiring the regulator to review prospectuses in detail, partly because of the amount of work involved and the risk that the limitations of any regulatory approval—in particular, that it is not a guarantee against loss—may not be apparent. But to avoid abuse, the structures would have to be precisely specified, including at least outlines of all the transaction documents involved. There would be frequent commercial pressures to circumvent the effect of the limitations, requiring continued vigilance by the regulator.

The suitability approach is at first sight more attractive, and it is relied upon in various areas of financial services. It does, however, require a high level of regulatory effort with supervisors of sufficient quality to be able to assess not only whether proper procedures have been followed but also whether they have led to well-founded and unbiased recommendations. This is easier said than done, and supervisors have been criticized in the past for failure to spot quite systematic misselling, despite having the appropriate rules in place and offering adequate access.

Another implicit assumption in an institutional market is that the investors are sufficiently knowledgeable and resourced to be able to assert their rights through the legal system, provided that this system is adequate in itself. This cannot be assumed in a retail market, although there may be alternatives through class actions or structures such as ombudsman schemes. These alternatives are, however, likely to be quite uncertain in their effect until jurisprudence is better developed, and small investors would be unwise to rely too heavily on them.

In many jurisdictions, therefore, the development of a retail (non-governmental) *sukuk* market is problematic, at least until there is market convergence on a limited number of structures, which can become well understood by investors, and perhaps the development of practical jurisprudence on areas affecting investors' rights.

New *Sukuk* Structures

Still more interesting regulatory issues will emerge if *sukuk* are launched in the future that have a greater element of asset or business risk. Conceptually, these might well be seen as better aligned with the principles of Islamic finance than many of the *sukuk* currently on the market. There are, however, important market issues here. In conventional markets, investors are used to taking either equity risk or credit risk. Although there are some intermediates in the market, such as in some of the subordinated debt instruments issued by financial services firms, the markets for them are relatively small.

Sukuk can, of course, be structured to have equity-like characteristics, but there is limited incentive to do so, since normal equity structures are acceptable within Islamic finance. The *sukuk* therefore need to offer something different. One fairly straightforward option would be to offer limited-term equity-like financing.[9] However, whenever an equity instrument can be traded, its holders already have an effective and more flexible right of exit, under most circumstances. They also have a right of voice, the ability to vote in the formal business of the company.

This is a valuable right because the market for control—the ability to sell shares to a possible bidder for the company—helps to underpin the value of the equity. It is a little difficult to see how this right of voice might be preserved in full within a limited-term equity structure, but without it the *sukuk* holders would rationally require a greater share of the returns than normal shareholders to compensate. This might be difficult to structure within the provisions of *Shari'ah*, however. All this suggests that, while simple limited-term equity-like *sukuk* could be structured fairly easily, they might struggle to find a market position that would work for both investors and businesses.

Thus, to offer something other than credit risk and remain economically attractive, new forms of *sukuk* will probably need to tap or develop a market somewhere between debt and equity, on the scales of both risk and return. It is as yet unclear whether there is a substantial market of this kind potentially available. If such a market does exist, it may well be for specialist applications such as project finance. There may, for example, be attractions in separating the risk and return of a particular project from the overall risk and return of the sponsoring business, as well as in offering a limited-term exposure to that project. These ideas are being explored particularly with an eye to infrastructure finance, where the existence (or

---

[9] The diminishing *musharakah* contract is suitable for this purpose; see Chapter 4 for a description.

creation) of tangible assets and the generally *Shari'ah*-compliant nature of their uses makes Islamic finance a natural avenue to explore.

Others have suggested that instruments could emerge that take a different kind of business risk—based, for example, on turnover or value added rather than profit.[10] This would take both regulators and investors into completely new territory (although developments in the conventional-bond world suggest that there may be markets, such as film finance, where investors might wish to take a position based on gross revenues). It would almost certainly take some years for the risks to be well understood and for the new instruments to be robust against, for example, manipulation of the accounts. Investors may well require a significant risk premium as the price of investing in untested instruments. In addition, there are likely to be elements of *Shari'ah* risk. It is highly unlikely that new instruments will use well-studied contract forms in well-tested combinations.

Scholars are therefore likely to take some time to become comfortable with these instruments, and this will inhibit commercial entities from using them for important transactions. It is also likely that any new instruments will be adopted on a small scale initially and in niche situations. (This is not necessarily a counsel of despair. In insurance, the catastrophe bond concept was developed on an essentially theoretical basis, and then some major firms used it in noncritical applications before it became an accepted business form. It is, however, less clear whether similar success will be achieved by the conventional bond that provides its return to investors in the form of chocolates.)[11]

Should hybrid or entirely novel *sukuk* emerge, the regulatory disclosures will be challenging. As suggested above, it seems likely that the first such *sukuk* will combine elements of equity and debtlike risk—for example, financing a project that will later be acquired by a known obligor. In such a case, one might expect that disclosures would be necessary about both the assets or project in question and the ultimate obligor. At prospectus level, this need not be too difficult.

There will, however, be issues in continuing disclosure. The easy course would be to specify a full set of disclosures for the project or assets and the obligor. This risks overburdening the markets with information, but more important, there is very little regulatory experience in requiring disclosures

---

[10] See, for example, Volker Nienhaus, *Stability Issues and Perspectives of Islamic Finance after the Global Financial Crisis*, paper, July 2009. Although the context is Islamic banking, the analysis could be applied equally well to *sukuk*.

[11] *Financial Times*, May 25, 2010, www.ft.com/cms/s/0/2a40a130–6802–11df-af6c-00144feab49a.html.

for a limited set of business assets. I suspect that the disclosures will initially be specified in very broad risk terms and that only as experience is gained will they be specified more precisely. However, given the limited experience in the market of making and enforcing the disclosures, there are bound to be some awkward troubles at first.

If the instruments are wholly new, the position would be somewhat different. It is difficult to discuss new instruments in the abstract, with very little idea of their characteristics. However, in such a case there are bound to be issues concerned with the initial prospectus disclosures. The risk disclosures are an obvious area that will require serious thought. There will also have to be financial disclosures that appropriately cover whatever is the basis of the return to investors and the various factors that influence it. The decisions made about initial disclosures will have to be carried over into continuing disclosures.

New structures and new bases for return may also create new opportunities for manipulation, or insider dealing, in any actively traded market. There is no reason to believe that these opportunities will be greater than in the conventional market—merely different. But market supervisors will need to be aware that different groups of people may have the opportunity for insider trading and different information may be capable of moving the market.

Longer-Dated *Sukuk*

At present, *sukuk* are concentrated in medium tenures, typically 5 years. There are some shorter-dated issues, most by governments, but few longer-dated ones, at least in the international markets. In 2010, the International Islamic Financial Market (IIFM) analyzed the *sukuk* issued in the international market between September 2001 and June 2009.[12] Of the 77 issues, it was able to identify fully 60 that had a maturity of 5 years. Another 8 were shorter, and only 2 had a maturity of more than 10 years.[13] The IIFM noted the contrast with the conventional market, where there is a full spectrum of maturities from three months to more than 30 years.

---

[12] I. A. Alvi, A. R. Mohammed, G. Z. Khan, U. M. Nasser, B. Naseer, and M. S. Khan, "*Sukuk* Report: A Comprehensive Study of the International *Sukuk* Market," in *The International Islamic Financial Market*, ed. I. A. Alvi (Manama, Bahrain: International Islamic Financial Market, 2010). There are some inconsistencies in the data, but they do not materially affect the line of argument.

[13] These were the issues by Tamweel (US$220 million with 30-year tenure) and Munshaat Real Estate (US$390 million with roughly a 20-year tenure).

More short-dated issues would be valuable in fostering the development of the Islamic finance industry, particularly in respect of its liquidity management, but these raise few questions from the standpoint of a financial markets regulator. The issues of prudential regulation will be covered below.

Longer-dated *sukuk* raise more interesting questions. There is a demand for longer-dated issues, particularly as long-term investment products, such as some family *takaful* (insurance) offerings, develop. In the conventional-bond world, governments, including both the United Kingdom and the United States, commonly issue bonds with tenures up to 30 years. In the corporate world, 7- to 10-year tenures are relatively common, and the United States has its municipal bond market, in which the tenure may be as long as 50 years. What are the prospects for such offerings to be made more frequently in the *sukuk* market?

One issue is structural. For most issuers, a long-term *sukuk* would imply finding assets with an appropriate lifetime. Although governments will commonly own infrastructure assets (e.g., roads and airports) with appropriate lifetimes, this will not always be the case for commercial entities, even some quasi-governmental ones. Furthermore, a long-term repurchase undertaking based on current value will transfer asset risk to the *sukuk* holders in a way that may not be acceptable in the market.

Nevertheless, there should be some scope for the origination of tradable *sukuk* structured under *ijara* or *istisna* and based on long-term assets. Even if these would not cover the full range of tenures offered in the conventional market, there seems to be no inherent reason why 10- to 20-year *sukuk* would not be possible. It may be, however, that buyers will need to become more comfortable with *sukuk* as a concept before they will be willing to invest at these tenures.

In general, longer-term *sukuk* pose few novel regulatory issues. There is one, however, that is difficult and does merit discussion: continuing *Shari'ah* compliance. In principle, there is clearly a risk that an issue that is compliant at the time of issue may become noncompliant later. For example, an impeccably compliant logistics firm may change its business model and move into arms manufacturing, or it may take on substantial conventional (interest-bearing) debt. The longer the tenure of a *sukuk* issue, the greater is the risk that this will happen.

In principle, some investors will have invested on the basis that the underlying activities, or the use of the assets, are and will remain halal. If it became known that this requirement had been breached, the effect might be a fall in the market value of the *sukuk* as Muslim investors divested. (Such a fall would, of course, also affect the interests of non-Muslim investors.) It has been suggested that the appropriate way to deal with this risk is to have some kind of *Shari'ah* board engaged throughout the lifetime of the *sukuk* to monitor continuing compliance. This is an expensive solution for what may be a limited risk. It would be likely to significantly inhibit the use of the *sukuk* market by firms that did not need an SSB for other purposes.

In such a situation, it may be that an action in tort by the *sukuk* holders offers the right remedy without imposing additional costs on all issuers. Such actions will, however, be easier in a common law than a civil law jurisdiction, and civil law jurisdictions may need to introduce specific provisions to permit them. It is unlikely that a business development sufficient in scale to affect compliance would go unnoticed, and a major development might have to be reported under continuous disclosure provisions.

Sukuk holders would thus be aware that their interests had been affected. The disadvantage of this approach is that it might, in a marginal case, lead to a secular court having to rule on an issue of what is or is not compliant. However, the SSB approach would also be likely to eventually lead to the courts, since in a non-Islamic firm an SSB would probably not have enough influence to prevent noncompliant business developments; the most it could do would be to blow the whistle for investors.

Pressure for More Trades on Exchanges

There are currently strong pressures to bring onto the market, or at least into central clearing, contracts that have previously been traded OTC. This derives from some of the failings observed during the global financial crisis and is being pursued energetically by the G20 through the Financial Stability Board and the international standard setters. The focus is primarily on derivatives, including asset-backed securities. There is, however, some risk that *sukuk* will be caught up in this inadvertently (because they fit the definition of asset-backed securities) and a somewhat greater risk that the general pressure toward exchange trading and/or central clearing will eventually extend to the *sukuk* market.

Central clearing should not, in itself, raise any new issues. It is intended primarily to reduce the risks associated with the default of a major market counterparty. Trading on exchange or (next best) central reporting of trades has a different purpose: improved price discovery. Should this become general in the *sukuk* market, regulators will be bound to devote more attention to ensuring that reported prices are fair. This will mean both increased scrutiny of market manipulation and increased attention to market disclosure. The issues in this area have already been discussed; the material change would be in the weight placed on them by regulators.

When *sukuk* are held by financial institutions, whether conventional or Islamic, the regulator may need to specify how they should be treated in the capital adequacy calculations of those institutions. At the time of writing, the revisions to the Basel Accord in the light of the global financial crisis have not yet been completed. However, there is no reason to doubt that the basic structure of Basel II will survive—that is, that there will remain a separation between trading and nontrading books and that in both regimens there will be a basic approach, with asset-risk weightings assigned by regulators, and more advanced approaches, in which internal models may be used subject to regulatory approval. There will also be patterns for supervisory intervention and enhanced market disclosures. [Basel III has been released and recommended. In it, an additional requirement has been introduced to increase the capital adequacy of banks to make financial institutions safer.]

The Basel model may be, in some jurisdictions, applied to some non-bank financial services firms. For insurance, the International Association of Insurance Supervisors is moving toward standards within a broadly similar structure, and this is paralleled in the European Solvency II regime, which may be taken up by non-European countries as the basis of their standards. The remainder of this section therefore assumes a risk-based capital regimen broadly along Basel II or Solvency II lines. Within such a regimen, how should *sukuk* be treated?

Fortunately, the standards produced by the Islamic Financial Services Board (IFSB) take us a long way toward answering this question. There are two relevant standards.[14] The earlier standard deals with market risk, in which *sukuk* are held for trading similar to conventional bonds and based on the credit rating and the residual term to maturity. The standard analyzes credit risk on the basis of the underlying contracts and any variations in the exposures over time (e.g., when an asset is being constructed under *istisna*). However, it implicitly assumes that the *sukuk* are fully asset-backed structures involving full transfer of legal ownership of the underlying assets.

The second standard covers those cases in which *sukuk* are asset-based (i.e., where the ownership rights over the underlying asset may not reliably result in an effective right of possession in the case of default, and where recourse to the originator therefore provides the primary protection for investors). It also deals with "pass-through" structures. Although the standards are aimed primarily at banks, the principles are transferable to other financial services regimes, including Solvency II–like regimens.

If new types of *sukuk* emerge, especially hybrid types, it cannot necessarily be assumed that any of the treatments defined in these standards will be applicable. The principles and form of the analysis should be transferable

---

[14] Islamic Financial Services Board, *Capital Adequacy Standard for Institutions (Other Than Insurance Institutions) Offering Only Islamic Financial Services*, report, December 2005.

fairly readily to new *sukuk* types, but they will require significant intellectual input from regulators. One of the lessons of recent years has been that financial institutions have strong incentives to engage in regulatory arbitrage, especially when it comes to capital adequacy. Thus, there will have to be capital charges that properly reflect the risks involved in an area where the analysis may not be trivial.

There are also capital adequacy issues when *sukuk* are issued by financial institutions, particularly with regard to whether the assets can be removed from the institution's balance sheet. These situations are relatively rare in practice and are dealt with in the second IFSB standard. This also covers retained securitization exposures, including those arising from the provision of credit risk mitigants to a securitization transaction and the extension of a liquidity facility or credit enhancement. Again, the principles are transferable to other contexts, but their application will require careful thought.

Payoff Structures and *Sukuk* Valuation

The Foundation and Principles of Islamic Finance

This chapter provides the general foundation and principles of Islamic finance. This discussion will place *sukuk* securities within the ambit of design features common to Islamic (participation) finance. The governing principles are profit and loss sharing, risk sharing, fee-based transactions (not discussed up to now), the prohibition of excessive uncertainty and ambiguity (*gharar*, *maysir*, and *qimar*), information symmetry, and the prohibition of *riba* (interest).

FOUNDATION

Shari'ah-based financial transactions have their roots in the Quran and the *Sunnah*, the body of practices of the Prophet Muhammad, refined over 1,400 years from the time his mission that began in 610 CE.[1] The Quran contains commandments prohibiting interest (considered as usury in contemporary interpretation) or contracts with excessive uncertainties (*gharar*), with speculation (*maysir*), or chance bets (*qimar*), such as gambling.

These highly developed financial practices lapsed around 1850 CE, following the introduction and consolidation of Western colonialism, with its laws, practices, secular banking, and capital markets that had disconnected with

---

[1] Some of these financial transactions were in practice before the advent of Islam and were merely approved by *Shari'ah*. For instance, the Prophet practiced the *mudarabah* contract with his wife Khadijah because this was the common practice before the inception of Islam. This form of business was then recognized and endorsed by *Shari'ah*.

religion. When political independence freed these colonies from Western financial practices after World War II, there was a collective urge to return to Islamic norms for financial transactions, which were considered more just and ethical.

Hence, Muslims started to avoid some, though not all, Western practices, and this movement developed into Islamic finance as interpreted by the newly evolving Islamic schools of thought in the second half of the 20th century. Existing modern financial practices were fine-tuned in accordance with the Quran and the *Sunnah*.

Contemporary Islamic finance is an attempt to revive some of the older practices while not rejecting modern financial instruments for modern times. It creates new products (*sukuk* as an example) or adapts existing ones to Islamic principles. Contemporary Islamic finance is only about 50 years old (participation banking started in 1963). It spread into many major areas of financial practices, and it borrows heavily from modern finance in order to serve modern needs.

Early attempts at Islamic finance attempted to revive the historical microfinance and community banking systems, but both of these failed to take root, though microfinance has been a fledgling part of finance in the last few years.[2] Then Islamic banking introduced the two-tier *mudarabah* (a savings account modified to suit profit-sharing deposits) as a permissible product under *Shari'ah* principles. Later, Islamic banking adopted other services of conventional finance. In this short time, the number of Islamic financial institutions (mainly banks) has grown to more than 390 in 76 countries. Table 12.1 summarizes the expansion of Islamic finance in the last 40 years.

PRINCIPLES

As a product of Islamic debt finance, *sukuk* must comply with the principles of Islamic finance. These principles have been explained in more detail in the 2011 work *Foundation of Islamic Banking: Theory, Practice, and Education* by Mohamed Ariff and M. Iqbal.

Profit and Loss Sharing

Profit and loss are two sides of the same coin; therefore, one must accept both possibilities in any investment decisions, as has been the historical practice right up to the time of modern banking with fractional reserves.

---

[2] The first known Islamic bank was established in Mit Ghamr, Egypt, in 1963 by Ahmad Elnaggar, and it operated until 1967. Also in 1963, Malaysia introduced the Malaysian Pilgrims Fund Board (Tabung Haji), which could be seen as the first Islamic investment fund. S. A. Shaikh, *A Brief Review and Introduction to Practiced Islamic Banking and Finance* (Hyderabad: University of East Pakistan, 2010).

TABLE 12.1 Expansion of the Islamic Financial Services Industry

1970s	1980s	1990s	2000–Present
Institution			
Commercial Islamic banks	Commercial Islamic banks	Commercial Islamic banks	Commercial Islamic banks
	Takaful	*Takaful*	*Takaful*
	Islamic investment companies	Islamic investment companies	Islamic investment companies
		Asset management companies	Asset management companies
		Brokers and dealers	Brokers and dealers; e-commerce
			Islamic investment banks
Products			
Commercial Islamic banking products	Commercial Islamic banking products	Commercial Islamic banking products	Commercial Islamic banking products
	Takaful; mutual funds	*Takaful*	*Takaful*
		Mutual funds or unit trusts	Mutual funds or unit trusts
		Sukuk	*Sukuk*
		Shari'ah-compliant stocks	*Shari'ah*-compliant stocks
		Islamic brokerage	Islamic brokerage
Area			
Persian Gulf, Middle East	Persian Gulf, Middle East, Asia Pacific	Persian Gulf, Middle East, Asia Pacific	Persian Gulf, Middle East, Asia Pacific, Europe, United States, global offshore

Source: Adapted and amended from N. Daryanani, *A Deeper Understanding of the Prohibition of* Riba (Nottingham, UK: University of Nottingham, 2008).

A capital owner who invests in a venture under conventional borrowing is subject to either the profit or the loss of the investment and cannot claim a loss from the borrower. If the venture is prosperous under *sukuk* borrowing, the profit is distributed between the parties in a prenegotiated ratio. If the venture turns out to be a failure, the capital provider loses his or her capital unless negligence or fraud is proven in a court, whereas the entrepreneur loses his or her efforts.

Risk Sharing

Related to the above, all parties to a contract share the risk associated with the contract, proportionate to the amount of each party's share in the venture.

Fee-Based Transactions

Shari'ah accepts some forms of fee-based financial transactions for specific purposes. These fees are fixed and predetermined and should not be based on an interest rate. *Murabahah* and *ijarah* are contract forms based on this principle. Mortgage financing is done in this manner in which the financier lends money to buy a property and adds fee, while the borrower makes regular payments for property or machine in order to defray the total loan while owning the assets.

The Prohibition of Excessive Uncertainty and Ambiguity

Gharar, ambiguity or excessive uncertainty in a contract, is strongly prohibited in *Shari'ah* because it may be a way for one party to take an unfair advantage of the others as a result of the one-sided effect of the uncertainty. Hence, any type of transaction in which the subject matter, the price, or both are not determined and fixed in advance is considered to contribute to uncertainty.

The most extreme form of uncertainty, speculation, is called *maysir* and is also strongly condemned in *Shari'ah*. Uncertainty can ultimately turn into a chance-based game, or gambling (*qimar*). This, too, is prohibited as sinful activity in Islam. Although the Quran does not totally deny the fact that there are advantages in these activities, the disadvantages are greater. Thus, these speculative activities are forbidden.

Information Symmetry

Islamic principles require the disclosure of information and the removal of asymmetrical information in a contract by all parties. A contract that has not revealed how disputes are to be resolved in the absence of a clearly defined court system would be considered an asymmetric contract and would be technically void. Similarly, a contract that specifies a term introducing uncertainty at the time of liquidation of the contract would also be an asymmetric contract.

The Prohibition of *Riba*

Riba (interest or usury) is any return, reward, or compensation charged on a loan contract or in rescheduling debts. According to the currently accepted majority opinion in Islamic law, interest is not allowed in a contract. Islamic scholars believe that money is only a medium of exchange and does not have any intrinsic value as did Aristotle even before the advent of Islam.

As a result, charging interest on loans (starting with consumption loans, at least) is considered unjust; hence, all transactions should be interest-free and based on profit sharing, if there is risk involved. This is essentially aimed at preventing the exploitation of the weak by those who possess money and power. From the prohibition of *riba*, one may infer that a return from a loan contract, the compensation-based restructuring of debts, and trade in debt contracts at a discount are also prohibited. Even when a lender receives some kind of favor from the borrower, it is considered *riba* and hence forbidden. Scripture-based principles are aimed at lending to individuals, and the scholars have confused this with production loans, which had profit shares.

However, as described in Chapter 3, there is a difference of opinion despite the majority consensus. For example, would a rate of reward that is very close to the rate of inflation be considered usurious if given after an entrepreneur and the financier share the risk? Some scholars say no. It is the risk sharing and then profit sharing that is the issue.

CONCLUSION

To these six fundamentals, common to all Islamic financial instruments, one may add asset backing as a major component of *sukuk* industry practices. Asset backing, or its softer version, asset-based *sukuk*, provides a degree of joint financing between the financier and the entrepreneur so that the contract is evenhanded instead of being one-sided like the conventional banking practices of interest and no risk sharing.

Hence, the *sukuk* industry, as part of the wider Islamic financial industry, offers participation financing consistent with the ethical and fair principles central to the Quran's call for just and fair dealings among people.

Cash-Flow Identification and Pattern Recognition for Theoretical Valuation Models

In this study, a couple of assumptions have been made to simplify the calculations or generalize the findings. These assumptions may affect the applicability of the findings, to some extent, but they are necessary at this stage. We try to keep assumptions to a minimum, however.

The first assumption made in this study is that the interest (more correctly for *sukuk* the discount) rate is fixed for the whole tenure of a security. This assumption contradicts reality, but it is used in the examples because it simplifies the mathematical processes.

The second assumption is that the risk characteristics (i.e., risk rating) of a particular *sukuk* security is stable for the whole tenure of the security. The most common *sukuk* has a five-year tenure, during which time the nature of the firm may change; hence, the rating may not be stable. Again, this might not be the case in reality, but it has been assumed to make the mathematical calculation simpler. There are cases in which a security's rating has been upgraded or downgraded at a specific but unknown point in time before maturity. Changes in the risk characteristics and rating of a particular security will directly influence the investors' expected yield and, subsequently, the discount rates applied.

ZERO-PROMISED REGULAR-PAYMENT *SUKUK*

The theoretical valuation of *sukuk* can be achieved by following the same approach and rationale used for conventional bonds. Therefore, the value or price of a *sukuk* security will be equal to the present value of all expected cash flow generated by it, taking into account the value of possible embedded options. In this section, the same approach used with conventional bonds

FIGURE 13.1   Zero-Promised Regular-Payment Cash-Flow Pattern of *Sukuk* Securities

is applied to *sukuk* securities while considering the unique and distinctive features of the latter.

The simplest form of cash flow generated by a *sukuk* security is obtained from those securities that pay a lump-sum amount of cash at a certain and predetermined time in the future (i.e., the maturity date). There is no cash payment to investors before maturity (see Figure 13.1). Various *sukuk* contracts that can result in such cash flow are explained in Chapter 4 . This type of cash flow can be from *mudarabah sukuk*, *musharakah sukuk*, *bai muajjal murabahah sukuk*, *salam sukuk*, and *istisna sukuk* securities.

Two of these are tradable under Islamic law, and others are nontradable, which means that they either should be kept until maturity or sold at par value. The tradable zero-promised regular-payment *sukuk* are *bai-muajjal murabahah* and *musharakah*. The difference between them lies in the amount of maturity payment, which is predetermined for the former and undetermined for the latter. However, the market practice of *musharakah sukuk* is for a predetermined amount of funds to be paid at maturity. Hence, both types of securities might be modeled similarly.

Zero-promised regular-payment *sukuk* with a predetermined amount of maturity payment is typical of a *bai muajjal murabahah sukuk* or a *musharakah sukuk* in which the maturity payment is predetermined and known at the time of the *sukuk* issuance. This form of cash flow is the same as that of a conventional discount bond. Thus, the same valuation process is applicable. The valuation of these forms of *sukuk* could be carried out using the conventional pricing approach. The current price of *sukuk* is the maturity payment (i.e., face value) discounted to the present time, similar to discount bonds.

In Equation 13.1, P is the price of the *sukuk*, M is the maturity payment (i.e., the face value), T is the maturity date, t is the time, and r is the discount rate, which should not be based on any interest-bearing benchmark.

$$P = \frac{M}{(1+r)^{T-t}} \tag{13.1}$$

FIXED-PROMISED REGULAR-PAYMENT *SUKUK*

Sukuk securities may be designed to have periodical payments to investors. The interval between two consecutive payments (i.e., duration of the period) is fixed for the whole tenure of the security. However, it may vary from one payment per year to one payment per month (e.g., 1, 2, 3, 4, 6, and 12 payments per year are common in different markets). The simplest form of *sukuk* with promised regular payments are those with a fixed number of promised payments. Such a cash-flow pattern might fit three forms of *sukuk* securities: diminishing *musharakah sukuk*, *bai bithaman ajjal sukuk*, and *ijarah sukuk*.

Fixed-Promised Regular Payments and Zero-Promised Maturity Payment

The diminishing *musharakah sukuk* payment structure may be to have some promised regular payments at certain times with a zero maturity payment. The number of promised regular payments is fixed and predetermined. The cash-flow pattern of such a security is depicted in Figure 13.2.

The cash flow here is identical to a constant annuity. Thus, in order to evaluate the price of a diminishing *musharakah sukuk*, the present value of the annuity is applicable. This results in Equation 13.2.

$$P = \sum_{t=1}^{N} \frac{R}{(1+r)^t} = \frac{R}{r}\left[1 - \frac{1}{(1+r)^N}\right] \qquad (13.2)$$

Here P is the price of the diminishing *musharakah sukuk* security, R is the amount of the periodical promised payment, r is the discount rate, and N is the number of periods remaining to maturity.

FIGURE 13.2   Fixed-Promised Regular-Payment Cash-Flow Pattern of *Sukuk* without Promised Maturity Payment

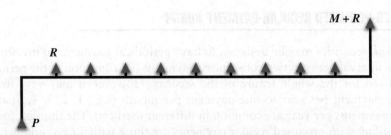

FIGURE 13.3   Cash-Flow Pattern for *Sukuk* with Fixed-Promised Regular Payments
and Promised Maturity Payment

Fixed-Promised Regular Payments and Promised Maturity Payment

Bai bithaman ajjal sukuk may generate a cash-flow stream of some fixed-promised and predetermined-promised regular payments and promised maturity payments. *Ijarah sukuk* has fixed and predetermined rental payments (i.e., rewards) and a market-valued maturity payment. However, in practice, the maturity value of the property is fixed and predetermined for both sides of the contract. Therefore, the cash-flow pattern of an *ijarah sukuk* would be similar to that of a *bai bithaman ajjal sukuk*. The cash-flow pattern of such securities is depicted in Figure 13.3.

The valuation of these forms of *sukuk* is similar to that of a conventional bond because of the similarity of cash-flow patterns and the tradability. Thus, *sukuk* can be priced by using Equation 13.3.

$$P = \sum_{t=1}^{N} \frac{R}{(1+r)^t} + \frac{M}{(1+r)^N} = \frac{R}{r}\left[1 - \frac{1}{(1+r)^N}\right] + \frac{M}{(1+r)^N} \qquad (13.3)$$

Here, P is the price of the *sukuk* security, R is the amount of the periodical promised payment, M is the amount of the predetermined maturity payment, r is the discount rate, and N is the number of periods remaining to maturity.

VARIABLE-PROMISED PAYMENT *SUKUK*

Some forms of *sukuk* securities have a variable cash-flow pattern. They can have a growing or declining pattern of promised payments. *Sukuk* with variable-promised regular payments are *bai bithaman ajjal*, *ijarah*, and diminishing *musharakah*.

Growing-Promised Regular Payments and Predetermined Maturity Payment

Bai bithaman ajjal sukuk may be designed so that the periodical promised payments follow a constant growth model; however, their respective amounts are predetermined. The amount of the maturity payment is fixed and predetermined, while the amount of the promised regular payment in a given period follows a predetermined constant growth model. In *ijarah sukuk*, the maturity payment should be based on the market value (hence, a priori undetermined), while the amount of the promised regular payment (i.e., rental fees) in a given period follows a predetermined constant growth model.

In practice, however, the maturity payment of *ijarah sukuk* is predetermined and mentioned in the contract. Therefore, its cash flow is similar to *bai bithaman ajjal sukuk*. The cash-flow pattern of these *sukuk* securities is depicted in Figure 13.4.

This cash-flow pattern of *sukuk* consists of a growing annuity of promised regular payments and a promised maturity payment. Thus, using the formula for calculating the present value of an annuity, one can formulate the price of a *sukuk* security as shown in Equation 13.4.

$$P = \sum_{t=1}^{N} \frac{R}{(1+r)^t} + \frac{M}{(1+r)^N} = \frac{R_1}{(r-g)} \cdot \left[1 - \left(\frac{1+g}{1+r}\right)^N\right] + \frac{M}{(1+r)^N} \quad (13.4)$$

Here, P is the price of the *sukuk*, r is the discount rate, N is the number of periods to maturity, g is the growth rate of promised regular payments, and R_1 is the amount of the first promised regular payment. It is assumed that the promised payments are growing at a constant rate of g; thus, $R_2 = R_1(1 + g)$.

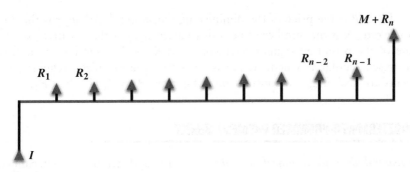

FIGURE 13.4 Growing-Promised Regular-Payment Pattern with Predetermined-Promised Maturity Payment

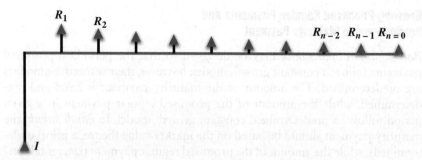

FIGURE 13.5   Declining-Promised Payment Cash-Flow Pattern

Declining-Promised Regular Payments and Zero-Promised Maturity Payment

In diminishing *musharakah sukuk*, the amount of the promised regular payment in a given period follows a predetermined constant negative growth (i.e., declining) model with growth rate that is a negative number. In other words, the cash flow of regular payments declines to zero at maturity. This cash flow is presented in Figure 13.5.

The same formulation approach used for the valuation of *bai bithaman ajjal sukuk* is applicable for the case of diminishing *musharakah*, with consideration of the negativity of the growth factor. Thus, the price of a diminishing *musharakah sukuk* can be formulated as shown in Equation 13.5.

$$P = \sum_{t=1}^{N} \frac{R}{(1+r)^t} = \frac{R_1}{(r-g)} \cdot \left[1 - \left(\frac{1+g}{1+r} \right)^N \right] \tag{13.5}$$

Here, P is the price of the diminishing *musharakah sukuk*, r is the discount rate, N is the number of periods to maturity, g is the negative growth rate of the promised regular payments, and R_1 is the amount of the first promised regular payment. It is assumed that the promised regular payments are declining at a constant rate of g; thus, $R_2 = R_1 (1 + g) < R_1$.

UNDETERMINED-PROMISED PAYMENT *SUKUK*

Musharakah and *mudarabah sukuk* securities distribute undetermined amounts of payments. The amount of a promised payment in such *sukuk* securities is calculated based on the venture's performance in each specific

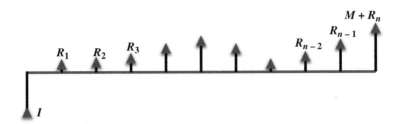

FIGURE 13.6 Undetermined-Promised Payment Cash-Flow Pattern

period. Moreover, the amount of the maturity payment is not predetermined. It is based on the value of the venture at maturity. However, the distribution ratio of payments is fixed and predetermined. The cash-flow pattern of such *sukuk* securities are charted in Figure 13.6. Since the *mudarabah* contract is a debt contract, this type of security is not allowed by *Shari'ah* to be traded at any price other than par value.

The valuation of *musharakah sukuk* requires summation and the discounting of stochastic variables. The value of such *sukuk* can be expressed as shown in Equation 13.6.

$$P = f(M, R_i;\ r, T, d) \tag{13.6}$$

Here, P is the price of the *musharakah sukuk*, M is the stochastic variable representing the market value of the venture at maturity, R_i is the stochastic variable representing the amount of the periodical promised payment, r is the discount rate, T is the time to maturity, and d is the distribution ratio.

CONCLUSION

This chapter translated the structures of different *sukuk* contracts into their basic payment patterns. This enables us to see the fundamental principles of the payment structures, which can be used to build mathematical models and coherent valuation theories for the industry practices. This is similar to the attempts in the 1930s and 1960s to build valuation models for conventional finance instruments, such as the bonds by Professor J. B. Williams in 1938.

We believe that valuation is a necessary condition for providing objective market advisory services as the *sukuk* market grows bigger in more and more financial centers. Serious students of Islamic finance can use these models to value as well as refine the formulas.

CHAPTER 14

A Matter of Choice: *Sukuk* or Bond?

The market for *sukuk* securities described so far is about a new class of corporate and sovereign debt instruments that are increasingly being viewed as an alternative to conventional interest-based issuances. This new security is increasingly being issued across the world by both private firms and governments and their agencies. This funding is for production, not consumption. In fact, the first public issue in this market was by an international firm, the Shell Oil Company. In recent years, the World Bank issued medium-term *sukuk* to raise capital for its development financing. Available statistics further suggest that there are slightly more sovereign debt issues than private-sector debt issues in the *sukuk* markets (not counting over-the-counter contracts).

The question that arises is why *sukuk* is chosen by borrowers to raise money instead of common bonds. This question is especially interesting because AAA yields of private *sukuk* instruments are significantly *lower* than the yield of equivalent conventional bonds, which makes this form of funding slightly less expensive for borrowers. What the attraction is of a funding mode that offsets the lowered cost of *sukuk* financing is a pertinent question. Zero-risk *sukuk* yields are higher than common zero-risk bonds. In this chapter, we speculate on the economic logic behind the choice of this new profit- and risk-shared financing over the one-sided, prenegotiated, interest-based financing.

This chapter first provides a description of the conventional bond-based debt market before examining some of the alleged (since there is no agreement on these claims) advantages of *sukuk* as an alternative form of debt funding—especially since the world is currently trying to grapple with the debt overload of the private sector, governments, and households, particularly in developed economies.

The chapter ends with an answer by way of stating a serious emerging public policy on debt overload around the world. We point to a growing consensus that asset-backed, risk-shared financing has the advantage of synergizing the joint interests of the entrepreneurs, with their skills, and the financier, with the necessary capital for sustainable economic activities, on a fairly equal basis. Interest-based funding does not synchronize entrepreneurial skill with the search for fair rewards through economic activities.

THE ECONOMICS OF CONVENTIONAL BOND-BASED FUNDING

History teaches us that human societies have come to accept debt financing for personal loans, private ventures, and government ventures, including, in the last case, to conduct wealth-destroying wars. Archival evidence made available during the last 80 years suggests that borrowers, especially rulers of empires, accessed considerable loans through interest-based borrowing. Nevertheless, it has also been very common throughout history for most economic activities to rely on contracts in which risk, profit, and loss are shared.

Christopher Columbus's navigation adventures were based on such contracts, with Queen Isabella and King Ferdinand of Spain as the financiers and Columbus as the entrepreneur. However, on society's margins, there were widespread instances of common people being exploited through lending based on usurious rates of interest, which all societies have rejected as evil and which Islam and early Christianity gave a scriptural basis for rejecting (*riba*).

King Hammurabi of Babylon (modern-day Iraq) passed a law five millennia ago banning loans that charged 33.33 percent interest. Usurious loan is a vicious form of exploitation, which, according to the Quran (3:130), is "the doubling of the loan amount at the end of a period of loan, and then doubling again if the loan is unpaid at the end of the second period." The Quran specifically defines this form of loan as exploitative, and it has been banned for Muslims since 629 CE. The Tang (618–907) and Sung (960–1280) dynasties each passed laws to lessen the usurious burden on the Chinese people from the exploitative interest rates then in practice. Most societies, including the United Kingdom before the jurist Jeremy Bentham campaigned to remove usury law in the 19th century, have passed laws to extinguish usurious interest. Human societies have generally considered normal interest to be between 3 and 5 percent per year and have agreed that usurious rates of interest are harmful for the welfare of society.

Although rulers conducted wars using borrowed money, most economic activities relied upon sharing risk, whether in shipping, camel caravans, mule trains, trade, agriculture, and commerce. Money is lent, and then profits and losses are shared, such as when family members make capital available to start a business using equity funding in family business. Profits are shared.

Throughout history, kings conducted wars financed through interest-based loans while desperate individuals relied on interest-based loans just to fulfill their basic personal consumption needs. Napoleon, the Sung emperors relied on loans, and so did the Athenians in their wars with the Persians. The Sung emperors spent vast sums of money on expensive maritime expeditions to subjugate the peoples of northern Asia and Southeast Asia in the 16th century. A bankrupt empire was quickly dispatched by the invading Manchus, who ruled China till 1905.

With the birth of modern fractional banking around the middle of the 19th century, lenders began to write contracts with no risk sharing and slowly initiated the process of charging very low (or normal) interest rates on such loans—but *without* contracting to share in the risk and the profits, which had been a customary business practice to that point.

Societies gradually began to rely on bank lending using an unbalanced contract, which means with no provision for risk sharing. The borrowers bore the risk of the financing as well as the other risks of entrepreneurship. Lowering interest to what is now considered a normal rate arose for two reasons. The first was the direct refusal of banks to share in the risk of lending. The second reason was much more circuitous.

Banks started to create money under a fractional reserve system, and governments recognized this in law. At first, the loans made by a bank were dependent on the amount of money deposited by the bank's customers. Banks then became able to create more loans through the fractional reserve system, which creates money itself so that it is possible for a bank to lend more money than it has in deposits. In a sense, fractional banking, with the lowered interest multiplied by the manifold loans on a dollar of deposit, actually gave the banks returns closer to or more than usurious rates.

In 1994, major economies permitted banks to take the loan book value out of the balance sheet by securitizing part of the loan book as collateralized debt obligations to further qualify for a reduction of equity capital below 4 percent. As we now know, this was the main reason for the global financial crisis.

From 1656 to the 19th century, full asset backing dropped from 100 percent to about 50 percent. It slowly fell further, to the current 4 percent equity plus 4 percent tier 2 capital. A 4 to 6 percent liquidity capital was added on top, and has been widely followed by most nations since the 1990s. Thus, for more than 250 years to date, banks have been able to forgo risk sharing, create money using fractional banking, and then lend more money than they had because full loan book asset backing was diluted under a fractional system.

Hence, the 100 percent asset backing for loans that existed in the 17th century banking in Amsterdam slowly gave way to unbacked loans, leading to the 21st century practice of about 8 percent capital backing a dollar of loan in 2013. Banks helped to keep interest rates very low, since there is no need to take financial risks in lending. The widespread usurious practices could not survive the low-interest lending started by modern fractional banks.

The economic forces at work led to the divorce of risk sharing in a production loan from the growth of multiple dollars of loans that is now possible from one dollar of deposit using the money multiplier: $1/(0.08 +$ safe liquidity). Today, with a voluntary liquidity rate of around 15 percent, banks can create \$6.67 of loans for each \$1 deposit. In a sense, the banks reaped greater rewards using the multiple dollars of loans, although each loan dollar was yielding a smaller normal interest payment compared to the prevailing profit-sharing rewards.

Low interest and no risk sharing slowly began to dominate the world in the last century as lenders and borrowers agreed to write a debt contract this way. The new special lender could create free money on which to earn more, under the fractional lending principle. For firms with limited liability recognized in law in the late 19th century, the low interest rate was appealing because there would be no interference from the lender on the specific use of the debt, giving rise to the general purpose loan in conventional bond markets.

Profit-sharing contracts would require the lender to monitor loans made to the firm (as in the German and Japanese banking systems). The lender had legal claim to all assets of the borrower through the courts in case the borrower went bust. This is a softer form of the asset-backing principle under Islamic debt contracting.

Corporate tax was introduced in 1903 in the United States and later spread around the world. It had a significant effect on the actual cost of loans for firms (but not individuals) by permitting the tax deductibility of interest expenses. The actual borrowing cost became \$Loan(1 − Tax rate). Hence, with a 30 percent tax rate, a \$1 loan was reduced by 30 percent, so firms benefited from a lowered cost while individuals paid tax on interest income.

An argument could be made that the adoption of lower and lower reserve backing of the loan book under a fractional banking system engineered the right conditions for prodigious borrowing by firms. The limited liability feature and the tax deductibility of interest costs made bond-based lending a lot cheaper than would have been the case in previous centuries under profit and loss sharing.

The cost of equity capital began to widen in favor of debt more and more as the tax rates went up and the fractional reserve rate fell to the 4 percent equity capital provision. This made it possible for producers to be attracted to take on as many loans as they could muster and leverage the return on equity for shareholders as much as possible.

The consequence in the 20th century from these economic forces was that firms took on loans amounting to about 40 percent of the total assets of a typical nonfinancial firm. The developing countries, starved of a high savings rate, racked up loans to a total assets rate of 70 percent. Firms experiencing high growth, such as in the fast-growing economies of South Korea and Japan, took on even more debt resulting, in about 70 to 80 percent of the total assets being debt capital.

The natural consequence of this long historical process was that the practice of profit- and risk-shared lending slowly disappeared, and interest-based conventional lending, with no risk shared by fractional reserve banks began to dominate the capital markets of the world about a century ago.

WORLD MARKETS FOR CONVENTIONAL LOANS

The total debt burden of societies in 2013 is US$52 trillion or US$8,500 per capita, which is 72 percent of the world's gross domestic product (GDP), according to the *Economist*. The G7 nations' debt burden is estimated to be 130 percent of its GDP. The World Bank's guidelines suggest that debt at 80 percent of the GDP is unsustainable. Should this splurging in debt be continued without a reform of the foundation of modern lending practices? A chorus of voices is suggesting key reforms to current lending practices to bring the worldwide debt burden to a sustainable level.

Since *sukuk* securities are becoming prevalent as a new source of debt capital only in a few minor economies, it is worth noting that the 57 members of the Organization of Islamic Countries (OIC) have a total debt of US$903 billion in the form of conventional debt capital against their total US$-based GDP of US$5,300 billion. The debt burden of the OIC members is therefore US$360 per capita, while the world's per capita debt is US$800. At the end of this chapter, we will examine how debt restructuring of conventional bonds could be done slowly to enable the OIC members to return to profit-shared and risk-shared *sukuk* debt.

How big is the conventional bond market? A reasonable estimate of the outstanding value of *sukuk* debt in the 12 markets was US$1,200 billion in 2013 (excluding the unknown over-the-counter market size). The worldwide conventional bond market assets, including short-term and long-term loans of financial corporations, added up to US$154,000 billion in 2011. However, the world's debt burden is even higher if we include short-term trade loans and loans of financial corporations, which are not for production activities alone.

Before the birth of fractional banking, one could observe a clear preference for the sharing of risk, profit, and loss in debt by firms while unfortunate rulers and those without assets preferred interest-rate borrowing. Fractional reserve banks, using the cheaper interest-based rate (devoid of risk), slowly encouraged producers to prefer interest-based debt. Institutional changes such as corporate tax law, accounting rules permitting interest tax deductions, and the legal registration of firms with limited liability all had the effect of introducing a favorable environment to make interest-based loans cheaper than the sharing of profit and loss in debt.

Obviously, the conventional bond-based market is too big to compare with the minuscule *sukuk* debt market. But compare we must, since the attractive feature of *sukuk* is its ability to link the entrepreneur with wealth-producing economic activities in a joint venture with the financier willing to share his or her capital to make the economic production process safer. Some statistics are given here on the conventional bond market before we discuss in the ensuing section how debt overload and seasonal wasting of assets at each business-cycle downturn could be avoided by the more balanced features of Islamic or participation debt contracting.

The total money lent by banks in 2013 was US$14 trillion, and the amount lent in local currency in local bond markets across the world was US$39 trillion. International loans made in six foreign currencies in 10 eurodollar centers amounted to US$8 trillion. Hence, the total loans in all forms used by both financial and nonfinancial entities were much higher than the sovereign private-sector debt of US$52 trillion. In fact, the total is US$61 trillion, which is nearly $10 trillion more.

THE CASE AGAINST INTEREST-BASED DEBT WITH NO RISK SHARED

The damaging effect of the global financial crisis has been felt since 2007 in all economies. This is particularly so in the developed economies, which from 1980 to 2013 shifted production to cheaper locations. This basically hollowed out their own economic activities, impoverishing their own citizens, while the nations offering cheap labor have become more prosperous. Obviously the capital providers in developed countries have become richer with profits going up from shifting productions to cheaper locations.

Concurrently, the producers and financiers in the developed countries are reaping huge returns because of reduced labor costs. The result is an unprecedented ballooning of loans in the private sector and the public sector across the world. As we noted, the debt burden of the G7 countries is 130 percent of their GDP; these are the countries hit by the transfer of technology and production to countries with cheap labor. That level of debt burden is unsustainable for any balanced economic activities. Judged from another angle, as a percentage of the export value of these rich countries, the debt burden exceeds the optimum of 80 percent.

There are about 128 developing countries, and their combined debt is US$5 trillion, which is about 23 percent of their GDP. Judged by export value, this debt burden is just approaching the optimum level of 80 percent, unlike in the case of G7 nations, for whom it has already passed the optimum level. The OIC group of 57 members has the lowest debt burden, US$903 billion, which is 17 percent of their GDP. Judged against export value, this level of debt is far below the optimum of 80 percent.

These statistics show that the three groups of countries had significantly different debt burdens in 2013.

There is growing disquiet in the policy circles of the G7 and G20 countries, as well as among applied economists like Paul Krugman, about the threat to world growth posed by debt overload. The political changes in 2011–2013 brought on by the disclosure of debt burden in several of the core EU-currency nations (Greece, Ireland, Portugal, Spain, and Cyprus) makes a strong case for rolling back the debt burden in the Eurozone.

Sovereign debt in excess of about 60 percent of the GDP and government deficit financing in excess of 3 percent have received widespread condemnation in those countries and led to the extolling of a growth-retarding policy of cutting debt at all costs. This twin policy is likely to be the way things would happen in the Eurozone.

In addition, the world needs to tame the banks with new regulations, such as the very timid Camel III regulations from Basle for BIS II or the New Zealand law that threatens to deregister a bank that has more than 10 percent of its loans with heavily indebted firms.[1] The pressure is on to bring down debt burden slowly.

In the United States, the sovereign debt was about 105 percent of the GDP in 2013. The proposed new fiscal policy would bring sovereign debt down to below 80 percent of the GDP by 2019 through voluntary cuts and tax increases. There is thus a recognition that debt is a bad thing in our world's largest economy.

The developing country debt has reached 72 percent of the GDP, which is very close to the optimum recommended by the World Bank. Among these countries is China, which has a huge debt overload, past the optimum level, at both the central and provincial levels as well as at the household level. Policy initiatives in such countries are moving toward the kind of reforms that the more developed countries have taken on or are in the process of taking on.

In some seriously indebted countries within the OIC group, active debt restructuring is being pursued to reduce the high levels of debt. Overall, this

---

[1] The fourth party to be restrained is the investment banks, such as Goldman Sachs, which can borrow billions and take the loans off the books in derivative trades.

group has debt at just about 17 percent of the GDP, although a few countries, such as Indonesia and Turkey, have excessive debt.

Are the existing practices of conventional lending with some policy adjustment the right way to deal with the debt burden of the world? Several writers and influential thinkers have increasingly voiced opposition to interest-based lending with no risk shared as fundamentally flawed. There is an incentive to take more debt if debt taking is not (1) tied to the ability of the borrower (the producer) to service the loan, and (2) tied to sharing the risk of financing with the risk of business failure or asset-backed.

It appears that so many years of fractional banking and low-interest lending has whetted the appetite for leveraging equity with more debt to earn more for the shareholders. All financial crises are perpetrated by explosive credit based on interest rates: Korea had a 470 percent rate of loans supported by $1 of equity capital in the private sector when the economy suffered in the Asian financial crisis. Such heavy indebtedness was also registered in Russia, Thailand, Indonesia, and the Philippines then.

The 110-year history of corporate tax deductibility of interest costs has further lowered the cost of debt to producers. The economic agents have become hooked to creating debt, especially since the limited liability law makes firms go to bankruptcy to offload too much debt by incurring huge losses to lenders at the time of the bankruptcy. Society throws away useful production technology each time this bankruptcy occurs.

It is well-known that easy credit breeds more debt, which spirals as assets bubble and leads to a financial crisis with debtors going bankrupt, creditors losing money, and taxpayers' money rescuing the banks. Debt overload results from easy credit policy followed, over a long period, by a loose monetary policy. If easy credit is potentially destabilizing sustainable economic activities, as amply evidenced in the studies of financial crises, obviously the instability from easy credit can be said to lead to debt overload (associated with asset bubbles).

While debt overload is 72 percent of the GDP, sovereign debt is estimated to be about half this amount. What is disturbing is that the revenue to government is 32 percent of the GDP. That is, the ability to service the debt at 72 percent of the GDP is certainly questionable. Several studies of U.S. credit levels suggest that private-sector firms had nearly quadrupled their debt rate, from about 31 percent of assets in 1994 to about 120 percent of assets in 2006.

Household debt in 1960 was 15 percent of the GDP and rose to 95 percent of the GDP in 2011 in core economies. That is a more than sixfold increase in household debt, driven mainly by the asset bubble in the housing sector brought on by easy monetary policies. In the case of the private sector, the guidelines of the Bank for International Settlements suggest that household debt is in excess of 30 percent of household income, which is considered unsustainable. UK statistics suggest that one in six households has passed this limit.

The story is even worse in the Eurozone, China, Hong Kong, Japan, New Zealand, Singapore, and the United States. Facing such a housing bubble, the Reserve Bank of New Zealand introduced a rule in 2013 to curb further debt. Lending exceeding 10 percent of loans beyond 80 percent of a household's asset values (known as the 10/80 prudential rule) will lead to the cancellation of the bank's license.

In summary, there was a disturbing trend in the world economy from 1990 to 2010 to quadruple debt through an easy monetary policy that led to an easy-credit policy in the financial sector. The result is that debt overload was built in by 2005 in all three sectors: households, governments, and the private sector. Although the global crisis arose from the design and sale of dubious financial derivatives that failed, it also occurred as predicted from a long period of credit expansion through easy monetary and credit policies initiated by the United States and the United Kingdom and followed by others.

Is there an alternative method of debt structuring that would prevent or curb this historical tendency to surpass the limits of debt (80 percent of the GDP, 80 percent of the export value, and debt service cost exceeding 30 percent of household debt)? A number of writers insist that the financial system must be drastically restructured in order to prevent this backsliding of economies from debt overload.

ARE *SUKUK* AN ALTERNATIVE TO BONDS?

Among the solutions suggested to revamp the financial system, there are two radical solutions. One is the abolition of fractional banking, which is at the root of creating voluminous loans. Once 100 percent backing of the loan book is mandated, the problem of easy credit would disappear. Greg Manikov of the Harvard School of Economics has voiced this solution. *Sukuk* is that sort of security, based on asset backing without removing fractional reserve.

The second solution is to tackle the regulatory capital's weakness: low-equity capital, which is the source of the problem. Banks would be treated simply as another form of firm, so they would have to have about 30 percent equity capital compared to their 4 percent in 2013 to attain financial stability.

A less radical solution is available if debt is structured under *sukuk* principles. Two characteristics of *sukuk* address debt overload. First, risk sharing before reward helps to minimize the urge of a lender to sell off debt when a firm faces a temporary loss of income, especially during economic downturns.

Second, profit sharing is an incentive to stay connected to the firm in hard times as well as good times in the hope of earning higher returns than would be the case in conventional lending or by just depositing the capital in a bank to earn a return no more than the inflation rate. Togetherness in production activity via profit-risk-sharing promotes stickiness of capital to the project.

To these two desirable features, one can add another: *sukuk* lending is based on the transfer of ownership of part of the assets of a borrower to a special purpose vehicle that would service the loan and help redeem the principal. In a sense, it insulates the producer firm, since the bulk of the assets are not under the control of the borrower. In reality, only part of the assets are under the control of the lenders, who feel safe owning part of the assets.

A fourth desirable feature is that the most the producer can borrow in a *sukuk* contract is the value of the assets in place. This arises from the full asset backing of loans, a requirement in *sukuk*. If, for example, assets are worth about 70 percent of the market value at a point in time (conventional banks actually estimate assets at that value for computing collateral value), the most a firm could borrow under *sukuk* principles is about 70 percent of the value of its total assets. There is an automatic limit for loans; no further loans can be asset backed when a producer's loans reach about two-thirds the value of assets of the firm.

We believe that a return to this more balanced—some say more equitable and symmetric—way of contracting debt would eventually yield two desirable outcomes. First, the market would discipline the creation of debt linking debt to a project's profit or loss experiences and thus avoiding the excessive periodic asset abandonment through court-ordered bankruptcy when economies experience recessions or crises. Current bankruptcy laws yield huge incomes to accountants and lawyers.

Second, there would be an automatic limit to profligate loans. This automatic limit would occur at 70 to 80 percent of the asset value: the World Bank number for sustainable debt. There would be no need for the World Bank or the government to police the debt levels; the market would do it automatically. The issue of how much loose or tight monetary policy the country would follow is outside the limits imposed by the design features of *sukuk* securities.

It is our view that fractional banking is here to stay. Radical suggestions to increase capital backing for deposits or dramatically increasing regulatory capital would lead to massive shortages of capital. Responding to the call to fix the banks after the 2008 global crisis, the Basel Committee was reluctant to increase capital adequacy until 2021.

Not only would the cost of money for banks go up, the cost of borrowing would jump to the detriment of price stability if solutions are sought through dismantling fractional reserve banking. Even if all countries adopted the *sukuk* way of creating debt, it would take perhaps half a century for loan levels to come down to the level that we predict in our studies.

CONCLUSION

In this chapter, we described the problem of debt overload in all three sectors of the economy (households, government, and the private sector). Wage incomes of households account for 30 percent (in exploitative economies) to 72 percent (in developed economies) of the GDP. Government revenues account for 11 percent (in poor nations) to 32 percent (in rich nations) of the GDP. Corporations keep anywhere from almost 50 percent (in socialist countries) to 20 percent (in capitalist countries) of the GDP as retained earnings. Against this background, one has to devise ways of controlling the debt overload in any of these sectors to relieve the world of too much debt and hence too little growth.

The easy credit policy within conventional lending was made economically possible by fractional reserve banking once the cost of interest-based (as opposed to profit-shared) borrowing was further reduced by limited liability and the tax deductibility of interest costs under corporate tax laws.

Although the innate conservatism of borrowing kept the debt far below the levels of danger (e.g., in the OIC group and some of the developing countries), recent banking developments in the last quarter century have led to excessive debt by all.

The remedies suggested, such as an increase in the full backing of bank deposits or the abolition of fractional reserve banking, may prove very costly if adopted quickly. We suggest that *sukuk* security design is ideally suited to lead to a balanced debt policy, given risk sharing, profit and loss sharing, and asset-backed lending. We endorse the growth of this form of lending as likely to lead to sustainable debt and greater resilience of the economies to grow, create jobs, and be financially stable. At least the OIC members are taking this new pro-growth policy direction.

CHAPTER 15

Challenges and Future Developments

Since their introduction in the early 1990s, *sukuk* securities have emerged from being a small-scale niche industry to becoming a relatively sizable force around the world as both private issues and in publicly traded markets. In 2013, the outstanding value was variously estimated to be US$1,200 billion. *Sukuk* securities have unique features that fit the market practitioner's targeted fund needs and hence help the industry to become an important niche player in the huge lending-based investment markets.

However, in order to sustain the high growth, some critical developments are essential. This chapter discusses some of the major challenges of the global *sukuk* markets that, if not addressed as the markets are growing larger, will become potential obstacles and limit future growth. An important challenge to *sukuk* trading centers is from London as it enters the market this year (2014). Given London financial market's long history of nurturing new products such as insurance, investment banking, and Islamic banking, the entry of London to the *sukuk* market is by far the most important development to date. These challenges are discussed in this chapter.

VALUATION

Practitioners use existing conventional bond valuation models for pricing *sukuk* securities. Such estimates are used by investors to make decisions. However, these models are not entirely suitable for the valuation of *sukuk*, as was shown in Chapter 13. First, *sukuk* and bond securities have fundamental differences, ranging from the risk-sharing features of *sukuk* to the role of the special purpose company (SPC) in risk transfer to the variation in periodic payments. Second, our tests proved that there is a significant difference in the yield to maturity of *sukuk* compared to that of bond securities of the same risk, term, issuer, and coupons.

Hence, the absence of proper models for valuation is likely to limit the usefulness of advisory services on different types of *sukuk* securities.

Consequent lack of precision in investment advisory is likely to hinder investors from using this source for funding. For more than two centuries, investors used the market-clearing prices of bonds as an indication of their values. Only in the 20th century did scholars and experts work out the mathematics of bond valuation. We need such progress in *sukuk* valuation.

Although *sukuk* trading is already a reality, we have not yet devised methods to estimate the worth of *sukuk* based on cash flow, ratings, and tenure. This is an urgent task waiting to be done as the market is growing; thus, accurate valuations are needed to provide advisory services to investors in this market.

LIQUIDITY

Liquidity, or the speed of converting a security to its money value, is the litmus test of any financial market meeting its function of price clearance. Therefore, exchanges have always paid special attention to improving liquidity in order to ensure that a given new securities market will survive in the long run. Liquidity is also a requirement for the speedy entry and exit of participants, so that delayed trading does not create an impediment to trading or to cashing securities.

There are two main strategies adopted by market makers to spur liquidity. The most common method is to interpose a market maker to hold the inventories to be sold to investors in the market maker's books. A second method is to create a discount house that participates in the initial public offering market as the wholesaler, then resell the securities to retail investors for a small profit, usually no larger than four to six basis points. A third method, less common, is to mandate specialist brokers to be market makers to the counterparty to make trades continuous. The specialist is tasked to be the counterparty when trading is sluggish and the counterparty to a bid or an asking price is absent.

To date, none of the *sukuk* markets in any country have adopted these structures to spur liquidity. Liquidity, as pointed out in this book, is a serious problem in all *sukuk* marketplaces (also in bond markets in some countries). *Sukuk* securities' volume of trade in the secondary market is very low compared to that of conventional bonds. The majority of *sukuk* markets suffers from illiquidity to the extent that 70 percent or more were not traded, as of 2011. That means that some of the securities have never been publicly traded, from their issuance date until their maturity. This is due to the mutuality of this form of funding, and investors tend to be more picky in not wanting to trade this instrument at this initial small size of the market.

MARKET WIDENING AND MARKET DEPTH

Sukuk markets are relatively young and small compared to conventional bond markets around the world. An exception is the Malaysian market, where the size of the *sukuk* market is comparable to that of the conventional bond market there. In order for the *sukuk* markets to grow further, two types of activities should be initiated: widening the investment options to new forms of *sukuk* and deepening the size of the existing types.

Market-deepening activities should be undertaken to improve the market size. For example, 80 percent of issues in Malaysia are one type of *sukuk*. Not only more *sukuk* securities should be issued, but also in larger sizes. The issuance of more *sukuk* securities can add to the reputation of this form of fund-raising and and bring more investors to the market. Consequently, when the demand increases for *sukuk*, the issuers, the fund users, may get better economics from the market. Larger *sukuk* issues should be offered to the market because widespread ownership would spur more trade.

Larger issues are typically those offered by sovereigns or those for funding megaprojects. Governments of Muslim countries may choose *sukuk* as a vehicle for their infrastructure fund needs. The World Bank has a policy directive to use this form of fund-raising for development financing. Some of the larger projects in the Persian Gulf states or in Malaysia or in United Arab Emirates have already been financed through *sukuk* issues, and megaprojects in two regions of Germany have similarly relied on *sukuk* issues. This form of activities will add to the depth of the *sukuk* markets. The World Bank's borrowing through this market is also a large funding exercise in US dollars.

Market-broadening activities are also required to further develop the *sukuk* markets. Introducing more securities targeted at the specific needs of the customers would help introduce a broader list of securities. For example, the *sukuk* market has 6 traded securities, although conceptually there are 14 different types. A combination of two or more types of existing contracts would result in a new security to address the unique needs of the issuer. More efforts should be put into the financial engineering of *sukuk* securities.

COST OF ISSUANCE

The conventional bond-issuance markets developed in the post–World War II period with a great deal of standardization of contracts. This resulted in lowering the issuance cost to a firm, and it also lowered the transaction costs of traders. A bond issue of US$1 billion can be arranged by a syndicate of banks with very little securitization cost: About US$4–5 billion can be raised in a day. The costs in major centers range from as low as 25 basis points to 100 basis points. Given the uniqueness in conceptualizing the *sukuk* securities to fit the needs of the firms, the number of embedded contracts and terms in a *sukuk* contract increases the cost of new issues. Besides that concern, there is also the difference of opinions of the *Shari'ah* boards.

The result is that the cost of the issue increases, sometimes prohibitively, and the *Shari'ah* scholars make huge profits as fees. The standardization of contracts would strengthen the convenience of the securitization process. That boosts the cooperation among the regulatory bodies of different centers, which leads to one-stop servicing of primary market making and lessens the cost burdens of the issuance process.

VARIATION IN SCHOOLS OF THOUGHT

One of the elements hindering the standardization process is the variation in *Shari'ah* opinions in terms of the different Islamic schools of thought. Some of these schools strictly follow the practice of the Prophet Muhammad and base a fatwa (a scholarly opinion) on such strict grounds. In cases with no historical evidence to support a transaction, the fatwa will most probably be against it. This will result in a more conservative approach toward *Shari'ah* issues and required compliance.

There is another school of thought that follows a rationalization of the historical evidence and extracts the rationale to apply the idea to the new phenomenon. A relatively more dynamic or liberal interpretation of *Shari'ah* can be anticipated from such an approach, which has been emerging in recent years. In reality, the rational school is the most predominant school of legal interpretation and decision making, followed by almost 85 percent of Muslims. The conservative school is followed in much less modernized countries with long historical roots to conservative thinking.

Historically, every 100 years *Shari'ah* scholars used to come together to debate the new phenomena of the times, and at the end they would renew the application of *Shari'ah* accordingly. This enabled *Shari'ah* to address the relevant issues of every period, when a new environment would require a fresh interpretation of existing dogmas. The last time this happened under the watch of a central authority was during the second half of the 19th century by the Ottoman legal scholars, who had undertaken this task for several hundred years.

Modern banking developed around that time, and the capital base of banks at that time was closer to 80 percent of assets (compared to 8 percent in 2014). Since then, there has been no such central authority to systematically codify and amend the laws in light of changed financial environments.

A world academy was funded by the Saudis for this purpose, but critics point to its inadequacy because of the bias of this body toward entrenched conservatism and opposition to modernity. Hence, there is a need in Islamic finance to make a new attempt to provide guidance that will be accepted by all Muslim countries and all schools of thoughts in Islam.

In this manner, a harmonized and coherent approach would be developed. However, such a gathering never took place after the middle of the 19th century. The absence of such harmony among *Shari'ah* scholars in the past century has caused conflicting *Shari'ah* rulings made by different scholars. Some may argue that the task of the harmonization of different schools of thought rests on the *Shari'ah* committee of the Organization of Islamic Countries. The outcomes of this committee, in practice, did not bring that much harmonization to the various financial phenomena that have emerged in the past few decades.

Harmonization thus remains a key issue. The lack of harmonization has led to market organizers shopping around for more lenient locations for issues (commonly known as "fatwa shopping"). As the market grows, competition is based on the economics of the market process and not on regulatory subterfuge. Damage to the reputation of *sukuk* as a feasible financial instrument for targeted funding has to be avoided through greater degree of harmonization. Financial instruments have died off quickly as they came to market when the reputation of the instrument was damaged: think of the collateralized debt obligations (CDOs) and the global financial crisis.

At the time of the global financial crisis of 2008, we witnessed the death of CDOs, which, during their heyday, had a value equal to US$12 trillion just in JP Morgan alone. The harmonization of regulations and opinions on the rules governing *sukuk* will help to preserve the prestige that *sukuk* appears to have at the present.

EDUCATING MORE EXPERTS IN *SUKUK*

Education is another critical area that needs more attention in order to ensure the continuity and sustainability of the *sukuk* markets. Currently, education and training efforts around the world are highly uncoordinated. The standardization of education and training in Islamic finance in general and *sukuk* securities in particular is absent. There is no internationally agreed accreditation for different programs offered to the public.

Although an international accreditation body for educational programs would be ideal, national accrediting bodies may serve the need for the time being. The existence of accreditation for Islamic finance programs would not only ensure the quality of the programs but would also be a vehicle for the standardization of these programs.

Although a limited number of institutions (e.g., INCEIF [International Centre for Education in Islamic Finance] in Malaysia) offer specialized programs that train their students in both finance and *Shari'ah*, most universities do not offer Islamic finance programs. There is limited demand from a small emerging market, and they often do not have the resources to effectively conduct such a program, which requires special expertise in both finance and *Shari'ah*.

The underlying reasons for the shortage of qualified experts should be further investigated. Some reasons might be the lack of a sufficient syllabus, the lack of demand for such programs, or a lack of mastery of the English and mathematics demanded in financial markets.

To address this issue, higher-education institutions and the central banks should take the lead. Universities may collaborate and share their resources to develop a market intelligence database, which can be used to identify potential programs, courses, and syllabi. For instance, special programs may be developed to train *Shari'ah* board members; currently about 300 qualified people are catering to a huge market demand for such expertise, and these experts are so thinly spread that many of them sit on 20 or more boards.

REGULATORY SUFFICIENCY

Dispute resolutions relating to the enforcement of contracts have posed serious problems for two important reasons. The first is that the legal jurisdiction of where the dispute is resolved is left up to the parties in the case. Because most countries do not recognize *Shari'ah*, dispute settlement by their courts necessarily rely on laws applicable in the country where the resolution is settled. That is fine, since there is a legal tradition for this viewpoint in both historical and contemporary times. There are even several cases (not mentioned here) in which the disputants came from offshore financial centers where the SPCs were registered, so the disputes were taken to courts in the United States or the United Kingdom.

In such instances, notwithstanding the nonapplicability of *Shari'ah*, the courts interpret the intentions behind the contractual terms. Any settlement must take cognizance of the laws of the land in interpreting whether a contract violation has occurred in the case within a given civil jurisdiction. To call for the imposition of other laws would be inappropriate. For practical reasons, the use of the laws where the malfeasance occurs is an age-old practice and should be respected by the disputing parties. This requires careful development of dispute settlement process in each of the *sukuk* marketplaces.

This brings us to the second reason that dispute resolutions pose problems. Even where *Shari'ah* applies to a case (e.g., Nakheel Holdings in the UAE) and a breach of promise has occurred, should the parties seek redress in another legal jurisdiction? The Nakheel case was sent to the United Kingdom, and an out-of-court settlement was made. This poses a number of questions. Did the litigants perhaps have a greater trust in the outside court? Or was this a way for the plaintiff to shop around for a more lenient jurisdiction?

It appears to us as researchers that this and similar cases pose an important dilemma for dispute resolutions that must be addressed carefully. The criterion to be applied in such cases is whether the interests in an Islamic financial dispute are better settled to the satisfaction of litigants through recourse to the principle of domicile applied widely. Should not the case be settled in the place where the malfeasance occurred? Or should the parties be permitted to shop around? A discussion of this aspect is needed, as the market for *sukuk* gets larger and the possibility increases of more cases coming to court.

CONCLUSION

A whole new way of meeting the funding needs of producer firms and governments (not consumption loans for individuals) is now available through the emerging *sukuk* securities market. The design and operating principles of this new instrument is targeted to different economic activities and tailored for safety for both parties. The asset backing put in place with the SPC limits the debt of a borrower from going beyond the capacity of the firm to fund, while the risk sharing makes the parties loyal to each other in the lending and borrowing process.

The synchronous nature of the contracts makes it possible to reduce the adversarial relationship that is very common between lenders and borrowers in the world's debt markets. Every time something goes wrong, the adversarial behavior goads the parties to court with costly litigation. Having profit-sharing contracts ensures that lenders will try to avoid going to court as the first recourse or going to the market to dump the security at the slightest bad news.

The targeting of the contracts to specific aspects of a firm's funding needs and the backing of assets to a loan make this form of lending desirable for firms. Perhaps these are the reasons that this market is growing very fast around the world. London's entry into this market in 2014 was an eagerly awaited development, expected to create innovations that will take this form of lending in new directions. This is welcome news exactly as the world has become reluctant to take on more debt (personal, state, and corporate) since the European Union debt crisis that started in October 2011.

There is worldwide recognition that debt at the corporate, government, and individual levels has increased too much under the one-sided interest-based debt contracting. Participatory debt through *sukuk* offers an automatic end to profligate borrowing by firms, governments, and individuals. The optimal debt cannot be over the value of the assets of the borrowers—a historical marker that, when breached, often leads to financial crisis. The debt-to-equity ratio of firms in the countries affected by the 1997–1998 Asian financial crisis was close to 400 percent of the equity values. That was the fundamental weakness that led to the crisis.

The desirable feature of asset backing before a loan can be made makes *sukuk* funding tame the appetite for debt. The appetite for debt has been associated with the financial fragility of economic agents throughout history and is a root cause of major financial crises, including the 2008 global financial crisis and the 2011–2013 Eurozone debt crisis.

Addressing the challenges identified in this chapter is an urgent task that each of the 12 (Hong Kong is a late entrant) *sukuk* markets must make a priority. The *sukuk* market is growing quickly at 22 to 25 percent per year, yet the impediments to its efficiency will remain unaddressed if this task is not undertaken. Addressing these challenges will lead to better-functioning Islamic debt markets.

There seems to be a strong competition among the major financial centers to attract the huge Middle Eastern clientele to this new niche growth market. Countries such as Malaysia, the UAE, and Bahrain, which currently enjoy the benefits of first-mover advantage in the *sukuk* market, will soon face new entrants with hundreds of years of experience in bond trading. These competitors are better organized and have the commitment to emerge as frontrunners. The organizers of *sukuk* markets have to seriously address the challenges listed in this chapter to ensure that they cater to the investors' search for an efficient and low-cost alternative to the bond market. Only then will the market move, slowly and surely, to the more efficient marketplaces such as London.

BIBLIOGRAPHY

Abdel-Khaleq, A. H., and C. F. Richardson. "New Horizons for Islamic Securities: Emerging Trends in *Sukuk* Offer Earnings." *Chicago Journal of International Law* 7, no. 2 (Winter 2007): 409–26.

Abd Razak, D., and M. A. Abdul Karim. "Development of Islamic Finance in Malaysia: A Conceptual Paper." Paper presented at the Eighth Global Conference on Business and Economics, Florence, Italy, October 18–19, 2008.

Abdul-Gafoor, A. L. M. "Islamic Banking and Finance: Another Approach." Paper presented at the Islamic Hinterland Conference on Critical Debates among Canadian Muslims, Toronto, Canada, September 3–5, 1999.

———. "Mudaraba-Based Investment and Finance." *Journal of Islamic Banking and Finance* 23, no. 4 (2006): 78–98.

Abdul Majid, Abdul Rais. "Development of Liquidity Management Instruments: Challenges and Opportunities." Paper presented at the International Conference on Islamic Banking: Risk Management, Regulation, and Supervision, Jakarta, Indonesia, March 9–10, 2003.

Accounting and Auditing Organization for Islamic Financial Institutions (AAOIFI). *Guidance Statement on Accounting for Investments and Amendment.* Financial Accounting Standard 17. Manama, Bahrain: AAOIFI, 2008.

———. *Resolutions on* Sukuk. Manama, Bahrain: AAOIFI, 2008, http://islamicbankers.files.wordpress.com/2008/09/aaoifi_sb_sukuk_feb2008_eng.pdf.

———. Shariah *Standard No. 18 on Investment* Sukuk. Manama, Bahrain: AAOIFI, 2002.

———. Shariah *Standards for Financial Institutions.* Manama, Bahrain: AAOIFI, 2004.

Adam, N. J., and A. Thomas. *Islamic Bonds: Your Guide to Issuing, Structuring, and Investing in* Sukuk. London: Euromoney Books, 2004.

———. "Islamic Fixed-Income Securities: *Sukuk.*" In *Islamic Asset Management: Forming the Future for Shari'a-Compliant Investment Strategies,* edited by S.Jaffar. London: Euromoney Books, 2004, pp. 72–81.

Ahmad, Z. "Islamic Banking: State of the Art." *Islamic Economic Studies*, 2, no. 1 (1994): 1–34.

Ainley, M., A. Mashayekhi, R. Hicks, A. Rahman, and A. Ravalia. *Islamic Finance in the UK: Regulation and Challenges*. London: Financial Services Authority, 2007.

Al Amine, M. "The Islamic Bonds Market: Possibilities and Challenges." *International Journal of Islamic Financial Services* 3, no. 1 (2001): 18.

Albuolayan, A. "Rapid Surge in *Sukuk* Market." *Arab News*, July 17, 2006.

Al-Jarhi, M. A., and M. Iqbal. *Islamic Banking: Answers to Some Frequently Asked Questions*. Jeddah, Saudi Arabia: Islamic Development Bank, 2001.

Al-Masri, R. Y. "Market Price of *Salam* on the Date of Delivery: Is It Permissible?" *Journal of Islamic Economics* 16, no. 2 (2003): 29–32.

Al-Omar, F., and M. Abdel-Haq. *Islamic Banking: Theory, Practice, and Challenges*. Karachi, Pakistan: Oxford University Press, 1996.

Alsayyed, N. A., and F. Malik. *Sukukization: Islamic Economic Risk Factors in the Shariah View*. Kuala Lumpur, Malaysia: International Shari'ah Research Academy for Islamic Finance, 2010.

Alvi, I. A., A. R. Mohammed, G. Z. Khan, U. M. Nasser, B. Naseer, and M. S. Khan. "*Sukuk* Report: A Comprehensive Study of the International *Sukuk* Market." In *The International Islamic Financial Market*, edited by I. A.Alvi. Manama, Bahrain: International Islamic Financial Market, 2010.

Alvi, I. A., A. R. Mohammed, and U. M. Naseer. "*Sukuk* Report: A Comprehensive Study of the International *Sukuk* Market." In *The International Islamic Financial Market*, 2nd ed., edited by I. A.Alvi, Manama, Bahrain: International Islamic Financial Market, 2011, pp. 1–75.

Amado, S. "Malaysia: An Islamic Capital Market Hub." International Monetary Fund, September 18, 2007, www.imf.org/external/pubs/ft/survey/so/2007.

Amin, M. "The New UK Tax Law on *Sukuk*," January 1, 2008, www.newhorizon-islamicbanking.com/index.cfm.

Amislamic Capital Market. "The Bright Side of Downturn." *Islamic Finance Bulletin*, July–September 2009.

Anwar, M. "Islamic Banking in Iran and Pakistan: A Comparative Study." *Pakistan Development Review* 31, no. 4 (Winter 1992): 1089–97.

Archer, S., and R. A. A. Karim, eds. *Islamic Finance: Innovation and Growth*. London: Euromoney Books and AAOIFI, 2002.

Ariff, M. "Ethics-Based Financial Transactions: An Assessment of Islamic Banking." In *Foundation of Islamic Banking: Theory, Practice, and Education*, edited by M.Ariff and M.Iqbal. Cheltenham, UK: Edward Elgar, 2011, pp. 11–39.

Ariff, M., F. F. Cheng, and V. H. Neoh. *Bond Markets in Malaysia and Singapore*. Kuala Lumpur, Malaysia: University Putra Malaysia Press, 2009.

Ariff, M., M. Iqbal, and M. Shamsher. *The Islamic Debt Market for Sukuk: Theory, Practice, and Issues*. Cheltenham, UK: Edward Elgar, 2012.

Asad, S. "The Business of *Shariah* Advice." *Dawn* (Karachi newspaper), October 11, 2009.

————. "An Overview of the *Sukuk* Market." *Jang* (Karachi newspaper), March 19, 2009.

Aseambankers. *Capitalising on Opportunities in the Sukuk Industry*. Kuala Lumpur, Malaysia: Aseambankers, 2005.

Ayub, M. *Understanding Islamic Finance*. Hoboken, NJ: John Wiley & Sons, 2008.

Baljeet, K. G. "Raising Capital through Labuan IOFC." Paper presented at the Labuan Offshore Financial Services Authority, Labuan, Malaysia, December 12, 2006.

Bank Negara Malaysia (BNM). *A Guide to Malaysian Government Securities*. 2nd ed. Kuala Lumpur, Malaysia: BNM, 2007.

————. *Malaysian Sukuk Market Handbook: Your Guide to the Malaysian Islamic Capital Market*. Kuala Lumpur, Malaysia: RAM Rating Service, 2008.

Bank Negara Malaysia (BNM) and Securities Commission of Malaysia (SCM). *Malaysian Debt Securities and the* Sukuk *Market: A Guide for Issuers and Investors*. Kuala Lumpur, Malaysia: BNM and SCM, 2009.

Bashir, A. H. M. "Risk and Profitability Measures in Islamic Banks: The Case of Two Sudanese Banks." *Islamic Economic Studies* 6, no. 2 (1999): 1–26.

Bose, S. Sr., and R. W. Mcgee. *Islamic Investment Funds: An Analysis of Risks and Returns*. Social Science Research Network eLibrary, 2008, http://papers.ssrn.com/sol3/papers.cfm?abstract_id=1310449.

Box, T., and M. Asaria. "Islamic Finance Market Turns to Securitization." *International Finance Law Review* 24, no. 7 (2005): 1–22.

Braudel, F. *The Mediterranean and the Mediterranean World in the Age of Philip II*. Vol. 2. New York: William Collins Sons, 1973.

Cakir, S., and F. Raei. *Sukuk vs. Eurobonds: Is There a Difference in Value-at-Risk?* Washington, DC: International Monetary Fund, 2007.

Chapra, U. M. "The Major Modes of Islamic Finance." Course in Islamic Economics, Banking, and Finance series, Islamic Foundation, Leicester, UK, 1998.

————. *Muslim Civilization: The Causes of Decline and the Need for Reform*. London: Routledge, 2010.

Cizakca, M. "Domestic Borrowing without the Rate of Interest: *Gharar* and the Origins of *Sukuk*." Paper presented at Symposium on *Sukuk* Financial Instruments, Dubai, UAE, May 3, 2010.

Damak, M., E. Volland, and K. Nassif. "Standard & Poor's Approach to Rating *Sukuk*." *S&P's Islamic Finance Outlook 2008*, September 17, 2007.

Dar Al Istithmar. Sukuk: *An Introduction to the Underlying Principles and Structure*. Oxford, UK: Dar Al Istithmar, 2006.

Daryanani, N. *A Deeper Understanding of the Prohibition of* Riba. Nottingham, UK: University of Nottingham, 2008.

DiVanna, J. "Will Islamic Banking Appeal to Non-Muslims?" In Alexander G. Leventhal (ed.), *Convergence: New Directions in Islamic Finance*. Cambridge: Harvard University Arab Financial Forum, 2008, pp. 1–87.

Dommisse, A., and W. Kazi. *Securitisation and* Shariah *Law*. Emerging Market Special Report Fitch Rating Agency, March 24, 2005, p. 4.

Dubai International Financial Centre (DIFC). Sukuk *Guidebook*. Dubai, UAE: DIFC, 2009.

Dusuki, A. W. "Challenges of Realizing *Maqasid al-Shariah* (Objectives of *Shariah*) in the Islamic Capital Market: Special Focus on Equity-Based *Sukuk*." Paper presented at the International Islamic Management Conference on the Islamic Capital Market, Penang, Malaysia, October 28–29, 2009.

Ebrahim, M. S. "Integrating Islamic and Conventional Project Finance." *Thunderbird International Business Review* 41, nos. 4–5 (July-October 1999): 583–609.

El-Gamal, M. A. *A Basic Guide to Contemporary Islamic Banking and Finance*. Plainfield, IN: Islamic Society of North America, 2000.

———. *Islamic Finance: Law, Economics, and Practice*. Cambridge, UK: Cambridge University Press, 2006.

———. "Mutuality as an Antidote to Rent-Seeking *Shariah* Arbitrage in Islamic Finance." *Thunderbird International Business Review* 49, no. 2 (2007): 187–202.

El-Ghazali, A. H. *Profit versus Bank Interest in Economic Analysis and Islamic Law*. Jeddah, Saudi Arabia: Islamic Development Bank, 1994.

Enders, W. *Applied Econometrics Time Series*. New York: John Wiley & Sons, 1995.

Erik, U. "Islam Is Not the Only Driver for *Sukuk* Popularity." *Financial Times*, April 30, 2007, www.ft.com.

Fadeel, M. "Legal Aspects of Islamic Finance." In *Islamic Finance: Innovation and Growth*, edited by S. Archer and R. A. A. Karim. London: Euromoney Books and AAOIFI, 2002, p. 91.

Faisal, A. "Overview of Malaysian *Sukuk* Market." *Malaysia Islamic Finance (MIF) Monthly*, February 2008.

Farook, R. "Global Financial Crisis Unthinkable Under Islamic Banking Principles." *Sunday Observer* (Sri Lanka), March 1, 2009.

Fitch Rating Agency. *Rating* Sukuk: *Cross-Sector Criteria Report*. New York: Fitch, 2012.

Floor, W. "*Čak* (Legal Document, Testament, Money Draft, Check)." In *Encyclopedia Iranica*, edited by E.Yarshater. New York: Columbia University, 1990.

Fuad, A., and A. Mohammed. *Islamic Banking: Theory, Practice, and Challenges*. London: Zed Books, 1996.

Gait, A. H., and A. C. Worthington. *A Primer on Islamic Finance: Definitions, Sources, Principles, and Methods*. Wollongong, Australia: University of Wollongong, 2007.

Gambling, T., R. Jones, and R. A. A. Karim. "Credible Organizations: Self-Regulation versus External Standard-Setting in Islamic Banks and British Charities." *Financial Accountability and Management* 93 (1993): 195–207.

El-Quqa, O. M, Faisal Hasan, Bikash Rout, and Abdelkarim Joubaili. "*Sukuk*: A New Dawn of the Islamic Finance Era." *Global Investment House* (January 2008): 1–36, http://www.menafn.com/updates/research_center/regional/special_ed/gih0108.pdf.

Granger, C. W. J. "Investigating Causal Relations by Econometric Models and Cross-Spectral Methods." *Econometrica* 37, no. 3 (1969): 424–38.

Gurgey, U., and Keki, E. "*Sukuk* in Turkey." *International Financial Law Review* 27 (November 2008): 111–12.

Haneef, R. "From 'Asset-Backed' to 'Asset-Light' Structures: The Intricate History of *Sukuk*." *International Journal of Islamic Finance* 1, no. 1 (2009): 103–26.

Hanif, A. "Islamic Finance: An Overview." *International Energy Law Review* 27, no. 1 (2008): 168.

Hasan, Z. *Islamic Finance: What Does It Change, What Does It Not*. Kuala Lumpur, Malaysia: International Centre for Education in Islamic Finance, 2010.

Hassan, M. K., and M. K. Lewis. *Handbook of Islamic Banking*. Cheltenham, UK: Edward Elgar, 2007.

Heck, G. W. *Charlemagne, Muhammad, and the Arab Roots of Capitalism*. Berlin: Walter de Gruyter, 2006.

Hesse, H., A. A. Jobst, and J. Sole. "Trends and Challenges in Islamic Finance." *World Economics* 9, no. 2 (2008): 175–94.

Hettish, K. "*Sukuk* Bond Issue on the Rise." *Daily Times*, May 2007, www.bluechipmag.com/subarticledet.php?id.

Homoud, S. H. "Progress of Islamic Banking: The Aspiration and Realities." *Islamic Economic Studies* 2, no. 1 (1994): 71–80.

Hossain, A. "Granger Causality between Inflation, Money Growth, Currency Devaluation, and Economic Growth in Indonesia, 1951–2002."

International Journal of Applied Econometrics and Quantitative Studies 2, no. 3 (2005): 23.

Ibn Rushd (Averroes). *The Distinguished Jurist's Primer.* Vol. 2, *Bidayat al-Mujtahid wa Nihayat al-Muqtasid.* Translated by I. A. K.Nyazee. Reading, UK: Garnet, 1996.

Ijlal, A. A. "*Sukuk*: Developing a Secondary Market." Paper presented at the Fifth Islamic Finance Summit. Dubai, UAE, 2006.

International Financial Services London. "Bond Markets 2009," www.ifsl.org.uk.

International Islamic Fiqh Academy. *Resolutions and Recommendations of the Council of the Islamic Fiqh Academy, 1985–2000.* Jeddah, Saudi Arabia: Islamic Development Bank, 2000.

Iqbal, M. "Islamic Banking." In *Lessons in Islamic Economics,* edited by M. Kahf. Jeddah, Saudi Arabia: Islamic Development Bank, 1998, pp. 261–71.

Iqbal, M., and P. Molyneux. *Thirty Years of Islamic Banking: History, Performance, and Prospects.* New York: Palgrave Macmillan, 2005.

Iqbal, Z. "Financial Engineering in Islamic Finance." *Thunderbird International Business Review* 41, nos. 4–5 (1999): 541–59.

Iqbal, Z., and A. Mirakhor. *An Introduction to Islamic Finance: Theory and Practice.* Singapore: John Wiley & Sons, 2006.

Iqbal, Z., and H. Tsubota. *Emerging Islamic Capital Markets: A Quickening Pace and New Potential.* The World Bank: Euromoney Institutional Investor, 2006.

Ishrat, H. "The Surge in Islamic Financial Services." *Dawn,* 2006, www.dawn.com/events/ifs/ifs.

Islamic Finance Asia. *Islamic Finance Asia Ratings: How Do They Do It?* Kuala Lumpur, Malaysia: REDmoney Group, 2008.

Islamic Financial Services Board (IFSB). "Capital Adequacy Requirements for *Sukuk*, Securitizations, and Real Estate Investment." Kuala Lumpur, Malaysia: IFSB, 2009, www.ifsb.org/standard/ifsb7.pdf.

Ismail, M. I. "Rating of *Sukuk*." Workshop at Conference on Structuring Innovative *Sukuk.* Jakarta, Indonesia, June 19, 2007.

Jabbar, H. S. F. A. "Islamic Finance: Fundamental Principles and Key Financial Institutions." *Company Lawyer* 30, no. 1 (2009): 23–32.

———. "Sharia-Compliant Financial Instruments: Principles and Practice." *Company Lawyer* 30, no. 6 (2009): 176–88.

Jalil, A. "Islamic Bonds Issues: The Malaysian Experience." In *The 6th Asian Academy of Management Conference,* edited by T. Ramanayanah, M. Sulaiman, H. Harun, R. Ali, A. M. Nasurdin, N. A. Wahid, and I. Osman. Perak, Malaysia: Asian Academy of Management, 2005, pp 1–8.

Jamelah, J. "Liquidity in the Malaysian *Sukuk* Market," *Malaysian Islamic Finance Monthly*, June 2008.

Jerry, U. "Banking on Allah." *Fortune*, June 10, 2002.

Jobst, A., P. Kunzel, P. Mills, and A. Sy. "Islamic Finance Expanding Rapidly." International Monetary Fund, September 9, 2007, www.imf.org/external/pubs/ft/survey/so/2007.

John, I. "*Sukuk* Key to Meeting $1.5tr Infrastructure Needs of ME, Asia." *Khaleej Times* (Dubai), July 22, 2007.

Kahf, M. *Instruments of Meeting Budget Deficit in the Islamic Economy.* Jeddah, Saudi Arabia: Islamic Development Bank, 1997.

Kamali, M. H. "A *Shari'ah* Analysis of Issues in Islamic Leasing." *Journal of Islamic Economics* 20, no. 1 (2007): 3–22

Karimzadeh, M. "Role of *Sukuk* in the Islamic Capital Market: Experience of Iran (1994–2011)." *Arabian Journal of Business and Management Review* 1, no. 7 (February 2012): 94–105.

Khan, M. A. *Islamic Economics and Finance: A Glossary.* London: Routledge, 2003.

Khan, M. M. *Interest-Free Finance: The Islamic Banking and Finance Movement in Pakistan (1980–2002).* Melbourne, Australia: University of Technology, 2003.

Khan, M. M., and M. I. Bhatti. "Development in Islamic Banking: A Financial Risk-Allocation Approach." *Journal of Risk Finance* 9, no. 1 (2008): 40–51.

———. "Why Interest-Free Banking and Finance Movement Failed in Pakistan." *Humanomics* 22, nos. 3–4 (2006): 145–61.

Khan, T., and H. Ahmed. *Risk Management: An Analysis of Issues in the Islamic Financial Industry.* Jeddah, Saudi Arabia: Islamic Development Bank, 2001.

Kharazmi, A. A. "Mafatil al-Ulum." *The Keys to the Science.* Ed. G. V. Vloten. Leiden, Netherlands: E. J. Brill, 1895.

Lewis, M. K. "Islamic Banking in Theory and Practice." *Monash Business Review* 3, no. 1 (2007): 1–8.

Lewis, M. K., and L. M. Algaoud. *Islamic Banking.* Cheltenham, UK: Edward Elgar, 2001.

Liquidity Management Center (LMC). *Guide to the Sukuk Market.* Manama, Bahrain: LMC, 2008.

Malaysian Rating Corporation (MARC). *Rating Approach to Sukuk.* Kuala Lumpur, Malaysia: MARC, 2008.

Maurer, B. "Anthropological and Accounting Knowledge in Islamic Banking and Finance: Rethinking Critical Accounts." *Journal of the Royal Anthropological Institute* 8, no. 4 (2002): 645–67.

———. "Form versus Substance: AAOIFI Projects and Islamic Fundamentals in the Case of *Sukuk*." *Journal of Islamic Accounting and Business Research* 1, no. 1 (2010): 32–41.

McKenzie, D. *Islamic Finance 2008*. London: Islamic Financial Services, 2008.

———. *Islamic Finance 2009*. London: International Financial Services, 2009.

———. *Islamic Finance 2010*. London: International Financial Services, 2010.

———. *Islamic Finance 2012*. London: International Financial Services, 2012.

McMillen, M. J. T. "Asset Securitization *Sukuk* and Islamic Capital Markets: Structural Issues in These Formative Years." *Wisconsin International Law Journal* 25, no. 4 (2008): 703–72.

———. "Contractual Enforceability Issues: *Sukuk* and Capital Market Development." *Chicago Journal of International Law* 7, no. 2 (Winter 2007): 427–29.

Metwally, M. M. "Economic Consequences of Applying Islamic Principles in Muslim Societies." *International Journal of Social Economics* 24, nos. 7, 8, 9 (1997): 941–57.

Mirakhor, A. "Islamic Finance and Globalization: A Convergence." *Journal of Islamic Economics, Banking, and Finance* 2, no. 2 (2007): 11–72.

Moghul, U. F., and A. A. Ahmed. "Contractual Forms in Islamic Finance Law and *Islamic Investment Company of the Gulf (Bahamas) Ltd. v. Symphony Gems N. V. & Others*: A First Impression of Islamic Finance." *Fordham International Law Journal* 27, no. 1 (2003): 150–88.

Mohd, A. N. "The Effect of Islamic Private Debt Securities Rating Changes on Firm's Common Stock Returns." *Journal of Muamalat and Islamic Finance Research* 1, no. 1 (2004): 25–38.

Mokhtar, S. "A Synthesis of *Shari'ah* Issues and Market Challenges in the Application of *Wa'd* in Equity-Based *Sukuk*." *International Journal of Islamic Finance* 1, no. 1 (2009): 139–45.

Muhammad Al-Bashir, M. "*Sukuk* Market: Innovations and Challenges," *Islamic Economic Studies* 15, no. 2 (2008): 1–22.

Nasr, S. H. *The Heart of Islam: Enduring Values for Humanity*. New York: HarperOne, 2002.

Nassif, K., J. Manley, and M. Wilkins. "Project Finance *Sukuk*." *Standard and Poor's Rating Direct*, November 9, 2007.

Obaidullah, M. *Islamic Financial Services*. Jeddah, Saudi Arabia: Islamic Economics Research Centre, 2005.

Obiyathulla, I. B. "Adapting *Mudarabah* Financing to Contemporary Realities: A Proposed Financing Structure." *Journal of Accounting, Commerce, and Finance* 1, no. 1 (1997): 26–54.

Olson D., and T. A. Zoubi. "Using Accounting Ratios to Distinguish between Islamic and Conventional Banks in the GCC Region." *International Journal of Accounting* 43, no. 1 (2008): 45–65.

Pearl, D. *A Textbook on Muslim Law*. London: Croom Helm, 1979.

Pomeranz, F. "The Accounting and Auditing Organization for Islamic Financial Institutions: An Important Regulatory Debut." *International Journal of Accounting, Auditing and Taxation* 6, no. 1 (1997): 123–30.

Rating Agency Malaysia. "Market Statistics." *Islamic Finance Bulletin*, July–September 2009.

———. "*Sukuk* Rating: General Approach, Criteria, and Methodology." *Islamic Finance Bulletin*, July–September 2009.

"Record *Sukuk*—Islamic Bond Offering—by Pakistan." *Khaleej Times*, January 26, 2005.

Richard, K. *A Closer Look at Ijara Sukuk*. Dubai, UAE: Standard & Poor's, 2005.

Rosly, S. A. "The Islamic Capital Market: *Shariah* Stocks, *Sukuk*, i-Reits, and Islamic Unit Trust Funds." Workshop on Islamic Finance, International Center for Education in Islamic Finance, Labuan, Malaysia, November 14–16, 2007.

Rosly, S. A., and M. M. Sanusi. "The Application of Bay' Al-'Inah and Bay' Al-Dayn in Malaysian Islamic Bonds: An Islamic Analysis." *International Journal of Islamic Financial Services*, 1, no. 2 (1999): 1–16.

Saeed, A. *Islamic Banking and Interest: A Study of the Prohibition of Riba and Its Contemporary Interpretation*. Leiden, Netherlands: E. J. Brill, 1996.

Safari, M., M. Ariff, M., and M. Shamsher. "Do Debt Markets Price *Sukuk* and Conventional Bonds Differently?" *Journal of Islamic Economics*, 26, no. 2 (2013): 113–49.

Salah, O. "Islamic Finance: The Impact of the AAOIFI Resolution on Equity-Based *Sukuk* Structures." *Law and Financial Markets Review* 4, no. 5 (September 2010): 507–17.

Saleh, N. A. *Unlawful Gain and Legitimate Profit in Islamic Law: Riba, Gharar, and Islamic Banking*. Cambridge, UK: Cambridge University Press, 1986.

Saqqaf, L. "Middle East Debt: The New *Sukuk*; Innovative Structures Are Changing the Face of Islamic Bonds." *International Finance Law Review* 10, October 2006.

Securities Commission of Malaysia. "Malaysia Islamic Capital Market." *Quarterly Bulletin* 4, no. 3 (September 2009): 8–11.

———. *Resolutions of the Securities Commission Shariah Advisory Council*, 2nd ed. Kuala Lumpur, Malaysia: Securities Commission, 2006.

Shaikh, S. A. *A Brief Review and Introduction to Practiced Islamic Banking and Finance*. Hyderabad: University of East Pakistan, 2010.

Shamsher, M., H. Taufiq, and M. Ariff. "Research in an Emerging Malaysian Capital Market: A Guide to Future Direction." *International Journal of Economics and Management* 1, no. 2 (June 2007): 173–202.

Shankar, S. "Global Capital Flows," 2007, www.findarticles.com/articles/mi_qa3715/is_2007.

Shinsuke, N. "Beyond the Theoretical Dichotomy in Islamic Finance: Analytical Reflections on *Murabahah* Contracts and Islamic Debt Securities." *Kyoto Bulletin of Islamic Area Studies* 1, no. 2 (2007): 72–91.

Siddiqi, M. N. *Issues in Islamic Banking*. Leicester, UK: Islamic Foundation, 1983.

———. Riba, Bank Interest, and the Rationale of Its Prohibition. Jeddah, Saudi Arabia: Islamic Development Bank, 2004.

Siddiqui, R. "Contributing to the Development of the Islamic Capital Market: The Dow Jones Citigroup *Sukuk* Index." *Dow Jones Islamic Market Indexes Newsletter*, December 2008.

Sundararajan, V., and Errico, L. *Islamic Financial Institutions and Products in the Global Financial System: Key Issues in Risk Management and Challenges Ahead*. Tehran: Central Bank of the Islamic Republic of Iran, 2002.

Tariq, A. A. *Managing Financial Risks of Sukuk Structures*. Leicestershire, UK: Loughborough University School of Business and Economics, 2004.

Tariq A. A., and H. Dar. "Risks of *Sukuk* Structures: Implications for Resource Mobilization." *Thunderbird International Business Review* 49, no. 2 (2007): 203–23.

Thomas, A., S. Cox, and B. Kraty, B. *Structuring Islamic Finance Transactions*. London: Euromoney Books, 2006.

Udovich, A. L. "Bankers without Banks: Commerce, Banking, and Society in the Islamic World of the Middle Ages." In *The Dawn of Modern Banking*. Ed. UCLA Center for Medieval and Renaissance Studies. New Haven, CT: Yale University Press, 1979, pp. 255–75.

———. "Trade." In *The Dictionary of the Middle Ages*, Vol. 12, ed. J. R. Strayer. New York: Charles Scribner's Sons, 1989, pp. 750.

Usmani, M. T. *An Introduction to Islamic Finance*. The Hague, Netherlands: Kluwer Law International, 2002.

———. *Principles of* Shari'ah *Governing Islamic Investment Funds*. Bahrain: AAOIFI, 2001.

———. *Sukuk and Their Contemporary Applications*. Manama, Bahrain: AAOIFI, 2007.

Van De Graaff, S., and B. P. Gallogly. *Opportunities in the Islamic Finance Market: International Securitization and Finance Report*, 11, no. 22 (2008): 220–32.

Vishwanath, S. R., and S. Azmi. "An Overview of Islamic *Sukuk* Bonds." *Journal of Structured Finance* 144 (2009): 58–67.

Wan Abdullah, W. R., J. Roudaki, and M. Clark. "The Evolution of the Islamic Capital Market in Malaysia." Paper presented at the Accounting History International Conference on Accounting and the State, Wellington, New Zealand, August 2010.

Warde, I. *Islamic Finance in the Global Economy.* Edinburgh, UK: Edinburgh University Press, 2000.

Wilson, R. "Innovation in the Structuring of Islamic *Sukuk* Securities." *Humanomics* 24, no. 3 (2008): 170–81.

———. "Islamic Finance in Europe." *Journal of Islamic Economics, Banking, and Finance* 3, no. 2 (July–December 2007): 73–104.

———. "Overview of the *Sukuk* Market." In *Islamic Bonds: Your Guide to Issuing, Structuring, and Investing in* Sukuk. Ed. N. J. Adam and A. Thomas. Durham, UK: Euromoney Institutional Investor, 2004, pp. 3–17.

Zaher, T. S., and M. K. Hassan. "A Comparative Literature Survey of Islamic Finance and Banking." *Financial Markets, Institutions, and Instruments* 10, no. 4 (2001): 155–99.

Index

A

Accounting and Auditing Organization for
Islamic Financial Institutions (AAOIFI),
20, 22, 27, 40, 44, 52, 54
Accreditation, 193
Al-Ghazali, 33
Al-Juwaini, 33
Amsterdam, 179
Annuity, 7
Approaches to Islamic finance, 40–41
idealistic, 40
liberal, 40
pragmatic, 40
Asset-backed, 15, 25, 114
asset-based contract, 178
unbacked contract, 179
Asynchronous contract, 7
Athenians, 179
Autorite Marches Financiers, 152

B

Bahrain, 196
Bahrain Monetary Authority, 68
Central Bank of Bahrain, 73
Liquidity Management Centre, 107
Banks, 179
Basle, 183
BIS, 183
Bond rating agencies
Fitch, 118–119
MARC, 121
Moody's, 22, 115–118
RAM (Rating Agency Malaysia), 8, 22,
119–121
Standard & Poor's, 22

C

Cash flow patterns, 169–178
declining payments, 174
fixed promised, 171
fixed regular, 171
fixed regular at end (balloon) payment,
172
growth stream payment, 173
undetermined payments, 175
variable payments, 172
zero-promised, 169
Cairo *Genizah*, 42
Cheque vs. *Sakk*, 43
China, 179
Colombus, Christopher, 4, 178
Commenda, 8, 13
Conventional bond, 7–10, 12, 20, 22, 81–95
AAA-rated, 22, 82
government, 82
yield difference, 81, 82–90
yield to maturity, 86–90
Conventional debt size, 182
Country-of-domicile, 128
Credit reputation, 8
Cyprus, 183

D

Debt burden
economics of, 177, 181
G7 debt, 183
household debt, 184
world debt burden, 181, 182, 183
Depository markets, 10
Developing countries, 183
Dividends, 16
Dubai International Financial Centre, 127

E

Education, 194–195
Ethics in financial transactions, 3, 6
Christian ethics, 7
Islamic ethics, 7
Europe, 42
Eurozone, 183

F
Farooq, Mohammad Omar, 39
Fatwa, 99
   shopping, 193
Ferdinand, King of Spain, 4
Fractional banking, 79, 181
Funding
   production, 4, 8

G
Gold, 37
Greece, 183
Gross domestic product, 184

H
Hadith, 37, 196
Hong Kong, 185
Human societies, 178, 179

I
Individual investors, 142
Indonesia, 125, 127
Interest versus *riba*, 39
International Centre for Education in Islamic
   Finance (INCEIF), 194
International Islamic Financial Market
   (IIFM), 59
Ireland, 183
Isabella, Queen of Spain, 4, 178
Islamic Development Bank, 22
Islamic finance principles, 35
   fiqh al mu'amlat, 110
   gambling, 4
   gharar, 35, 39
   halal, 45
   information asymmetry, 167
   Islamic debt securities, 4
   mark-up fee, 167
   profit sharing, 166
   qimar, 36
   riba, 35, 38, 41, 66, 167 189
   risk sharing, 4, 7, 13
   schools of thought, 192
   uncertainty, 167
Islamic Financial Services Board (IFSB),
   40–45
Islamic jurisprudence (*fiqh*)
   Council of the Islamic Fiqh Academy, 43
   fiqh, 33

ijma, 32, 35
ijtihad, 32–34
   legal scholars (*fuquha*), 6
   qiyas, 32
Islamic mutual funds, 5

J
Japan, 185
Jewish merchants, 42

K
Khazanah Holdings, 74, 81
Krugman, Paul, 183
Kuwait Financial Authority, 125

L
Latin America, 80
Liquidity, 175
Liquidity, trade days, 138–139, 158–159,
   180, 190
London as financial center, 10,
   189, 196
London Inter-Bank Offered Rate (LIBOR),
   24, 66, 74
Luxembourg, 10

M
Malaysia, 38, 127, 71
   Ministry of Finance, 71
Market maker, 191
Masai tribesman, 10
Mecca/Medina, 33
Middle Ages, 42
Middle East, 13
Mudarib, 57–58
Musharaka, defined, 58

N
Nahan Airline Company, 75
Nakheel Holding, 195,
   74–75 142
Napoleon, 178
New York, 10

O
Oman 9, 125, 127
Organization of Islamic Countries (OIC),
   181, 192

P

Pakistan, 127
Papal lending by the Church, 8
Paper currency, 10
Participation finance. *See* Islamic finance
  principles
Payoff structures, 11, 163–172
Pope Francis, 3
Portugal, 183
Private negotiation, 10
Product development, 31, 185
Professional advisors, 142
Profit ratio, 16
Public auction, 10

Q

Qatar Central Bank, 74
Qatar Financial Centre, 21
Quran, 8, 13, 32, 33, 35, 164,
  167, 178

R

Rabbal mal, 55
Regulating *sukuk,* 99–105
  Accounting and Auditing Organization
    for Islamic Financial Institution
    (AAOIFI), 100
  International Islamic Financial Market
    (IIFM), 100
  NASDAQ Dubai, 110
  number of sellers, 100
  retail market, 152
  Shari'ah board, 99–100, 103–104
Regulatory sufficiency, 194
  New Zealand, 15

S

Saad Group, 142
Saudi Arabia, 9, 125, 127
Securities Commission of Malaysia, 109
Securitization, 107–125
  country risk, 133
  disclosures, 109
  initial public offering (IPO), 197
  investor requests, 108
  issuing cost, 191
  public profile, 108
  register, 111
  Shari'ah regulation, 143–145

sukuk vs. conventional, 107
trading/listing, 108–109, 110, 111,
  147–150
Shari'ah, defined, 3
  riba (usury), 28
Shell, 9, 43, 71, 177
Silver, 37
Singapore, 130
South Asia, 179
Southeast Asia, 199
South Korea, 181
Spain, 183
Special purpose company (SPC), 7, 9, 15, 16,
  17, 18, 22, 45, 48, 50, 51, 60, 65, 69,
  108, 189
Standardization, 193
Sukuk markets, 125–141
  classification, 22–29
  defined, 5, 14, 44
  worldwide, 125, 129, 135
Sukuk products
  bai bithaman ajjal, 16, 23
  diminishing *musharak*a, 61
  discount *sukuk,* 23
  history, 41
  hybrid, 48
  ijara, 21, 23, 64, 69–70
  manfah, 77–78
  mudarabah, 24, 62–63
  muqarasah, 77–78
  murabaha, 24–25
  musaqa, 77–79
  qard hassan, 8
  salam, 25, 66–67
  savings, 126
  wakala, 52, 77
Sukuk structures, 31, 45–47
  design, 57–70, 77–80
  specific needs, 76
  structures, 145–146
Sung Dynasty, 178
Sunnah, 32, 164
Sydney (Australia), 10

T

Takaful, defined, 5
Tokyo, 10
Turkey, 6
Two-tier *mudarabah* bank savings, 164

U

UAE (United Arab Emirates), 59
UK Islamic Financial Council, 100
UK Listing Authority, 109
United States of America, 4, 185

V

Valuation matters, 10, 169

W

Williams, John Burr, 175
World Bank, 9, 177, 181
Worldcom Inc., 17

Z

Zurich (Switzerland), 10